THE AUTISTIC CHILD
Language Development
Through Behavior Modification

THE
AUTISTIC
CHILD

LANGUAGE DEVELOPMENT
THROUGH BEHAVIOR MODIFICATION

By O. Ivar Lovaas

IRVINGTON PUBLISHERS, INC., NEW YORK

Distributed by HALSTED PRESS, Division of
JOHN WILEY & SONS, INC.
NEW YORK   LONDON   TORONTO   SYDNEY

Distributed by HALSTED PRESS
A division of JOHN WILEY & SONS, Inc., New York

Library of Congress Cataloging in Publication Data
Lovaas, Ole Ivar, 1927–
    The autistic child.
    Bibliography: p.
    1. Autism. 2. Handicapped children—Education—
Language arts. I. Title.
RJ506.A9L68   371.9'2   76-5890
ISBN 0-470-15065-3

Printed in The United States of America   Photos by Allan Grant

To my children
Randi, Lisa, Kari, and Erik

CONTENTS

THE AUTISTIC CHILD
Language Development
Through Behavior Modification

FOREWORD

Ten years ago we began a comprehensive morning-to-evening project of treating autistic children by means of behavioral modification procedures. Considering the minimal behavioral development of autistic children, we were in a sense trying to build individuals starting with a *Tabula rasa*. Language was a crucial behavior both because it seemed the most complex one to tackle and because the children needed it in order to become more normal. It is difficult to be a normal person without possessing some form of language with which one can affect, or be affected by, the society in which one lives.

As language is strikingly complex behavior, to try to build it is a good test of how much we, as psychologists, know about behavior. Ten years ago not a great deal was known about how to build language. We read lengthy texts on the acquisition of language and then went back to face our children without having learned how to help them talk. We were altogether alone in trying to help these children; in a sense we lacked professional skills. If a child psychologist cannot teach a child to talk, what can he do?

This book will present some of the language programs we have developed since that time. It was obvious from the begin-

1

ning that even though psychology knew very little about how to build language, it did know something about how to build behavior. In particular we knew of the operant work on animal shaping, and we were familiar with modern learning theory. The language programs were derived from this literature, particularly from the area of discrimination learning.

The programs were most often conceived on the spot, without much forethought. Fourteen days after we had hospitalized the first group of children in 1964, we ran out of treatment programs; we had no choice but to invent and improvise. We were determined that the children were going to learn and that we were going to teach them. The programs will reflect this lack of adequate preparation.

Attempting to build all the language a child needs, we became Jacks-of-all-trades, amateurs in a way; it might have been more gratifying to have worked in a limited area, such as teaching grammar or conversational skills or helping the child increase his use of spontaneous language. But our goals for the children were essentially therapeutic: to make them as normal as possible. This goal precluded the mere building of isolated behaviors. Our global goals left many of our efforts with inadequate data and in need of more extensive analysis. But our efforts are a beginning of more detailed analysis of the conditions which help nonlinguistic children to speak.

Most of our efforts have been directed toward the autistic child who, in the more extreme manifestations of the condition had the motor development and the exterior physical appearance of a normal child but showed few if any of the behaviors that would help define him as a social individual. The less developed children did not give evidence of language (expressive or receptive), play with toys, or form emotional attachments to other people.

In all likelihood our findings have generality beyond the autistic child. We have already employed the same procedures to teach language skills to retarded children with Down's Syndrome. Other investigators report on the application of similar procedures to other forms of retardation, as well as to more normal children. Some investigators have even taught quite complex language to subhumans, using procedures which are strikingly similar to those used with disturbed children. The procedures we have helped develop, which we describe in detail in this book, will be useful in helping a wide variety of children to talk.

Beyond the practical benefit from these programs for children seriously lagging in language development, one may also entertain the possibility that these procedures represent the way "nature" ordinarily teaches language to normal children. These studies, then, should increase our understanding of language acquisition in general. We shall present some data contrary to certain theories of language development, particularly those which place a heavy emphasis on organic determinants.

This book is intended to help those working with children who are seriously behind in their language development. A variety of persons are so involved: parents, teachers, psychologists, speech therapists, psychiatrists, psychiatric nurses, and aides. The book should be easy reading for upper division and graduate psychology students, but it may prove quite difficult for parents with no background in psychology. Yet it is crucial that parents learn the principles we describe in this book, because the parents are the child's primary language teachers. We have been unable to help a child meaningfully in language development without the parent's active involvement. If we were to present this material in a less technical, more informal manner, so much precision would be lost that the text would be relatively useless, as it is extremely difficult to build complex language.

Throughout this book the reader will be introduced to the largely operant learning theory which has formed the basis for our language work up to the present. As many readers may want a deeper understanding of these learning concepts and processes than we can provide here, it may be desirable to supplement this book with auxiliary texts on operant work. There are several excellent texts, which will help, two of which are Fred S. Keller, *Learning: Reinforcement Theory,* and Sidney W. Bijou and Donald M. Baer, *Child Development, Volume 1: A Systematic and Empirical Theory.* A slightly more advanced text is G. S. Reynold's *A Primer of Operant Conditioning.* There are also several more "practical" but excellent books on the subject, such as Patterson and Gullion's *Living with Children,* Sulzer and Mayer's *Behavior Modification Procedures for School Personnel,* R. Vance Hall's *Behavior Management Series,* and Whaley and Malott's *Elementary Principles of Behavior.*

A good foundation in learning theory is basic, but not sufficient, for helping children learn to talk. One has to be familiar with the intracacies of children, their affect, what pleases them, and so on, in order to teach them. Such familiarity can be gained only by being around children.

Speech therapists have often written about how to help children talk. Most of this material deals with the more normal child, but some reference is made to the psychotic or retarded child. A number of suggestions are made in these writings on how to facilitate language development, and although there is little, if any, data to back up most of these suggestions, the reader may want to familiarize himself with them. In teaching our children to talk, we have often supplemented our own programs with material and suggestions from other language programs, such as the Monterey Program (Grey and Ryan, 1971, 1973). Several texts on speech pathology are also available, but it's beyond the realm of this book to try to evaluate those texts.

From what has just been said, and from what will become apparent as we present our programs, there is a great deal which we do not know as yet about language learning. I would single out in particular such areas as the effect of a child's emotions on the rate and kind of his language learning, the conditions under which receptive language facilitates expression or the optimal order (sequencing) of teaching language tasks.

Despite such ignorance, it is appropriate to publish this book because the information we provide is necessary for language learning. A psychotic or retarded child with severe limitations on expressive and receptive language will in all probability not learn language unless his therapist/teacher knows how to teach him according to the principles laid out in this book.

The book is organized to introduce basic learning principles in Chapter 1, with the application of these principles in building the first words and meanings given in Chapter 2, leading to progressively more complex language in Chapters 3 and 4. Chapter 5 states the theoretical implications of our work, and will be important primarily to professionals interested in language *per se*. Chapter 6 contains the language training manuals, which are referred to throughout the earlier chapters. Chapter 7 presents three illustrative case histories of children who have undergone our language training. Although these case histories are placed last in the book (because they can best be understood at that point), the reader may want to read Chapter 7 first, because the case reports help make sense of the basic principles as well.

References

Bijou, S.W., & Baer, D. M. *Child development, Volume I: A systematic and empirical theory.* New York: Appleton-Century-Crofts, 1961.

Grey, B., & Ryan, B. *Programmed conditioning for language: Program book.* Monterey, California: Monterey Learning Systems, 1971.

Grey, B., & Ryan, B. *A language program for the nonlanguage child.* Champaign, Illinois: Research Press, 1973.

Hall, R.V. *Behavior management series.* Lawrence, Kansas: H & H Enterprises, Inc., 1972 (No. 1-6).

Keller, F.S. *Learning: Reinforcement theory.* New York: Random House, 1954.

Lovaas, O.I., Berberich, J.P., Perloff, B.F., & Schaeffer, B. Acquisition of imitative speech by schizophrenic children. *Science,* 1966, *151,* 705-707.

Lovaas, O.I. *Behavior modification: Teaching language to psychotic children.* Instructional film, 45 min., 16 mm.-sound, Appleton-Century-Crofts, New York, 1969.

Patterson, G. R., and Gullion, M. E. *Living with children: New methods for parents and teachers.* Champaign, Illinois: Research Press, 1968.

Reynolds, G.S. *A primer of operant conditioning.* Glenview, Ill.: Scott, Foresman and Co., 1968.

Sulzer, B., & Mayer, R.G. *Behavior modification procedures for school personnel.* Hinsdale, Ill.: The Dryden Press, Inc., 1972.

Whaley, D.L., & Malott, R.W. *Elementary principles of behavior.* New York: Appleton-Century-Crofts, 1971.

ACKNOWLEDGMENTS

An enormous amount of work has gone into the data we present here, from a number of extremely bright, highly motivated, socially committed people who contributed at all levels; the project could not have succeeded without their help and effort. As we worked around the clock, we got to know each other quite well, and what is presented here is as much theirs as mine. In the early years, I had the help of several students who have since received their doctorates. I am particularly grateful for the contributions of Drs. John Berberich, Lorraine Freitas, Bijan Guilani, Irene Kassorla, Joan Meisel, Edward Nelson, Bernard Perloff, and Benson Schaeffer. As the language programs developed and we had the opportunity to investigate more analytical aspects of the acquisition process, I received much help from Mrs. Meredits Gibbs and Drs. Robert Koegal, Buddy Newsom, and Laura Schreibman. Perhaps more than anyone else, Dr. Judith Stevens-Long's help, both in organizing the data on spontaneous language and in relating our data to the normal child's language development, was critical. The training manuals in Chapter 6 of this book were organized by Dr. Steven-Long and Mrs. Meredith Gibbs. Finally, Ms. Cathy Graves and Ms. Sheryl Nisenson have edited and otherwise helped make this manuscript more readable.

I was fortunate to meet Dr. James A. Simmons, Associate Chief of the Mental Retardation and Child Mental Health Programs at the U. C. L. A. Neuropsychiatric Institute, early in my work with autistic children. From 1964 to 1968, we worked closely together, and much of the data presented here were collected at that time. We reinforced each other in what we thought was important to autistic children, and we have published together on these efforts.

The National Institute of Mental Health (MH 11440) and the Office of Education (0E 4-6-061188-0614) have supported our work on language. The organization and writing of this book were also facilitated by a Guggenheim Fellowship.

Aspects of this research were presented as early as 1965, as papers at the Western Psychological Association (Honolulu) and the American Psychological Association (Chicago). Those papers described the acquisition of abstract verbal behavior and our beginning efforts in building syntax. It formed the basis for an invited address to Division 7 of the American Psychological Association meeting in San Francisco in 1968. An overview of the language program was presented on film (Lovaas, 1969), which should provide a good introduction to the studies we present here. However, with the exception of a publication on the acquisition of verbal imitation (Lovaas, Berberich, Perloff, & Schaeffer, 1966), this is the first time our language studies appear in print.

Chapter I
BASIC PRINCIPLES

Most children acquire language without anyone knowing how they do so. It is a "natural phenomenon", and knowledge of the process is usually not needed. Unfortunately, some children do not learn to talk on their own; they need help. The benefits which come from knowing how language is acquired might be shared by many, as language is central in human life. Many consider it a unique characteristic of human behavior and feel it contributes in a major way to human thought and reasoning.

Despite the importance of language in human existence, no one knows how language is acquired. We do not as yet possess laws about language which would tell us what variables to manipulate to obtain a certain progress in language development. When linguists and psychologists have studied language in the past, they have confined themselves largely to descriptive accounts of language development; their studies describe the order in which normal children develop certain language behaviors and the content of these behaviors. On the basis of such observations,

the investigators have often guessed at why and how children acquire language. These guesses have not as yet been experimentally verified.

The same lack of systematic empirical evaluation characterizes the efforts of professionals directly concerned with teaching or otherwise facilitating language development. Such
teachers have no proven procedures to guide them. The
techniques they have suggested for teaching language are offered
without empirical evidence of their merits. Some of their
techniques may be useful, others may hinder. In short, then, if
one seeks facts and information on how to develop language in
persons who have no language, one finds no empirically validated
procedure.

We present in this book a technology and data on how to
teach language to nonspeaking children. This is a practical text
that reports on techniques we have developed over the last 12
years in our attempt to teach language to mute and echolalic autistic children. We also present studies which have used procedures similar to ours by investigators working with other types of
children, such as culturally disadvantaged and retarded children.

The intent behind this book is highly practical. We are concerned with helping the teacher or parent teach children to com-
municate more effectively. Being pragmatic clinicians and
teachers first, we wanted to use whatever procedures helped children learn to talk. Unfortunately, not enough is known about the
nervous system at this time to manipulate it with the precision
needed to produce language. Therefore, when one tries to help
children learn to talk, one is fairly well restricted to attempts to
manipulate the child's environment. Furthermore, if one seeks to
manipulate the child's environment to facilitate language learning, then one is largely restricted to those operations specified
within modern learning theory, certainly if one wants to base
one's teaching efforts on experimentally validated procedures.
Within modern learning theory, it is those operations which
define operant conditioning or reinforcement theory that have
been most explicitly related to the acquisition of human behavior. It is probably the case, then, that we have no choice at
this time but to work within modern learning theory to try to
teach language.

Once our procedures and data have been presented, we relate
our studies to current theoretical positions about language. To relate our findings to these theoretical positions, is almost unavoid-

able since they are so central in the history of psychology. For example, it has been considered by many that certain aspects of language such as grammar or syntax are so complex that they could not be acquired through experience, but had to come about because of certain innate neurologically based language abilities which generate language with minimal environmental assistance. From this point of view, our efforts to teach children language should fail. The data we present in this book support some theories of language more than others and may suggest certain directions for future research on language. We examine these theoretical considerations after we present our method and data. Let us now introduce the basic framework we used in teaching language.

Learning Theory and Language

Since we will draw heavily on learning theory, introducing certain learning concepts at this point will supply some order to our presentation. If we approach the problem of language acquisition from a learning theory framework, we see that a child who acquires language must acquire two events. First, he must acquire certain behaviors or *responses*, a differentiation of vocal output. These vocal or verbal responses correspond to various levels of language analysis within linguistics. One of these levels includes *phonemic* behavior (consonants, vowels); another level concerns *morphemic* behavior (words), another includes *syntactical* or *grammatical* behavior (arrangement of words in sentences).

When a child can produce only these verbal responses, his verbal output exists without meaning—it is not yet a language. One can observe such behavior in the form of imitation, or a parroting of words. Infants are said to pass through such a stage of imitating the utterances of others. Some psychotic and brain-damaged children come close to this in instances of echolalic speech, as when the child emits "How are you?" in response to the adult's question, " How are you?" In order for his vocal output to acquire meaning, the second event, his verbal behavior must occur within a certain stimulus context. Certain aspects of the child's environment must acquire certain stimulus functions which serve to regulate the occurrence of his verbal behavior. To accomplish this, a child must learn, first, what stimulus conditions, be they external or internal, give rise to verbal utterances and, second, what stimulus functions the utterance itself should possess—that is, what further verbal or nonverbal behavior, in himself or others, may be elicited by that utterance. In linguistics the term *semantics* most closely resembles our use of the term *stimulus functions*. This definition of language, of identifying the stimulus and response properties of language, is most closely associated with Bloomfield (1933) within the field of American linguistics; Skinner (1957) is its best-known contemporary spokesman.

Whether this view of language is correct or not, it is convenient for those who want to build language, for it relates one's efforts to some rather well-known principles of behavior change, those of discrimination learning. Perhaps it does not attribute enough novelty or uniqueness to language, since any response can be described in similar terms. A smile, for example, shares the same properties; it is a behavioral topography which acquires meaning to the extent that it acquires stimulus properties over other behaviors and comes to be controlled by stimulus events which surround it. Skinner has argued this repeatedly ("Verbal behavior is operant behavior."), and this argument is considered the most unique and radical in his position on language.

We repeatedly use the terms *stimulus* and *response* in describing our procedures, and also provide data which help to define these terms functionally and empirically. We do not state *a priori* how large or small a linguistic unit can be before it becomes or ceases to be a response. Are phonemes, morphemes, and sentences responses? Can they function as stimuli? We take the position that we can find out whether they are or not. We know that we have isolated a stimulus or a response when we can relate one in an orderly (lawful) manner to the other. It is likely that the study of language, more so than the study of any other behavior, will help us better to understand these terms at the human level. Such a functional-empirical definition of the terms stimulus and response is the defining feature of empirical behaviorism (Skinner, 1953).

Overview of Language Program

The goal of our research was to teach, to developmentally retarded (autistic) children who appeared to have little or no understanding or use of language, a language which approximated normal adult language. In working with nonlinguistic children, one soon realizes how handicapped they are without language. Instead of our being able to tell them what to do, they had to be moved physically through the desired behaviors. If one has to delay meeting their needs, there is no effective way to tell them to delay gratifications. When they became emotionally attached to us, there was no way to tell them when we left for the day that we would return the next day. If they wanted something, they had no easy way to tell us what they wanted. Language was to become a means to facilitate social interaction, to help the child to deal better with his feelings. There were other goals.

We were interested in learning how the child's language might regulate his own behavior. In the back of our minds we had some notion that if the child learned to talk, somehow a conception of himself would emerge, that he might become more defined as a person, that he might show more self-control.

Starting with the mute children, we first devised a program for them to acquire the first verbal utterances, simple morphemes such as "a" "b" and "mama". We did this by teaching the child to imitate sounds and words. Once this was done, we began to place those verbal responses in a more extended stimulus context, to label simple events around them. Simultaneously we taught them comprehension of those verbal utterances, to respond correctly to simple verbal requests from us. Gradually, we expanded the stimulus context controlling their speech, bringing it under increasingly abstract stimuli such as pronominal relations or temporal cues. At the same time, we expanded the child's verbal output to comprise grammar, the rules for combining words into sentences, and conversation with us.

To illustrate how some of these acquisitions may fit into a learning paradigm, let us consider our attempts to teach meaning. It so happens that these efforts roughly conform to two basic discriminations, as given in Table 1. In one discrimination the stimulus is verbal and the response is nonverbal; in the other discrimination the stimulus is nonverbal and the response is verbal.

Discrimination	Stimulus	Response
I. Receptive	Verbal	Non-Verbal
II. Expressive	Non-Verbal	Verbal

Although Table 1 presents two distinct discriminations, most discriminations are mixtures of both the verbal and the nonverbal. Rarely is the stimulus purely verbal without a nonverbal component; the response usually had both components too. For example, we may ask the child, "What's your name?" to answer this correctly, he has to discriminate both the verbal stimulus and his own person. When the stimulus is largely verbal and the response nonverbal, we label the discrimination as an instance of receptive language; we say that the child gives evidence of *comprehension*. When the response is verbal and the stimulus nonverbal, we may relate the interaction as an example of *expressive* language. When both the stimulus and the response are largely verbal, the interaction is specifically referred to as *conversation*. At times, the child may respond without any experimental stimuli immediately preceding his utterance ; we may refer to this as *spontaneous speech;* here the cues have to be inferred *post hoc*. Sometimes the child may provide himself with his own stimuli for his own subsequent behavior, as he does when he reads directions to himself, an exchange which many refer to as *self-control*. Sometimes he combines both verbal and nonverbal responses, both operants and respondents, as when he describes his behavior, "I am laughing," while laughing. We call such a child verbally *expressive*. One can think of many other parallels in everyday language. For purposes of building speech, however, it seemed helpful to consider that there were two kinds of discriminations, expressive and receptive.

At this point, we offer a brief outline of the more significant steps comprising the language program, before we describe it in detail. The language training became divided into several steps or programs, arranged in a hierarchy from "easy" to "difficult," such that we thought it would benefit a child to complete an early program before he was trained on a later one. We ended up with a large variety of programs, but we shall present only eight of them here, since these serve to illustrate the major steps in language training. There is some overlap between the various programs. For example, Program 2, the acquisition of labels for discrete events (object-terms, etc.) is a never-ending process that continues throughout the later programs, but we demanded some mastery of that program before the child was introduced to Program 3, which dealt with terms denoting the relationship between discrete events. What follows is an introduction of the major programs in our efforts to teach language.

Brief Outline of Language Programs

Program 1. Building verbal responses. The children who were mute and whose vocalizations were essentially limited to vowels and contained no discriminable words were first introduced to a program designed to teach them how to produce speech sounds or words. This became a program to facilitate phonological development, which we tried to accomplish by teaching the child to imitate the verbal utterances of others. We trained verbal imitative behavior in gradual steps, during which the child was reinforced for increasingly matching the verbal productions of others. Imitation, then, became a discrimination where the response (the child's vocalization) resembled its stimulus (the adult's vocalization). This training program gave the child the large range of complex verbal output he needed to begin the language training. At this level it existed as vocal output without meaning and resembled the echolalic child's verbal productions. We began to teach meaning in Program 2 (teaching labels). Programs 1 and 2 overlap in the sense that the child was introduced to Program 2 after he had acquired 10 recognizable words in Program 1.

Program 2. Labeling discrete events. The goal of this program was to teach the child the two basic language discriminations of certain discrete environmental events, such as everyday objects and activities. We wanted to give him a basic vocabulary, the nouns and verbs with which to answer questions like "What is it?" and "What are you doing?" As soon as he showed some mastery at this level, we made the vocabulary functional: Thus, he could tell us what he wanted (He had to ask or he was not fed), and we could begin to tell him what we wanted. We began to control him and he began to control us at a purely verbal level.

Program 3. Relationship between events, abstract terms. Once the child had acquired a labeling vocabulary of discrete events (objects and behaviors), we taught him the terms which described relationships between these events such as spatial relations (prepositions), temporal relations (time concepts), personal relations (pronouns), color, size, and shape. These concepts are called abstractions since the language which describes these events has come under the relatively narrow control of stimulus elements which may be shared by many objects. A child must know many of these abstract concepts in order to function at even the most minimal level in society.

Program 4. Conversation. As the training programs became
more and more elaborate, the interaction between the child and
his teacher increased in complexity, necessitating a more verbal
exchange between them, which we came to label "conversation
training." In general terms, this program was designed to teach
the child to ask and answer questions and to make comments
which would provide stimuli to which others could verbally
respond,—to exchange information, to "carry on a conversation."

Program 5. Giving and seeking information. What we tried to
accomplish in this program was to make language a short cut to
an enlarged experience. In other words, we wanted the child to
learn to seek information about his environment such as what we
were having for dinner or when school would be over. In the
laboratory, to untangle and build the basic mechanisms of information exchange, we placed the child in a three-person interaction. Person A asked the child a question. The child was taught
to seek the answer from Person B and return the information to
Person A. He also learned to discriminate between questions to
which he did or did not know the answer.

Program 6. Grammatical skills. Already during label training
and obviously during conversation training, the child's verbal responses required more than one-word answers, which necessitated
that we teach him certain basic rules on how to combine words
into sentences (how to make grammatical sentences). In the
grammatical skills program, we drilled him extensively on certain nuances of grammar, such as adjective-noun relationships,
subject-verb relationships, rules for transposing verbs from present to past, and so on.

Program 7. Recall. Once the child had mastered certain basic
temporal terms ("first," "last") and could transform verbs, we
moved toward one of the terminal goals of the project: teaching
the child to "enrich" the environment, his own or ours, by teaching him to recall his past. We began by teaching him to tell us
what he had just done some seconds before and then gradually
extended his descriptions to his past, such as what he had done
the previous day. We hoped that this would make his past more
real for him and that he could "rearrange" it to better suit himself. When a child verbalizes events which have occurred to him,
he also presents functional stimuli for persons who were not actually present when the events occurred. In a sense, others have
more "access" to him; it is an interpersonally enriching experi-

ence. At about this stage we also began programs for more extended and spontaneous descriptions of what he observed in his immediate environment.

Program 8. Spontanetity. Perhaps because of the highly-controlled nature of our language training and its reliance on experimental rather than "natural" reinforcers, many of the children showed verbal behavior that had come under very restricted environmental control. Too often his language occurred in response to the experimental situations, such as the teacher's questions, and very seldom otherwise. To help him become more free in his descriptions we became concerned with loosening this control, to shift the control to features of the environment not so specifically tied to the teacher's explicit requests for speech.

Informal training. With a base in the programs just discussed, using the same principles, we extended the language training on an informal basis into all or most aspects of the child's life. In working with children such as these, one has the opportunity, seemingly from the beginning, to teach logical thought and reasoning and to investigate questions of interpersonal motives and causation. We also taught the beginning of reading, arithmetic, and writing. We tried to relate these academic skills to the child's own everyday behavior, as when the teacher wrote down instructions for the child or the child himself wrote down his own experiences. Once the child got this far, we conducted "play school," as parents sometimes do with their own children before they leave for real school, except we had to be more systematic and careful.

In this book we describe these programs in detail. Suffice it to say that when we were teaching recall and description, the program extended in many directions. For example, we taught the child to use his imagination. We taught him games of "pretending"—to create stories enriched by comments about interpersonal motives and emotions. The rule of thumb was not to take for granted that the child could master a particular phase (for example, to move from recall to pretending or to begin asking questions about his environment) without being explicitly trained to do so. It also became apparent at this stage of the program that as language training and "therapeutics" began to merge, the behaviors and their controlling situation became very complex. Language became dynamically related to the child's experiences for example, in terms of what he wanted or did not want to recall. It is our contention that the mechanisms (learning steps) which brought him to this complex behavioral output were relatively simple, although very abstract. Let us look at them

Basic Training Principles

Discrimination Learning

Certain general concepts appear throughout the various training programs, which we will illustrate by first discussing discrimination learning. That part of learning theory which prescribes how behavior comes under the control of stimuli (whether externally or internally generated) is called *discrimination learning*. Discrimination learning underlies meaningful speech, and anyone who teaches language must understand this concept. In its most abstract sense, discrimination learning states that a behavior becomes controlled by certain features of its surrounding environment when its occurrence is reinforced in the presence of those features and is not reinforced in their absence. To illustrate from language teaching, we may expect that if we want the sight of the mother to reliably evoke the word "mother," then we have to reinforce the child for saying that word in the presence of the mother and withhold reinforcement if he says "mother " when she is not there. If we do so, the mother's presence should acquire discriminative stimulus (S^D) properties over the child's verbalization "mother." Of course, we want many other environmental and internal stimulus events to acquire such S^D control over his response "mother." For example, we may want a feeling of helplessness, the feeling of being protected and secure, of being loved, and numerous other events to evoke "mother." We want that word to become "meaningful" to him. Indeed, the range of events which may acquire S^D control over "mother" is truly amazing. I used to ski with some good friends who, as we approached the mountains and if it was sunny and warm, would look up at the white peaks and loudly proclaim "mother." Such highly personal meanings (such extensive idiosyncratic S^D control) do not prevent us from beginning to build meaning by teaching the child to say "mother" in the presence of his mother. And such meaning training is a problem in discrimination learning.

Let us just briefly sketch some of the procedures and problems associated with discrimination learning as we now know it. First, in order to reinforce the child for emitting "mother" in the presence of his mother (or some other appropriate stimulus), the child must first emit "mother" in her presence. It is unlikely that he will do so unless we help him. We may help him by *prompting* him to say "mother," and later remove that prompt. Discrimination learning, then, deals with problems such as discovering optimal strategies for presenting and removing prompts or, as others may say, for shifting stimulus control from one stimulus to another (from the *prompt* stimulus to the *training* stimulus). Exactly how one accomplishes such shifts in stimulus control is not fully understood. Discrimination learning deals also with procedures for finding appropriate contrasting (mother—not mother) stimuli in order to ease the discrimination task for the child. It may, for example, start out the training by maximizing the difference between mother (S^D) and nonmother ($S\Delta$) stimuli. Later in the training, one may want to diminish the difference between S^D and $S\Delta$ stimuli in an attempt to build more narrow discriminations. Discrimination learning has concerned itself with optimal procedures for facilitating the organism's responding to relevant stimuli, as in eliminating concurrent and irrelevant stimulus inputs, perhaps by randomizing the order or the position of the stimulus presentations. It deals with techniques for facilitating inhibition (nonresponding) to incorrect ($S\Delta$) stimuli and optimal reinforcement schedules during training. Discrimination learning also concerns itself with peculiarities in the sensory reception or attentional processing across organisms. Fortunately, much is known about discrimination learning from the animal literature. In order to understand the process of building a discrimination, it is useful to familiarize oneself with that literature through such chapters as those by Terrace (1966) and Blough (1966) and books such as those by Fellows (1968) and Trabasso and Bower (1968). These texts are somewhat advanced and may be best understood after an introduction to operant procedures such as that provided by Keller and Schoenfeld (1950), Bijou and Baer (1961), and Reynolds (1968).

Basic terms. Let us begin with some basic definitions. A *training stimulus* is a stimulus to which we train (help the child associate) a correct response. This stimulus can be either verbal or nonverbal. In most cases, the training stimuli we have used had both verbal and nonverbal components, so that when it is indicated in a manual that "*E* presents a training stimulus," this usually means that *E* presents some nonverbal stimulus such as an object, in conjunction with some verbal stimulus, such as the question, "What is it?"

Prompt and *prompt fading* are crucial parts of all training manuals. A prompt is a stimulus which cues the desired response prior to training or with minimal training. The prompt is presented in association with the training stimulus and assures that the child gives the desired response in the presence of the training stimulus. Prompting may be accomplished in a variety of ways—by E physically assisting the child to perform some response, or by E telling the child the correct answer, or by E serving as a model for the child's behavior. For example, if the desired response is nonverbal, like touching an object, E may pick up the child's hand and place it on the object. If S is imitating reliably, E may prompt the desired response by touching the object himself and then reinforce the child for imitating that act. If the response is verbal, E makes the response himself and reinforces the child for imitation.

After the response has been prompted for several trials and the response occurs reliably and with ease, the prompt is gradually eliminated so that only the training stimulus remains. This process of elimination is called "fading the prompt" and, as the term implies, it is usually a gradual process. Over a number of trials, E might move the child's hand only three-quarters of the way to the object, then half way, then simply touch the child's hand. If the prompt is verbal, E might gradually lower the decibel level of the prompt, then give only the initial sound, then voicelessly form the initial sound with his lips. After a number of trials E discontinues presenting the prompt entirely.

The rate of fading ought to be determined by the child. In some cases, very rapid, almost sudden, fading is appropriate and possible. In other cases, for certain children performing certain behaviors, fading is a slow process. The rule is to use the minimal number of prompts necessary to obtain the desired response. After 5 or 10 prompted trials, we presented the training stimulus once without the prompt. If the correct response was given, the prompt was, of course, no longer necessary and was removed altogether. If the correct response was not given, then E returned to prompting, using the smallest unit of the prompt necessary to elicit the correct response, and then proceeded to fade the prompt from that point, testing again without the prompt every 5 to 10 trials.

All is well so long as the prompt can be dropped entirely and the correct response occurs to the training stimulus alone. Often, however, a problem occurs in that the child's response won't "shift" from the prompt stimulus to the training stimulus. Technically, this is referred to as a problem in "shifting stimulus control." So far as we can see, little is known about how and why organisms do shift from one stimulus input to another; nor has the field of learning recognized how extensive and important this kind of learning is, particularly at the human level. When we encountered problems in shifting control, we tried to solve them in one or more of four ways: (1) to make the prompt stimulus "unreliable," so that it took effort for S to use it (while the training stimulus remained very salient and reliable); (2) to withhold reinforcement for responding to the prompt—in a sense, to make it difficult for S to eat or to avoid punishment unless he stopped responding to the prompt and began responding to the training stimulus; (3) to prompt within the same stimulus dimension as the training stimulus (to avoid cross-modality shifts); and (4) to drop the prompt altogether and "wait the child out." Schreibman's research (1975) has given some encouraging data on the ease with which psychotic children can shift stimulus control when such shifts occur within, rather than between, stimulus dimensions—that is, it is easier to shift control from a form stimulus to another form, rather than from a color stimulus to a form stimulus. Some day we will know how to use prompt techniques more efficiently.

A correct response occurs when the child makes the desired response to the training stimulus without prompts. This definition reads "to the training stimulus", and the complexities involved in this phrase are not immediately apparent. It is tempting to say that a correct response has been achieved when the child begins making the desired response without prompts upon the presentation of the first training stimulus in any training program, and indeed the term is often used in this manner. However, we learned repeatedly that we could not be certain that the child was responding to the relevant properties of the training stimulus merely because he emitted the desired response at the appropriate time (when E presented the object, asking "What is it?"). The child usually responded to some *other* aspect of the situation than the intended training stimulus. He may have been responding to the tone of E's voice or the way E looked at him. One can test what controls S's responding by deleting successive aspects of the total stimulus input. For example, if the training stimulus is an object like a cup and S has been taught to verbalize "cup" when E holds a cup in front of him, then it is always sober-

ing to hear *S* verbalize "cup" on the trial when *E* lifts his empty
hand. The response is as yet undiscriminated. Until a discrimination has been made, that is, until the child gives the desired response to the *relevant* stimulus and not to others, we have no
reason to believe he is responding to the training stimulus. In
this sense, a correct response is a discriminated response. The distinction is a subtle one, but the importance of discrimination
learning in almost every phase of language training is difficult to
overemphasize. We are more assured that *S* is emitting the correct
response when he can respond differentially to two training
stimuli, for example, a cup and a glass. In such a case, most or all
aspects of the training situation (such as *E's* movements) remain
constant between the two training stimuli; in order to be correct,
S has to learn to attend to (to *discriminate*) the relevant aspects of
the training stimulus. We tried to accomplish this through a procedure called "systematic stimulus presentation," which we will
describe, using steps from Expressive Discrimination Training.

Systematic stimulus presentation

Step 1. The process begins with the presentation of the first
training stimulus (TS1). *E* waits for *S* to attend to him visually,
or he may have pretrained *S* to respond to "Look at me". As soon
as *S* attends, *E* discretely and succinctly moves TS1 (for example,
an object such as a cup) into *S's* line of vision. *E* may or may not
ask, "What is it?" The question, "What is it?" may interfere with
S's response to more relevant parts of the training stimulus.
Through prompt (*E* says "cup") and fading *E* trains the correct R
(R1) to TS1.

Step 2. When *S* reliably gives R1 to TS1 (five out five presentations), a new training stimulus is introduced by *E* presenting a
second stimulus, TS2, such as an apple. It is almost a certainty
that the initial presentation of TS2 will evoke R1. The response is
not as yet discriminated. This being the case, *E* must correct *S*
and prompt the new desired response ("apple"). For example, *E*
accompanies *S's* mistake with "no," and a 5-second TO (Time
Out—meaning *E* looks away from *S*, ignoring him and being
unavailable). *E* then prompts the new R2 ("apple"), and the
prompt is then faded as in Step 1.

It is to be noted in the procedures we have just described that
S is allowed to make errors. There are procedures whereby one can
prevent or minimize errors, and these procedures may be impor-

tant to keep in mind. To illustrate: After we have trained R1 to
TS1 and we then present TS2, S will respond with R1, which is
an error, and E will in some way have to punish this (withdraw
his attention, tell S "no," and the like). Invariably, a succession of
errors will elicit tantrums from S or leave S unresponsive. To
avoid or minimize errors, we have experimented with procedures
whereby we try to teach S *not* to respond to TS2 when TS1 is
being trained. That is, while training R1 to TS1, we present TS2
in S's line of vision so quickly that S does not get a chance to
respond to it. Gradually we will present TS2 for longer and
longer duration and reinforce S for not responding with R1. We
are in essence teaching S to inhibit, withhold, or not to respond
with R1 to TS2. Exactly how this step will be worked in with
other steps remains to be seen. That is, once S has been taught *not*
to respond with R1 to TS2, it may be more difficult subsequently
to teach the correct R. But we do know that it is important to
keep S from making errors, since errors interfere so much with his
learning. Terrace (1966) has published extensively in this area of
"errorless" learning.

Step 3. When the child has mastered Step 2 (gives five out of
five correct R2's to TS2), E again presents TS1. When TS1 is
reintroduced, S will usually emit R2. During the early stages of
training, S gives an incorrect response each time E switches the
training stimulus. E should expect that as new stimuli are introduced, there will be a certain amount of loss in previously acquired responses. (We present some data on this later.) For example, when TS1 is reintroduced it will take the child fewer trials to
regain R1. In later stages of training, when one begins to work
with a third or fourth training stimulus, loss again occurs in the
previously mastered discriminations; however, the degree of loss
typically decreases as additional responses are acquired. This "savings over tasks" or "learning to learn" has been frequently reported in the learning literature in a wide variety of situations.

Step 4. Once TS1 again reliably evokes R1, E again presents
TS2, recovers R2, moves back to TS1, and so on. E now has to
become concerned about the *order* or sequence in which he presents stimuli. There are problems here which we have not
adequately solved, but we mention them so that the reader can
become aware of the problems involved and determine for a particular child how he will run a stimulus sequence.

Suppose S has become dependent upon the prompt. If E is not
careful, he may have taught him such dependency. For example,

E presents TS1, *S* gives R2, *E* then prompts R1, *S* now gives R1, *and E reinforces*. In such a procedure *S* is reinforced for responding to the prompt and may never have to attend to the relevant (important) stimuli (TS1 and TS2). In a general sense, *E* is so helpful that *S* never has to learn anything new. In a technical sense, TS1 does not acquire any S^D (discriminative stimulus) functions. To remedy this, *E* may simply have to wait for *S* to correct himself without prompts. This helps to minimize "prompt dependency", since the prompt does not always precede the correct R. This seems simple enough, but *S* may rapidly learn that if the first response he gives is unreinforced, he need only switch to the other response to gain reinforcement. That is, *E* presents TS1; *S* gives R2; *E* does not reinforce and does not prompt; *S* then gives R1 and is reinforced. *S* may, in a situation like this, learn to respond to the absence of reinforcement for one response with another response. Technically, the withholding of reinforcement for R2 becomes an S^D for R1. To prevent *S* from making this error, *E* may have to withhold reinforcement for the correct response, if it has been preceded by an incorrect response. For example, *E* must present TS1 twice in a row and *S* must respond correctly twice in a row before *E* reinforces. This step leads to other problems, because now *E* must guard against inadvertently reinforcing *S* for perseverating (repeating the same response). There are several ways in which *E* can build perseveration responding, and there are ways to avoid it. One way to minimize perseveration is to reinforce a correct R, if that R occurs on the first presentation of a stimulus in a series. For example, reinforce R2 if R1 was correct on the preceding trial. In general, it is wise to keep the trials as heterogeneous as possible, so as to maximize the discrimination of (attention to) the training stimuli. A similar problem occurs if *S* is allowed to discriminate a certain "order" of stimuli. For example, if TS1 and TS2 are systematically alternated (TS1, TS2, TS1, TS2, TS1, TS2), *S* may learn that alternating Rs bring reinforcement. Similarly, if *E* presents a particular stimulus more than once in a row (TS1, TS1, TS1, TS2, TS2, TS2), *S* may learn that by merely repeating a correct R at the next trial he is likely to be reinforced (a reinforced R becomes discriminative through its own recurrence). That is, *E* is teaching *S* to perseverate. Finally, *E* will minimize perseveration and other order effects by running a series of trials where the training stimuli are presented in a nonsystematic order. We refer to this as a "nonsystematic stimulus rotation." Non systematic rotation means that we avoid presenting the same training stimulus on more than two consecutive trials to avoid perseverative responding. We also avoided any specifiable order or pattern of presentation (such as TS1, TS2, TS1, TS2) to prevent a specific order to acquire S^D control. Again, our main concern is to insure that the child will be attending to the training stimulus for the appropriate response.

Other problems will arise, and the safest rule to apply is this: Whatever change in the environment is systematically present at the time a response is reinforced acquires S^D control over that response. Another safe rule to apply is this: If S can make the discrimination (give E the desired response) without attending to the cues which E *intends* for him to attend to, then S will do so. Some cues are more salient for some children than other cues; rarely are cues equally weighted for all children. The important message is that when E does reinforce, then S is learning, and one has to take great care not to reinforce the wrong discriminations. In this regard it is also important to point out that the problems we have enumerated here in the teaching of developmentally retarded autistic children are not unique to such children. Although much needs to be known about discrimination learning in young normal children or in retarded children, it is likely that one will encounter similar problems. Certainly, animal training literature abounds with examples of such problems (cf. Blough, 1966).

Let us return to Step 4. Once S has mastered that step, that is, when he can reliably on 10 successive trials give R1 and R2 to the first presentation of S1 and S2, given that S1 and S2 are randomly intermixed, then we can say for the first time that the child is making the correct response.

At this juncture a word should be said about selection of training stimuli. Both the stimuli themselves and the desired responses should be maximally different to aid in the discrimination process. It seems easier for the child to discriminate between objects that look different and words that sound different than between those that are similar. For example, the child will be able to discriminate more easily between the objects milk and bacon than between milk and juice (both of which generally come in glasses). It will be easier for S to learn the labels for "cup" and "ball" than "cup" and "car". Later in training, minimal differences may become important to sharpen S's discrimination. For example, one may want to expose S to numerous examples of an object in order to train or test generalization. But at first, the best results seem to be obtained with maximal differences among the training stimuli.

Most of the programs we present are generally concerned with expressive speech training because our interest focused on teaching the child expressive (productive) language. However, we began training on receptive speech (the adult would speak, the child would point) as a "pretraining" step to develop the child's own speech, because we felt that it would be easier for him to speak once he had learned to attend to many of the cues which would be relevant in acquiring expressive speech. Many consider it advantageous that receptive speech precede productive speech, but the whole problem of the interaction between receptive and productive speech is not known. Guess and Baer (1973) recently reviewed the empirical research in this area and present one of their own studies which failed to show interaction between the two forms of speech. According to their review, it is apparent that receptive speech may, under certain circumstances, facilitate productive speech, but it is by no means certain when such facilitating will occur.

Prompting and Shaping Behavior

So far, we have talked almost exclusively about discrimination learning—the kind of learning that relates behavior to an appropriate stimulus context. It will be more difficult to describe another kind of learning—how behavior itself is acquired. In terms of the language program, we will need procedures whereby a mute child will be taught to express verbal responses, that is, how to make words and sentences. In order to begin such training, we first need to know how to elicit the basic units of speech, the morphemes.

Let us illustrate the problems by an example from training. Suppose E is faced with a child who is mute, who never has uttered a word, as far as anyone can ascertain. The child may occasionally emit certain vowels, but his spontaneous rate of these productions may be so low that it is possible for him to be completely nonvocal in any one training session. E wants S to vocalize, because he can then reinforce these vocalizations and thereby increase their rate. Eventually, the child will undergo a shaping program which may turn these sound productions into more recognizable utterances, such as words.

E may now try to *prompt* *S* to help *S* vocalize, to break the silence. Essentially, *E* attempts to identify the unconditioned stimulus that elicits *S*'s vocalizations as respondent behaviors. Perhaps all operant behavior is initially respondent, vocal or otherwise. Certain respondents seem easily elicited—startle reflexes, rage, or the like. But little is known about how to elicit vocal behavior. Most likely, the unconditioned stimulus for vocal behavior is not a discrete event, as seems to be the case for startling or salivating. It seems instead to involve a certain *ordering* of many discrete stimuli. That is, a child must be in a good mood, rested, and not too hungry. *E* may reach over and stroke his stomach or tickle him gently under the arm, or he may feed him some small bites of food which increases the likelihood that *S* will vocalize. Sometimes *E* may try to elicit or induce the vocalizations by having the child jump, flap his arms, or engage in some other vigorous physical exercise. Or *E* may manually elicit a vocalization by closing the child's lips and suddenly letting the child release air. Once the first vocalization has occurred, *E* reinforces immediately to raise its rate. When he does reinforce, he must be careful to guard against the possibility that the reinforcing stimuli do not themselves inhibit or otherwise block further vocalization, as when the child is startled. Ideally, the reinforcing stimuli should themselves elicit more vocalization, which they seemingly do when a child is reinforced with food. The "spacing" of the trials probably is important, as the child appears to have a "rhythm" that will produce more vocalizations. Additionally, some vocalizations seem easier to control through reinforcement than others, but we do not know exactly which ones. *E* will probably also observe that the vocalization that becomes an operant (has come under reinforcement control) is slightly different in its topography than when it was a respondent, before it was reinforced.

In any case, little is known about how to elicit vocal behavior, and we do not know how or why such elicited vocal (respondent) behavior becomes operant through reinforcement. Segal (1972) has written on the problems of identifying the elementary units of operant behavior in general, and the reader may find her paper helpful. She suggests that operants initially exist as respondents. She also discusses certain broad variables that one can manipulate to elicit respondent behavior, such as the manipulation of emotional stimuli, deprivation, and induction by reinforcement. In recent times, learning theorists like Miller (1971) have also demonstrated reinforcement control over respondent behavior. But in general, this literature does not seem to contain a great deal of concrete information on the process whereby a respondent becomes an operant.

Once E was able to prompt a variety of sounds from the child and has increased the occurrence of these sounds through reinforcement, then the actual shaping of these sounds into words was accomplished through a training program in vocal imitation (Program 1). In that program, children were taught how to make words and sentences by first being taught to imitate the vocal behavior of attending adults. For the time being, let us say that the way in which we bring the first sounds from the child is poorly understood, and only a person who is familiar with a child (who knows how to play with him and otherwise care for him) will be able to elicit a full range of initial sounds.

Let us briefly describe one additional methodological problem before we go on. Once the child can produce a set of recognizable words and these words are brought into particular stimulus contexts, problems may occur. S may become almost inaudible, or he may begin to give combinations of two or more response alternatives—he may combine R1 (apple) and R2 (cup) into something like "cupapple" or "appcup." Sometimes (perhaps always) such a problem comes about because of E's eagerness to reinforce the child, which results in reinforcing approximations of the desired responses and may lead to a situation in which a response drifts away from criterion. E's job here is not much easier than the child's. If E is too liberal in his reinforcement, the child's responses remain undifferentiated and obscure. On the other hand, if E is too strict, the child's behavior will extinguish. Part of E's job is to keep the child behaviorally receptive. It is apparent that we do not know the exact procedure for shaping behavior, but we hope we know enough to begin the effort.

In the course of asking questions and prompting, special procedures are needed for dealing with echolalic children, since they repeat not only a verbal prompt but also the questions or comments that E makes to them. That is, echolalic children already have a verbal topography, which is often very extensive, but it is under socially inappropriate stimulus control. We have therefore developed a procedure for "breaking echolalia." In that program we teach the child to discriminate when it is appropriate and when it is not appropriate to echo. In general, we have attempted to "fade in" those parts of E's statement that we did not intend for imitation ("What is this?" is presented at a relatively low decibel level) and then "punish" whatever echolalia occurred at that time. At the same time we present the prompt ("cup") so loudly and quickly that it may block the echolalic repetition of the question, and then, of course, we reinforce S's repetition of the prompt. Technically speaking, we are teaching the child, through differentiated reinforcement, when it is appropriate to echo. The language film we produced (Lovaas, 1969) provides a good example of teaching the child to inhibit his echolalia. Teaching the child not to echo is an ongoing program, but in the later stages of training it requres less effort. As a child began to understand language, he was merely told, "Don't be echolalic."

In this section we have attempted to introduce some of the basic terms and operations that we employed in our efforts to build language. These terms and procedures will be further defined as we discuss the various language programs in more detail. Let us now describe the children to whom we taught language, so that the extent of their language deficit may be better understood.

The Children

Most of our research has dealt exclusively with those children who were sufficiently retarded in emotional, social, and intellectual development to be diagnosed as autistic or autistic with childhood schizophrenia. All of the children had been so diagnosed by at least one other agency not associated with this project. Also, the majority of the children had more than one diagnosis, usually being referred to as retarded and brain damaged, and had been rejected from one or more schools for the emotionally ill or retarded because their teachers could not control them and their behavior was so bizarre that it was disruptive. Clinically speaking, with three or four exceptions, they seemed void of anxiety. None had any awareness that something was wrong with him. We selected the most undeveloped of the children so as to virtually rule out the possibility that the children knew any language before we taught them.

Generally, the children we taught can be described as show-

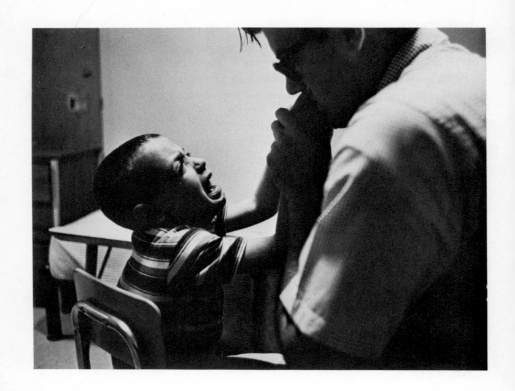

Picture A-1. Ricky, during an outburst of tears, screams and hits out at himself and the environment. Such tantrum-like behavior is typical during the early sessions and often seems triggered by the new demands which the teaching situation places on the child. There is a variety of ways in which one might try to treat such a tantrum. Sometimes it works to comfort a child; at other times such comfort may just serve to increase the tantrum. One may try to "work through" the tantrum, that is paying little, if any, attention to it and not allow it to disrupt the teaching situation. If this fails, one may try some procedures such as extinction or time-out where the therapist looks away from the child or places the child in isolation. Note that if the child's tantrum is an attempt to escape from the situation, then placing the child in time-out would merely worsen it. If everything else fails one may try aversive control, such as saying a loud "no" or one may have to give the child a slap on the bottom contingent on the tantrum. Note that if comforting the child did not help the first year, it may help the second year.

Picture A-2 Pam, self-stimulating, regarding her hand, and swishing saliva in her mouth. Such self-stimulation takes several forms, as in rocking, spinning, gazing, twirling, "sifting" sand, "inspecting" floating lint, etc. We try to suppress such behavior as much as possible, since the children appear inattentive during self-stimulation. On the other hand, we may let the children self-stimulate for a short period (3 seconds) as a reinforcer for being correct on the teaching tasks.

ing the following characteristics, all of which define autism: (1) the *language deficiency* was a salient feature. Thus *expressive* speech was missing or minimal. Half of the 20 children we trained were mute, that is, they produced no recognizable words. The other half were echolalic, which meant that they echoed the speech of others, either immediately or after a delay, giving the impression of nonrelated inappropriate speech. On occasion, some of the echolalic children would express a request (with the pronouns reversed) to an attending adult under the appropriate circumstances, such as "You want to get down?" if held in the adult's lap against his will or "You want some candy?" if there was candy available. Some autistic children have been known to use relatively elaborate language, but these were excluded from our study, since we were concerned with building spoken language in children who had little, if any, such behavior. In all the children *receptive speech* was missing or minimal. Some of the children would obey simple commands, such as shutting the door when asked to "Shut the door." It is not likely, however, that they understood this command, since they would also shut the door if one exclaimed "There's a window and a door." At best, they responded in a relatively undifferentiated way to language, using speech as a "go" signal. They could not identify (point to) their body parts or common objects around them if they were asked to do so. None of the children gave evidence of understanding abstract speech, such as prepositions, pronouns, and time.

In addition to this language deficiency, the children can be described as showing (2) *apparent sensory deficit,* which refers to the fact that most of the parents have described their children on the Rimland Checklist (Rimland Diagnostic Checklist for Behavior-Disturbed Children, Rimland, 1964) as (a) at one time appearing to be deaf and (b) looking through or walking through things as if they were not there. (3) *Severe affect isolation* was predominant, meaning that the parents described the children on the Rimland Checklist as (a) failing to reach out to be picked up when approached by people, (b) looking at or walking through people as if they weren't there, (c) appearing so distant that no one could reach them, (d) indifferent to being liked, and (e) not affectionate. (4) a high rate of *self-stimulatory behavior,* which refers to behavior that appeared only to provide the children with proprioceptive feedback (rocking, spinning, twirling, flapping, or gazing). (5) There was also an *absence of* or *minimal presence of social and self-help behaviors*—most of the children could not dress themselves, most were unaware of common dangers (they would walk out into busy streets), most could not wash themselves or comb their hair, some were not toilet-trained. (6) Some of these children were *self-destructive* or *self-mutilatory*. All had severe aggressive tantrum-like outbursts, scratching and biting attending adults when forced to comply with even minimal rules for social conduct. These are severe handicaps, indeed, but they do provide the investigator with the advantage of starting his work with as close to a *tabula rasa* as one can obtain.

The other problems these children display may be the cause of their language deficiency or its effect, or all may be caused by some third factor. Such an enumeration of "symptoms" as we have described serves to identify a certain number of children, but the behavioral grouping is probably quite arbitrary. For example, the absence of language, instead of being listed as a separate "symptom," could well be subsumed under the category of "minimal social behaviors," and all the behaviors may well be a consequence of "apparent sensory deficit." The relationships are not understood.

One has to make some changes in these children's behavior before one begins to teach them language, or it is unlikely that they will learn. It seems pointless to try to teach language to a child who is banging his head against the wall in self-mutilation or threatening to bite his teacher. So, before language learning could begin, we decided to remove these interfering behaviors by either presenting time out (TO) or other aversive stimulation contingent upon the behavior. It is surprising how quickly one can gain control over such interfering behavior (cf. Lovaas and Simmons, 1969).

One also has to suppress some of the self-stimulatory behavior (the rocking, spinning, twirling) before one will be able to go very far in the teaching of many of these children. The data we do have suggest that the self-stimulatory behavior delays or reduces the child's responses to auditory stimuli (Lovaas *et al.*, 1971) and does not allow for discrimination learning to occur (Koegel and Covert, 1972). Again, it was relatively easy to suppress self-stimulatory behavior by the use of contingent disapproval or other aversive stimuli.

The third, and probably the major, problem in dealing with autistic children centers on their deficient motivational structure. Without adequate reinforcers, we would lack a basic tool needed to effect the changes we hope for. There are two solutions to such a problem, but only one is available at this time. The one available to us presently entails the construction of an "artificial" or experimental motivational structure based on the use of food and physically aversive stimuli as reinforcers. This is a makeshift solution, with a number of drawbacks. Typically, the behavior one has built using an artificial reinforcer is extinguished when that reinforcer is removed. Such extinction often occurs when the child leaves the teaching environment. In order to prevent discrimination and to help him maintain the gains he has made, we must take pains to equalize treatment and nontreatment environments (Lovaas et al., 1971). Artificial reinforcers are obviously inadequate when compared to the immediacy, power, and availability of the natural daily-life reinforcers that probably serve to build the comprehension and the flexible speech of normal children. A normal child's speech can effect profound changes in his social and physical environment. He can make lights go on and off, he can control his playmates, he can make his parents laugh or weep. If such effects lost their reinforcing function for him, he might cease talking. One can say that the normal child speaks because he wants to, which is very much like saying that he speaks because he has to. We made sure that the psychotic children also had to talk in order to get along.

It is probably impossible to build flexible, highly articulated, "fluent" speech using food and other artificial reinforcement. Yet the alternative, trying to normalize the motivational structure prior to building speech, is simply not realistically available. Despite claims to the contrary (cf the large psychoanalytic literature on treating autism), no one has provided convincing evidence or a replicable method or data that would show us how to accomplish such an end.

There is one major advantage associated with this deficient motivational structure. In normal children, language is acquired so quickly and in so many circumstances that one does not get the opportunity to find out what is going on. Developmentally retarded, autistic children, on the other hand, develop very slowly. They are in a sense, like the bubble chamber in physics, giving us some measure of control over the process, slowing it down sufficiently to study the phenomenon of acquiring language in some detail. Normal child development in normal environments does not allow that.

For the purpose of contributing to a general theory of language development, we have assumed that the developmentally retarded, autistic child's failure to acquire language is based on his deficient motivational structure. If we can show that by "repairing" that structure the autistic child acquires language, then our assumption is supported. But one may also be alert to other peculiarities of the autistic child which would render him so unique that his language data would have limited generality. One can raise questions about organic damage and permanently altered ways of responding. For example, one may argue that there has been damage to a "language center," which has prevented "ordinary" language learning to occur. Or possibly, their failure to develop language is a function of certain sensory problems which distort incoming stimuli. Certainly, a limited deviation on the stimulus input side could well shut down the rest of the system, even if the rest were intact, and many other kinds of damage could be present. In fact, in initiating our venture, we found it best to ignore what others had said about organic damage and language acquisition. The prognoses one gathers from these arguments are so pessimistic that one would be unlikely even to start a language program if one attended to them.

References

Bijou, S. W., & Baer, D. M. *Child development. Vol. 1. A systematic and empirical theory.* New York: Appleton-Century-Crofts, 1961.

Bloomfield, L. *Language.* New York: Holt, 1933.

Blough, D. S. The study of animal sensory processes by operant methods. In W. K. Honig (Ed.), *Operant behavior: Areas of research and application.* New York: Appleton-Century-Crofts, 1966.

Fellows, B. J. *The discrimination process and development.* New York: Pergamon Press, 1968.

Guess, D, & Baer, D. M. An analysis of individual differences in generalization between receptive and productive language in retarded children. *Journal of Applied Behavior Analysis,* 1973, 6, 311-329.

Keller, F. S., & Schoenfeld, W. N. *Principles of psychology: A systematic text in the science of behavior.* New York: Irvington Publishers, 1950.

Koegel, R., & Covert, A.The relationship of self-stimulation to learning in autistic children. *Journal of Applied Behavior Analysis,* 1972, 5 (4), 381-389.

Lovaas, O.I. *Behavior modification: Teaching language to psychotic children,* instructional film, 45 min., 16mm.-sound, Appleton-Century-Crofts, New York, 1969.

Lovaas, O. I., Litrownik, A., & Mann, R. Response latencies to auditory stimuli in autistic children engaged in self-stimulatory behavior. *Behavior Research and Therapy,* 1971, *9,* 39-49.

Lovaas, O. I., Schreibman, L., Koegel, R., & Rehm, R. Selective responding by autistic children to multiple sensory input. *Journal of Abnormal Psychology,* 1971, *77* (3), 211-222.

Lovaas, O.I., & Simmons, J.Q. Manipulation of self-destruction in three retarded children. *Journal of Applied Behavior Analysis,* 1969, *2,* 143-157.

Miller, N. E. Instrumental learning of visceral responses. In N. E. Miller (Ed.), *Selected papers.* New York: Aldine & Atherton, 1971.

Reynolds, G. S. *A primer of operant conditioning.* Glenview, Ill.: Scott, Foresman & Co., 1968.

Rimland, B. *Infantile autism.* New York: Century-Crofts, 1964.

Schreibman, L. Within-stimulus versus extra-stimulus prompting procedures on discrimination learning with autistic children. *Journal of Applied Behavioral Analysis,* 1975, in press.

Segal, E. F. Induction and the provenance of operants. In R. M. Gilbert & J. R. Millenson (Eds.), *Reinforcement: Behavioral analysis.* New York: Academic Press, 1972.

Skinner, B. F. *Science and human behavior.* New York: Macmillan, 1953.

Skinner, B. F. *Verbal behavior.* New York: Appleton- Century-Crofts, 1957.

Terrace, H. S. Stimulus control. In W. K. Honig (Ed.), *Operant behavior: Areas of research and application.* New York: Appleton-Century-Crofts, 1966.

Trabasso, T., & Bower, G. H. *Attention in learning.* New York: John Wiley and Sons, Inc., 1968.

Chapter II
BUILDING THE FIRST WORDS AND LABELS

Let us now turn to the specific programs which illustrate our procedures. They are not exhaustive, nor are they presented in detail here. The reader who wishes to examine these training programs further can turn to the various training manuals in Chapter 6. In order to avoid discontinuity between these programs and the data relevant to each, data and program will be presented together. The data are illustrative, since it was both impossible and unnecessary to record all the language on all the children at all times. We employed the following rules for data collection.

First, we kept detailed data on a limited number of children (two to six Ss) throughout a particular program and then observed the rest of the children more informally on the same program. If a child deviated, we resumed detailed data recording.

Second, to help assess generality across Ss we took data from

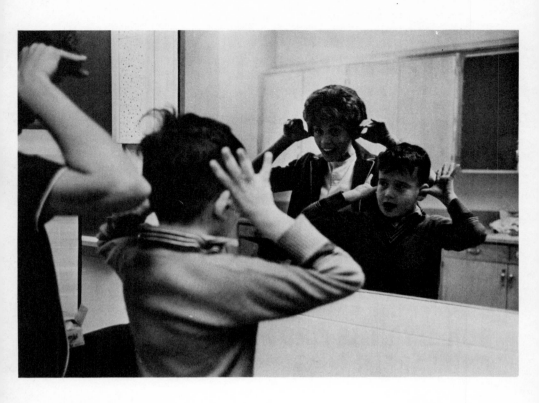

Picture B. One of the first tasks we try to teach the child is to imitate our nonverbal behavior. Nonverbal imitation may start out with imitation of simple behaviors such as raising arms upwards, followed by placing hand on the table, followed by patting head, etc. This is followed by behaviors which are more subtle to discriminate, such as facial expression which we see Billy practicing in this picture. We begin teaching the child nonverbal imitation since it is easier than verbal imitation. Once the child has made a beginning in nonverbal imitation, we try to gain verbal control over these behaviors and use them as a basis for teaching "following commands" (such as "raise your hands," "touch the table," etc.). This marks the first steps in receptive language training.

Picture C. Once the child has some control over his tantrums and self-stimulatory behavior, can sit in a chair and look at the therapists's face, and has made some progress in nonverbal imitation and receptive language, we begin verbal imitation. This particular scene shows Chuckie and his therapist practicing the vowel "oh," which has a distinct visual component also. We have felt that sounds which have distinct visual components (such as "oh," "a," "m," "p") help the child acquire verbal imitation. But there may be a problem in this use of such extra visual cues, since the child may become overly reliant on the visual cues and fail to attend to the verbal ones.

different children for the different programs. If Child A, B, and C
were recorded for Program 1, we tried to take data on Child D,
E, and F for Program 2.

Third, when the child's speech became particularly complex,
we recorded it verbatim.

Fourth, we tried to use larger Ns for the more advanced programs, since the advanced programs subsumed the introductory

Program 1: Building a Verbal Topography

Casual observation suggests that normal children acquire
words by hearing speech, that is, children learn to speak by imitation. The mute autistic children with whom we worked were
not imitative. The establishment of imitation in these children
appeared to be the most beneficial and practical starting point for
building speech. The first step in creating speech, then, was to
establish conditions in which imitation of vocal sounds would be
learned.

The method that we eventually found most feasible for establishing verbal imitation involved a discrimination training procedure. The child was rewarded only if his vocalization very
closely matched the adult's vocalization—that is, if it was imitative. Such verbal imitations were taught through the development of a series of increasingly fine discriminations.

During the training sessions the child and the adult sat facing
each other, their heads about 30 centimeters apart. The adult
physically prevented the child from leaving the training situation
by holding the child's legs between his own legs. Rewards in the
form of a single spoonful of the child's meal were delivered immediately after correct responses. Punishment (spanking, shouting by the adult) was delivered for inattentive, self-destructive,
and tantrum-like behavior which interfered with the training,
and most of these behaviors were thereby suppressed within one
week. Incorrect vocal behavior was never punished.

Four distinct steps were required to establish verbal imitation. In Step 1, we reinforced the child for every vocalization he
made, to raise the frequency of his vocal behavior. In order for us
to get vocalizations to reinforce, we tried to prompt or elicit them
in the manner we described in the section on "Prompting and
Shaping Behavior." That is, the child was kept content and in
good spirits and was frequently fondled, stroked, and tickled.
During Step 1 the child was also rewarded for visually fixating on

the adult's mouth. When the child reached a level of about one verbal response every five seconds without being fondled or otherwise manipulated and was visually fixating on the adult's mouth more than 50 percent of the time, Step 2 of training was introduced.

Step 2 marked our initial attempt to bring the child's verbal behavior under our verbal control, so that our speech would ultimately become discriminative for speech in the child. Mastery of this second step involved acquisition of a temporal discrimination by the child. The adult emitted a vocal response—for example, "baby"—about once every ten seconds. He would then passively wait for the child to vocalize, and if the child vocalized within five seconds after the adult's vocalization, he was reinforced. However, any kind of vocal response of the child would be rewarded in that time interval; he did not have to match the adult's speech. Vocalizations outside that five-second time interval were not reinforced. The next step, Step 3, was introduced when the frequency of the child's vocal responses within the five-second interval was three times what it had been initially.

Step 3 was structurally similar to the preceding step, but it included the additional requirement that the child actually match the adult's vocalization before receiving the reward. In this, and in following steps, the adult selected the verbalization to be placed in imitative training from a pool of possible verbalizations that had met one or more of the following criteria. First, we selected vocal behaviors that could be prompted; that is, vocal behaviors that could be elicited by a cue prior to any experimental training, such as by manually moving the child through the behavior. An example of training with the use of a prompt is afforded in teaching the sound "m." The training would proceed in three stages: (1) The adult emitted "m" and simultaneously prompted the child to emit "m" by holding the child's lips closed with his fingers and quickly removing them when the child vocalized. (2) The prompt would be gradually faded by the adult's moving his fingers away from the child's mouth, to his cheek, and finally gently touching the child's jaw. (3) The adult emitted the vocalization "m" only, withholding all prompts. The rate of fading was determined by the child; the sooner the child's verbal behavior came under control of the adult's without the use of the prompt, the better. The second criterion for selection of words or sounds in the early stages of training centered on their concomitant visual components (which we exaggerated when we pronounced them), such as those of the labial consonant "m" and of open-mouthed vowels like "a." We selected such sounds because we thought that the children could discriminate words with visual components more easily than those with only auditory components (the guttural consonants "k" and "g" proved extremely difficult to train and, like "l" and "s," were mastered later than other sounds). Third, we selected for training sounds that the child emitted most frequently in Step 1.

Step 4 was a recycling of Step 3, with the addition of a new sound. We selected a sound that was very different from those presented in Step 3 so that the child could discriminate between the new and old sounds more easily. To make certain that the child was in fact imitating and not attending to irrelevant aspects of the situation, we resorted to the discrimination training procedures we have described. That is, we systematically rotated the stimuli of Steps 3 and 4 and observed the other precautions we discussed in the section on "Basic Training Principles" to help the child to discriminate the particular sounds involved. There had been no requirement placed upon the child in Step 3 to discriminate specific aspects such as vowels, consonants, and order of the adult's speech; a child might master Step 3 without attending to the specific properties of the adult's speech. Step 4 is therefore a most difficult step to master. All steps beyond Step 4 consisted of replications of Step 3, but new sounds, words, and phrases were used. Each new introduction of sounds and words required increasingly fine discrimination by the child and hence provided evidence that he was in fact matching the adult's speech. In each new step, the previously mastered words and sounds were rehearsed on a randomized ratio of one mastered sound to every three new ones. A particular step or sound was introduced when the child had mastered the previous steps by making ten consecutively correct replications of the adult's utterances.

One hour of each day's training was tape-recorded. Two independent observers scored the child's correct vocal responses from these sessions. A correct response was defined as a recognizable reproduction of the adult's utterance. The observers showed better than 90 percent agreement. When the child's correct responses are plotted against days of training and the resulting function is positively accelerated, it can then be said that the child has learned to imitate.

The results of the first 26 days of imitation training on Billy and Chuck, both five years old and mute, are given in Figure 1.

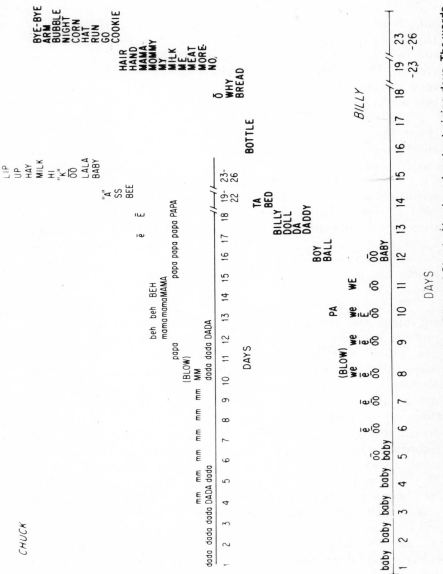

Figure 1. Acquisition of verbal imitation for Billy and Chuck. Abscissa denotes training days. The words and sounds are printed in lower-case letters on the days they were introduced and trained, and in capital letters on the days they were mastered.

Billy and Chuck were the first two children given the imitation training program. They were trained six days a week, seven hours a day, with a 15-minute rest period accompanying each hour of training. The abscissa denotes training days. The words and sounds are printed in lower-case letters on the days they were introduced and in capital letters on the days they were mastered. It can be seen that as training progressed, the rate of mastery increased. During the first two weeks of the program, the children took several days to learn a single word; whereas during the last two weeks, they would master several words in a single day.

The rate of acquisition varies enormously among the children. The performance of Chuck and Billy seems "average" for the 10 mute children we have worked with. We have seen some children who acquired in three days of training what Billy and Chuck mastered after 26 days. One can probably observe similar acquisitions with much less training. In other words, it is possible that there is little, if any, productive learning beyond two or three one-hour sessions spaced throughout the day. We do not know the optimal duration of training sessions or optimal rest between the sessions. There are times that we have done well with much less than the daily seven-hour regimen that Billy and Chuck underwent.

The errors which the child makes as new imitations (stimuli) are introduced may give some cue as to the underlying learning process. We recorded the amount of loss in an imitative sound as new sounds were introduced for Jose (a five-year-old initially mute child). He received two training sessions a day that lasted 50 minutes each. These sessions are plotted on the abscissa in Figure 2. The ordinate gives the percentage of correct responses (number of correct responses over the number of stimulus presentations—S^Ds per trial—$\times$ 100). As can be seen, we start recording when "ah" was laying at 100 percent correct reproductions. As soon as the second sound ("mm") is introduced (Session 3), the reproduction of "ah" deteriorates. Notice again the loss in "ah" when the third discrimination ("eh") is demanded in the seventeenth session. As each new sound is acquired, there is less and less loss in the previously mastered ones. The behavior gets "tougher" with training. We infer from these data that the child is learning to discriminate relevant features in the verbal behavior of the teacher.

After the child has been taught to imitate some of the adult's vocalizations, he becomes somewhat like the echolalic child; he

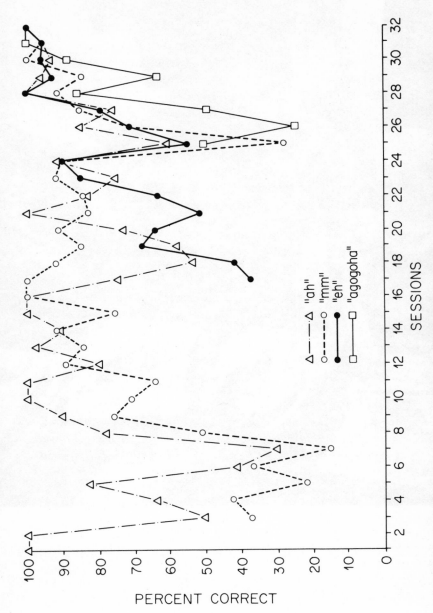

Figure 2. Errors during imitation training. The figure shows loss in amount of correct responding (on the ordinate) as new sounds ("mm" in Session 16, "eh" in Session 2, and "agogoha" in Session 27) are introduced.

Picture D. In this picture Corey and Doug are beginning some early pre-academic tasks, such as matching common objects, colors, shapes, etc. We include numerous tasks of this nature in an attempt to help the child to discriminate early concepts. Note that there is a large number of student-therapists present who meet with the child and parents on a weekly basis to review what the child has learned the preceding week, to spot potential errors in each others' teaching, and to formulate programs for the subsequent week.

has a repertoire of words, but he does not know what they mean. We begin this training in "meaning training" (semantics) during Program 2.

Program 2: Labeling Discrete Events

Discriminating environmental features. The goal of this program was to teach the child the names of common objects or events around him and the names of certain common activities and behaviors. We wanted to give him a basic vocabulary, the nouns and the verbs which answer questions such as "What is it?" and "What are you doing?" and to express wants such as "cookie," "water," and "out." We began with the names of objects (reinforcers) which seemed important to the child, such as foods. The child looked at these things and wanted them, and we took advantage of his attentiveness.

This program will basically describe a Type 2 discrimination procedure, but it is a classic example of a case where Discrimination 1 may be helpful as a "pre-training" procedure. The details of the program are presented in Manual A in Chapter 6. The training steps in Program 2 are similar to those in Program 1. Essentially, *E* begins the training by having the child point to or touch the objects he will later be required to label. For instance, *E* may place three objects (toast, bacon, and a glass of milk) on the table in front of *S*. *E* gives the command, "Touch the toast." *E* may prompt and reinforce the correct R. *E* proceeds with the training in accordance with the discrimination procedures outlined earlier. For example, he switches the position of the objects to prevent *S* from responding to position cues. He tries to facilitate *S*'s attention by having the child fixate on the objects before he presents the command. Also, since the onset of the trial might become a reinforcer, it is important to avoid presenting the trial just after tantrums or too much activity. It is often helpful to restrain *S*'s hands (keep them on *S*'s lap) at first, so that he makes a discrete response rather than reaching part of the way to several objects before making a complete response.

E begins the procedure for Discrimination 2 (labeling) once *S* has mastered Discrimination 1 (pointing) with three to six objects (or perhaps more). The first training stimulus (TS1, a glass of milk) is presented along with the question "What is it?" The desired response (R1, in this case "milk") is prompted. It is possible that the question "What is it?" should be deleted in the early phases of training, since it may block a good response to the prompt and conceivably also block S's perception of the training stimulus (the glass of milk). In general, the less E says at first, the better. ("John, look here, will you please, what do you call this?" is probably a good example of a stimulus which either has lost or is fast losing its S^D properties.)

In Step 1, E presents TS1 (milk), prompts, and fades until S gives R1 to TS1 as per criterion. Then E goes on to Step 2 and presents the second training stimulus (TS2, a piece of bacon) and prompts the desired response. E then reintroduces TS1 (milk, Step 3) and continues presenting milk until S is performing at criterion again. TS2 is then reintroduced (Step 4) and alternated with TS1 until S has made no errors, even though TS1 and TS2 have been alternated in random presentations on 10 successive trials. New training stimuli (TS3) may be introduced as rapidly as the child is able to handle them. Generally, it will be sufficient to begin with the introduction of the new training stimulus, as in Step 2, and then proceed immediately to stimulus rotation. In other words, E drills S on TS3 until S has reached criterion, then TS3 is immediately intermixed in a nonsystematic order with TS1 and TS2.

After S has mastered approximately 10 labels, it becomes cumbersome to review all the labels equally in every session. At this point one may begin to intersperse previously mastered stimuli with new stimuli. The ratio of old to new must be determined by how much review seems necessary in order to avoid loss of previous learning.

Before we present the data, let us make a procedural point. A great deal of research is needed in this area of elementary "labeling," and the data we present are to a large, but unknown, extent a function of the arbitrary procedures we use. For example, notice that the stimulus display for Discrimination 1 contained three objects (S had to point to toast, bacon, or milk). With three such objects, S will be reinforced 33 percent of the time if he is just guessing. A 33-percent schedule is more likely to extinguish guessing than a 50-percent schedule (using only two objects), but perhaps this is not thin enough for some Ss. The choice of three objects (as compared to two or four) was arbitrary; there are no data on optimum size of the stimulus display.

Let us now present some data which illustrate the results one typically obtains during the training of a labeling vocabulary. The acquisition of simple labels is presented in Figure 3. Both Ss were boys and were mute when training began; Kevin was seven years old and Taylor was five. They had received from three to six months of training in verbal imitation and had mastered three to six objects in Discrimination 1 (Ss could correctly point to the objects in various displays when asked to do so by E).

The labels are written in lower-case letters on the days they are introduced and practiced and in capitals when they are mastered. Although it took several days to learn a particular label in the beginning, the child acquired several labels in a single day later on in training. This positive acceleration of the learning curves ("learning to learn") has been present in all the children we have trained. With continuation of the training, many of the children eventually acquired new labels with a single trial per label, meaning that the correct response was prompted once (as they were told the correct label), and that was sufficient for acquisition.

The speed of learning varied enormously between children. Thus, several of the echolalic children could master within hours what Taylor (Figure 3) mastered after 40 days. For example, Rick (an eight-year-old echolalic) gave the correct response to TS1 after four trials in which he echoed the question "What is this?" before he began to give the correct response. When TS2 was introduced, he made two errors (he echoed two times) but maintained correct responding when TS1 and TS2 were intermixed. He echoed nine times when TS3 was introduced, but from TS4 on made no more errors, learning new labels by being prompted once. Pam (an eight-year-old echolalic) echoed 982 times on TS1, 14 times on TS2, 22 times when TS1 and TS2 were intermixed, and then was essentially errorless after TS4 had been reached. Rick was well on his way into label training the first day, but Pam's echolalia was more persistent and slowed her down. In the early stages of this program, prior to more objective data collection, we taught the alphabet (26 paired associates) to an eight-year-old echolalic child (who was diagnosed as having primary retardation, moderate range, with autistic features) in less than two hours. A performance like that, which may or may not be matched by a typical college freshman, can sometimes be observed among autistics. In some children, however, it may take months to teach that much.

Exactly how hard one has to work to accomplish the first dis-

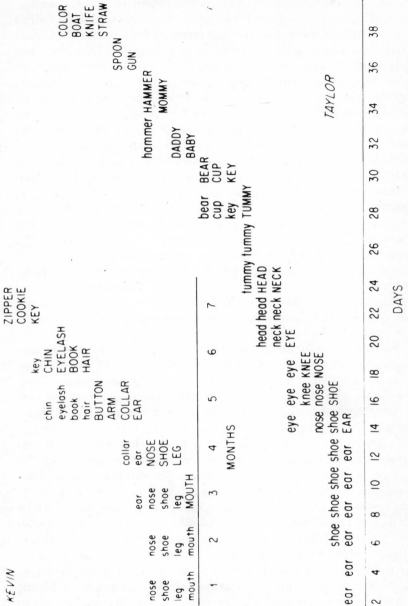

Figure 3. Acquisition of early labeling vocabulary in Kevin and Taylor. Abscissa denotes training days. The labels are printed in lower-case letters on the days they were introduced and trained, and in capital letters on the day they were mastered.

crimination is illustrated by Billy, a seven-year-old mute autistic, who was first taught verbal imitation (see Figure 1). In Billy's case, we had to work for 90,000 trials to bring about the first correct labeling (between "milk" and "bacon"). This does not imply that his acquisition consisted of 90,000 incremental steps or that "operant conditioning training" is slow by nature. Rather, Billy was the first mute child to undergo label training, and he taught us how easy it was to train the wrong discrimination. Some children become too dependent on prompts, others come to associate position rather than object cues, some perseverate, and others become barely audible or combine words, making it difficult for E to decide whether to reinforce or not. Billy showed all these problems. In his case, we ceased prompting altogether, presented the training stimulus alone, and waited for him to give the correct R on his own; if he gave the correct R upon the first presentation of the training stimulus, we reinforced him. We learned a great deal from Billy, but we are still a long way from understanding how to teach efficiently even simple discriminations to the children. Wasserman (1969), Koegel (1971), and Schreibman (1975) have described some of the problems that autistic children have in discrimination learning. We shall return to these problems later.

We have taught many behaviors that involve the child's discriminations of relatively simple stimulus aspects of the environment. In each case, the acquisition is positively accelerated. Consider the acquisition of correct nonverbal responses to simple verbal commands (which is Discrimination 1) such as "raise arm," "touch belly," "drop hands," "stand up," "touch nose," "tongue out," "touch eye," "touch ear," "pat head." For Michael, a six-year-old mute autistic, the number of sessions (a session was 50 minutes, with approximately six trials per minute) required for acquisition of these commands were 4, 3, 3, 2, 2, 3, 1, 1, 2, 1, 1, 1, respectively. For the correct response to simple questions such as "What do you want?" ("cookie"); "Do you want [name of food?] ("yes"); "What's your name?" ("Mike"); "What is this?" ("baby"); "How are you?" ("fine"); "Do you want me to hit you?" ("no"), the sessions required were 9, 8, 3, 4, 4, 3 respectively. The absolute numbers of sessions differ between children; Michael seemed "average" for the mutes. The accelerated rate of acquisition is representative for all.

The kinds of errors that the child makes during learning may give cues about the underlying learning process. Therefore, we recorded amount of errors that *S* made on a previously mastered label as new labels were introduced. These data are presented in Figure 4 for two children. Mike and Jose were initially mute, and

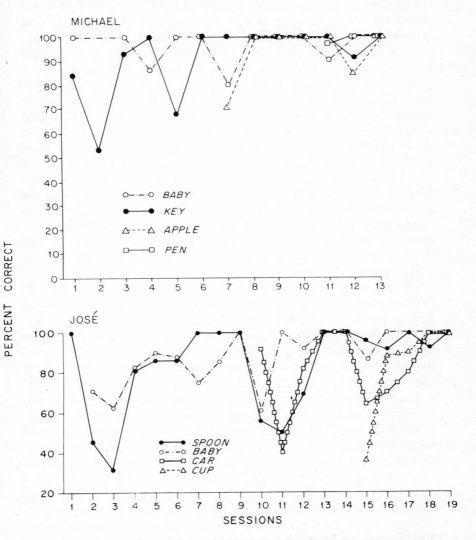

Figure 4. Errors during label training for Michael and Jose. Percent correct responding is given on the ordinate, and training sessions are shown on the abscissa. New labels were introduced in Sessions 1, 7, and 11 for Michael, and in Sessions 2, 10, and 15 for Jose.

both were approximately five years old. The number of sessions, which lasted 50 minutes and were given twice a day, are shown on the abscissa. The ordinate shows the percentage of correct responses (number of correct responses over the number of stimulus presentations—S^Ds per trial—× 100). It is apparent that whenever a new label is introduced, it interferes with the production of an older one, but this interference decreases as additional labels are acquired. An example is shown by the line that gives correct responding for TS1 ("spoon") in Jose's data in the upper half of Figure 2. He has been trained to 100-percent correct responding, and Sessions 1 and 2 show this mastery. When TS2 ("baby") is introduced in Session 2, his correct responding on TS1 drops to 30 percent, but recovers over the next sessions. It is back at 100 percent by Session 9, then drops again to 50 percent when TS3 is introduced in Session 10. It climbs back up once more, reading 100 percent by Session 14. It shows some loss (but much less) when TS4 ("cup") is introduced in Session 15. Similar effects can be seen in Mike's data in the lower half of Figure 2. Note the extensive similarity between Figures 2 and 4 (and Figures 1 and 3), which speaks of the commonality in the learning process underlying the two acquisitions.

A study by Newsom and Lovaas (1975) gives yet another illustration of the learning process underlying the acquisition of labels. In this study, echolalic children who had no labeling vocabulary were taught to give different labels to geometric forms with varying numbers of angles (3-, 4-, 5-, 6-, 7-, and 10-sided forms). They were first taught only one label, namely the label for the three-sided form "ah," and then were presented with the remaining (unlabeled) forms to test for generalization, that is, the extent to which the first label was given to the other forms. They were then taught a second label, "ee," to denote the 10-sided form, and again tested for generalization. Finally, they were taught to label the 6-sided form, "sh," and tested as before.

The data from one of the Ss (Jeff) in this study is presented in Figure 5. The ordinate gives the percentage of time a particular label is given to a particular stimulus (100 × the sum of particular label R/total number of the particular form presentation). The abscissa presents the various stimuli (3-, 4-, 5-, 6-, 7-, and 10-sided forms). If one examines the top part of the figure, it can be seen that the label ("ah"), which he was taught to the 3-sided form, is given equally often to all forms during the generalization tests. His generalization gradient is flat. When he is taught the second label ("ee") to the 10-sided form (middle of the figure), his

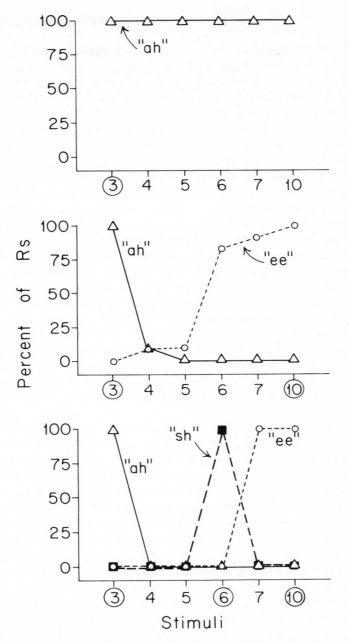

Figure 5. Generalization in label usage as a function of number of labels trained. Percent usage of a particular label is given on the ordinate, while the various stimuli (3, 4, 5, 6, 7, and 10) are given on the abscissa. The top part of the figure shows the use of the label "ah" across the different stimuli when it was the only label that was trained. It was trained to stimulus 3. The middle of the figure shows generalization when two labels had been trained, and the bottom when three labels had been trained.

generalization gradients are much steeper. When he is taught the third label ("sh" for the 6-sided form), the discriminations become quite sharp (bottom of figure). For example, the third label was not generalized to other forms; he used it much more discretely than he used the first label.

These data (Figures 1 through 5) are consistent with a discrimination learning model. Seemingly, the child learned to discriminate (attend to) those defining features of the environment to which we associate verbal behavior and not to respond to those features which are nondefining. Thus, in imitation learning, the child's verbal behaviors came under the S^D control of another person's verbal stimulus. In label training the child's verbal behavior came under the control of nonverbal stimuli. To focus or guide the child's attention to these various stimuli required differential reinforcement; extinction of R to nondefining ($S\Delta$) features and reinforcement for responding to defining (relevant, S^D) features.

When the child has mastered perhaps a dozen labels in Program 2, we begin generalization training on each one. By that we mean that the child must be trained to correctly label *members* of a class of objects, such as the different instances of the class of "chair" upon first presentation, before we can argue that he has a concept of the object. When we begin to train this concept, the child is exposed to numerous examples of the object and to similar objects which have different labels. For instance, the child may label anything with four legs "chair." He must therefore learn to discriminate between tables and chairs—that chairs may be any color, may be upholstered or not, may be made of wood, steel, or plastic, may have arms or not, or may be small or large. Obviously, such language is too rich in meaning (requires extensive discriminations) to be practically or effectively taught in a laboratory. It is practically impossible, and probably not necessary, to train formally any one concept to its full meaning. The child's day-to-day environment is full of all the necessary relevant (and irrelevant) stimuli, which is where the discriminations become "firmed up."

Let us make one more comment on how we informally extended the label training. Labeling is a continuous process which is never completed. While normal children may expand their vocabularies with minimal explicit adult assistance, autistic children need help, at least initially. In addition to arranging a teaching environment which facilitated the early discriminations, we also helped the children become more curious about the world around them. For example, autistic children typically do not ask for the names of objects around them as normal children often do. Therefore, to help them expand their vocabulary we taught them to ask questions about their environment, and we reinforced them for doing so. If the child did not know the name of an object, we prompted him to ask us "What is it?" and then gave him the label. Our film on language acquisition (Lovaas, 1969) illustrates such a method.

Building grammatical responses. From the very beginning, we built grammatical phrases and sentences as part of the programs we constructed, because the response we required from the children in these various programs soon extended beyond one-word answers. Even in the labeling program, we quickly began to demand more than a single word. We initially held the child to a one-word answer (like answering "cookie" to the question "What is it?"), and then demanded more elaborate answers ("It is a cookie"). Later, we required more elaborate descriptions that required combinations of words, such as verb-noun combinations (not just a "horse," but a "white horse"). The same requirement was placed on his demands to ask not just "bacon," but "I want bacon" or "I want (any number of things)." There are many other examples. When the children acquired prepositional speech (in Program 3), an example of criterion response would be: "I put the book under the table." More abstractly, we taught the children the sentence: "I put (x) under (y)," etc.

Use of phrases and sentences required that we teach the child to order words into grammatically correct sequences. This building of grammatical sentences did not involve a different process or set of techniques from that used for building single words. To move from simple sounds (like "m," "a," "i") to a combination of sounds (such as "mommie") involved the same teaching techniques we used in moving from a word to combinations of words, as in sentences. Combinations of sounds (words) and word combinations (sentences) all constituted verbal *responses* which we built through differential reinforcement to a variety of stimulus situations. The sound combination "t-o-p" was prompted and differentially reinforced in one kind of stimulus situation, while another combination of the same sounds, like "p-o-t", was reinforced in a different situation. The two verbal behaviors are different because the combinations of sounds are different and because their respective stimulus situations are different. The same is true of the sentence "I don't" as contrasted to "Don't I?" Technically, such shaping, when one vocalization provides part of the

S^D for the next vocalization, is known as response chaining. Therefore, we used the same prompt and fading procedures to build sentences as we had in building single words. Throughout, differential reinforcement was used to bring a particular verbal response under the control of either an external stimulus (as in labeling) or an internal stimulus (as in response chaining). In building chains, one typically starts with the last member of the chain and moves forward in gradual steps. Thus, if one wants to build the chain "I want bacon," one starts with "bacon," then goes on to "want bacon," and finally "I want bacon." One usually distinguishes between homogeneous and heterogeneous chains, and to move from a homogeneous chain (where each R looks like every other R, as in "ma-ma") to a heterogeneous chain composed of topographically different Rs (as in "mom-mie") is very difficult for the child. But apparently, once he can perform his first heterogeneous chain, new ones are acquired with greater ease.

We tried to teach heterogeneous chains in the following manner. Suppose "mommie" was the target R. If E initially presents "mommie" to the child, the child will give him back the *last* component of that stimulus such as "mie" or "ie" (which seems reasonable, since it is most recent for the child). To help the child reproduce or otherwise use the whole chain, E started by prompting each component ("mom" and "mie") separately. The size of the component was determined for each child; E used as large a component as S would give back intact. E then accentuated the first prompt ("mom") and gradually faded out the second prompt ("mie") while he tried to maintain both components ("mommie") for the child. In other words, E presents "mom" and the child now gives "mom-mie." E then gradually fades in the second syllable ("mie") while maintaining the child's "mom-mie," so that eventually E's "mommie" cues the child's "mommie." The same procedure is used to teach any heterogeneous chain such as "I want bacon."

By using prompt fading and reinforcement techniques, we built sentences as heterogeneous chains. What the child is *learning,* however, when he is taught sentences is probably different from what he is learning when he is reinforced for emitting single words. In general, if he is reinforced for producing sentences, he learns to order words into grammatically correct sequences. For example, if the child is prompted and reinforced for emitting the sentence "I want [bacon, candy, milk]" in a large variety of situations, then he will eventually emit "I want [x]" without being prompted when he is confronted with situation "x." He gives evidence that he can order words into a correct sentence. We return to a discussion of the conceptual issues involved in treating sentences as responses later in this book and present explicit data on the way in which we taught certain aspects of grammar, such as verb transformations.

But let us first illustrate how we taught the use of sentences by presenting verbatim transcripts of tape recordings taken during various stages in different programs. The following excerpt illustrates the training procedures with Billy, previously mute, who is being taught to ask for things, using phrases like "I want [object]." He had been taught verbal imitative behavior and mastered about 10 labels for different foods. He sits in front of his breakfast tray with *E*.

E   What do you want?
Billy   Egg.
E   No, what do you want? I . . . .
Billy   (No response)
E   I . . . .
Billy   I want . . . (*E*'s "I" cues Billy's "I want" on the basis of prior training).
E   Egg (pause). O.K., what do you want?
Billy   I want egg.
E   Good (feeds Billy).
E   What do you want?
Billy   Egg.
E   No, what do you want? I . . . .
Billy   I want egg.
E   Good boy (feeds Billy).
E   What is this? (shows Billy bacon).
Billy   Bacon.
E   Good, what do you want?
Billy   (No response)
E   I . . . .
Billy   I want bacon.
E   Good. What do you want?
Billy   I want bacon.
E   Good (feeds again). What is this? (shows milk).
Billy   Milk (*E* corrects pronounciation).
E   Good. I . . . .
Billy   I want milk.
E   You want what?
Billy   I want egg.
E   Egg (to improve enunciation).
Billy   Egg.
E   O.K. (feeds).

Billy   I want egg.
E   Good (feeds).

The data collected on phrase-building, like our other data, were positively accelerated. To illustrate, it took Dean (previously mute) two days to learn to chain "I go," whereas he acquired three two-word phrases—"swimming pool," "sewing machine," and "clap hands"—on the fifth day of training.

Michael's acquisition of "I want toast" is given in Figure 6.

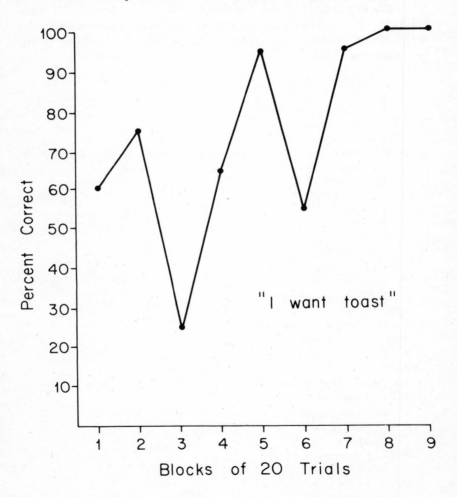

Figure 6. Michael's acquisition of the response "I want toast" to the question "What do you want?" at breakfast time.

Like Billy, the previously mute Michael sat in front of the breakfast table. *E* held up the toast and asked him, "What do you want?" Michael was scored correct if he answered "I want toast" to that stimulus without being prompted. As can be seen, his performance was errorless after 180 trials. He started at a high of 60 percent (in the first block of trials) since he had already had several sessions of training on other phrases.

References

Koegel, R. *Selective attention to prompt stimuli by autistic and normal children*. Unpublished doctoral dissertation, University of California, Los Angeles, 1971.

Lovaas, O. I. *Behavior modification: Teaching language to psychotic children*, instructional film, 45 min., 16 mm.-sound, Appleton-Century-Crofts, New York, 1969.

Newsom, C. D., & Lovaas, O. I. Stimulus control in the acquisition of labels. In preparation, 1975.

Schreibman, L. Within-stimulus versus extra-stimulus prompting procedures on discrimination learning with autistic children. *Journal of Applied Behavioral Analysis*, 1975, in press.

Wasserman, L. M. *Discrimination learning in autistic children*. Unpublished doctoral dissertation, University of California, Los Angeles, 1969.

Chapter III
BUILDING ABSTRACT TERMS

**Program 3: Relationships among Objects and Events, and
Other Abstract Terms**

Once the child had acquired a basic labeling vocabulary of objects, behaviors, and other seemingly concrete events, we introduced him to common abstract terms like prepositions, pronouns, and time concepts. These terms define simple relationships in time and space and relationships among people, objects, and events. The child must know many of these concepts in order to function at even the most minimal level in society. As these concepts must come under the relatively narrow control of stimulus elements that may be shared by many objects, these discriminations seem more difficult (more "abstract") than those involved in the acquisition of "simple" labels. However, even "simple" labels require "abstract" behavior: The second time a stimulus is presented, the situation is not identical to the first time (the angle of sensory input is slightly different, as are the background stimulation and possibly other factors), and no two members of a class of objects are just alike. Learning to label relationships between events thus often requires the prior acquisition of labels for the events themselves. Let us consider how we can teach some of these abstractions.

Prepositions

Prepositions denote the spatial relationships between objects. In teaching prepositions we had the underlying notion that we might thereby help the child to define and order space and locate himself within it. Eventually we did teach the child about his own position in space and the relationships between objects in space (the sugar placed *beside* the cereal, the child lying *on top of* his bed). A child can acquire comprehensive understanding of prepositional concepts only when he is continuously initiating and changing spatial relations among objects. Such an understanding can help him get along better, if for no other reason than that he will understand better what others say. As usual, we began to teach the basic concepts in the laboratory, using simple and easily manipulated objects, such as a penny placed *on top of* a cup. To facilitate the learning of the preposition and to prevent *S* from attending to irrelevant cues, *E* taught the spatial arrangements by using many different kinds of common objects (a block inside a dresser, a spoon beside a plate). That is, we tried to avoid a situation in which *S* would learn merely to place object A on top of B at the command "Place A on top of B," since the child may learn only that particular placement (A on B) and not the relational term. To break up such incorrect discriminations, we arranged for B to be put on top of A and for a variety of objects to be placed on top of each other.

The manual for prepositions is an example of a program which we always began with Discrimination 1 training. *E* instructed *S* to place an object, such as a penny, *in* a container, like a cup. The response was prompted (*E* moved *S*'s hand, holding the penny to the cup, and helped him release it). The prompt was faded, and the training proceeded along "basic principles." When the child had mastered this discrimination (*in*), *E* introduced a *second* container, a small box, and instructed the child to place the object *under* the box. Training proceeded through alternate presentations of TS1 and TS2 in the *systematic stimulus presentation* routine described earlier. Once the stimulus rotation had been completed, *E* gradually faded out the differences between the containers, teaching the child to respond appropriately to *in* and *under,* using only one container. Finally, new objects and containers are introduced. New prepositions, such as *beside* and *in front of,* were then taught by repeating the procedure, first with the introduction of a new training stimulus (TS3), then with alternate presentation of TS3, TS2, and TS1 through stimulus rotation, and finally with the introduction of new objects. Manual B in Chapter 6 describes the training method in detail.

When the child had mastered five or six prepositions at the level of Discrimination 1, *E* began Discrimination 2. The procedure was exactly the same as for Discrimination 1, except that now *E* placed the object *in* or *under* the container (or *E* instructed *S* to do so) and then asked *S,* "Where is it?" The desired response, *"in* the cup" or *"under* the box," was prompted. The procedure was repeated. *E* sometimes introduced TS2 using the same container as for TS1. Once *in* and *under* had been trained, *E* used many different objects and containers, as for Discrimination 1. We will present no formal data here on the acquisition of prepositional speech. A very comprehensive project, directed by Mansfield (1972) in our laboratory, has produced ample data showing the similarity between this kind of acquisition and the acquisition of other abstract concepts such as pronouns and time-related terms, which we will report on. One of Mansfield's findings was that successive prepositions were acquired with a decreasing number of trials, that is, the acquisition curve was positively accelerated. This observation is consistent with viewing the mastery of prepositional relations as the acquisition of a set of successive discriminations.

Pronouns

It is difficult to specify all the gains for the child who understands and uses pronouns appropriately. At one time we thought that such learning would help the child discriminate between himself and others, to form a body image, a concept of "self," and so on. Even if such ambitions are not achieved, the child who can be told what belongs to him and what belongs to others, who has to do what, or what is going to happen to whom will obviously make large gains in his social behavior.

Our program for teaching pronouns involved training in both the nominative and the possessive case. In the initial stages of training for the nominative case we employed a large number of ordinary daily behaviors (standing, sitting, jumping, laughing), while common objects (shirt, shoes, watch) and body parts (eyes, nose, arm, foot) were employed in training for the genitive case.

We first trained for personal pronouns in the nominative case. *E* began training by asking the child, "What am I doing?" while performing some discriminable activity, such as jumping. *S* was prompted to say "*You* are jumping." (If *E* initially pointed to himself while asking the question, of course, the additional prompt was faded as usual). *S* was now told to engage in the activity, and *E* asked "What are you doing?" The desired response was prompted, "*I* am jumping." The pronouns were exaggerated (made especially loud and distinct) to help the discrimination. *I* and *you* were alternated and then rotated as usual. *E* changed the activity from trial to trial once *S* had mastered the discrimination between *I* and *you* with the first activity. At this point a second adult was introduced, and appropriate responses to "What is *she* (*he*) doing?" were trained. We review the training of pronouns briefly later in this chapter, and a more complete description of the training can be found in Manual C in Chapter 6.

We next trained for possessive pronouns in the genitive case. Training for possessive pronouns began with Discrimination 1, that is, the child had to discriminate the referent of the pronoun used in *E*'s sentence. *E* began training with "Point to *your* ("nose", or some other body part)." Once the child had mastered "Point to *your* (body part)," the command "Point to *my* (body part)" was introduced. When this discrimination was completed, *E* began changing the body part over trials. A second adult was then introduced, and *his* or *her* was trained.

At this stage, training in Discrimination 2 was initiated. The child was required to give the appropriate verbal as well as the correct nonverbal response to the referent of *E*'s statements. Pronoun reversal sometimes occurred. *E* had labeled *S*'s nose "*your* nose" during Discrimination 1; now *S* had to label that same nose "*my* nose." Conversely, *S* had pointed to *E*'s nose, which *E* called "*my* nose"; but now *S* had to call it "*your* nose."

When the child had mastered both personal and possessive pronouns, we proceeded to train their combined use. For such training *E* engaged in some simple activity that involved a body part or possession. For example, *E* touched *S*'s nose and asked "What am *I* doing?" *S* was prompted to say "*You* are touching *my* nose." *E* then had *S* touch *E*'s nose and asked "What are *you* do-ing?" *S* was prompted to respond "*I* am touching *your* nose." Training proceeded as for individual pronouns. A third person was introduced once the first stage was mastered, and responses such as "He is touching his nose" were trained. As soon as *S* had mastered the correct pronoun use for a particular body part, new body parts were introduced to help insure that *S* acquired the broad abstraction rather than some concrete aspect of the stimuli.

We present some data on pronoun acquisition here. Although the training procedure is quite complex, the data do appear to be typical of the results we obtained in attempting to teach other abstract relationships. The acquisition of the possessive pronouns "your," "my," and "her" is presented in Figure 7. Data are presented on six children. The trials are presented in blocks of ten on the abscissa, while the percentage of correct responses within each block is presented on the ordinate. The child was required to re-spond nonverbally (Discrimination 1) by pointing to the object denoted by *E* ("Point to *your* (object)"). One can see how the commands "Point to *your* (object)," "Point to *my* (object)," and "Point to *her* (object)" were trained separately, intermixed, and rotated with each other (referred to as "your, my, her mixed").

When the child approached mastery, we made certain that in any one block of trials, a certain number of objects or possessions (more than two out of ten) had not been trained in the previous blocks. If the child was still responding at 100 percent correct, then we were assured that he was responding to the abstract rela-tionship between new stimuli rather than basing his answer on some irrelevant aspect of the training.

Looking at the data, one can draw two rather obvious infer-ences. First, the children did learn about the pronouns, but there is great variability in their acquisition rates. Tito (a six-year-old echolalic) apparently acquired the second pronoun "my" as he learned the first pronoun "your" (making no errors on the pro-noun "my"). He made only two errors in learning to discriminate between "your" and "my." (See the first block of "your, my, mixed.") Sheldon (a seven-year-old mute), on the other hand, was much slower than Tito, requiring 240 trials to learn "my." That they learned "about pronouns" is apparent when we look at the savings over tasks. The children were faster in the mastery of the third pronoun "her" than the first two pronouns, "your" and "my." Similarly, the discrimination of "your," "my," and "her"

Picture E. Mark with his mother, at home, in one of the more formal sessions. Mark is beginning to acquire pronouns, and in this particular scene points to his mother's nose on her request, "point to mom's nose," as contrasted to "point to Mark's nose." Later these requests may be more pronoun-specific, such as specifying "point to *my* nose," and "point to *your* nose." Notice that the mother has Mark sitting down in the chair in an attentive position, since these early acquisitions are difficult to acquire. Most language learning at home occurs informally, with the child free to move around.

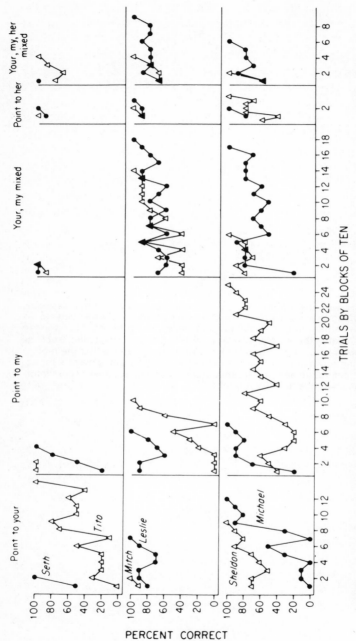

Figure 7. The acquisition of correct response to the possessive pronouns "your," "my," and "her" in six different children. Percent correct responding is given on the ordinate, and the abscissa gives trials in blocks of 10. Correct response to "point to your" was trained first, followed by training of correct response to "point to my." These commands were then intermixed, followed by training on "point to her," and so on.

intermixed required fewer trials than that of "your," "my" inter-mixed, even though the former involves more stimuli than the latter.

The data we have presented on pronoun learning represent only a fraction of the amount of training a child needs in order to use pronouns correctly. As soon as a child showed some mastery of pronouns in the controlled laboratory training session, he was moved to the outside environment ("Whose bed is this?" "Who is eating cereal?" "Is she your mother?"). Training in the correct use of pronouns was also imbedded in a number of other programs, as in conversation training, which we will illustrate shortly.

The complexities involved in teaching pronouns become ap-parent when we examine the conditions under which the child acquired Discrimination 2 in pronouns. The child had already been taught (as in Figure 3) to give a correct nonverbal response (he had to point to E's nose) to an essentially verbal stimulus (E says "Point to *my* nose."). This is Discrimination 1. Now, we wanted the child, while he was engaged in this nonverbal re-sponse, to label verbally (with the correct pronoun, "*your* nose") an essentially nonverbal stimulus (E's nose). That is Discrimina-tion 2. We ran Discrimination 1 and 2 concurrently. The difficulty in this acquisition arises when one considers that the verbalization "*your* nose" was used to refer to the child's nose when E spoke (Discrimination 1), while it is E's nose that is meant if the child says the same phrase. S has to discriminate the relationships of verbalizations to the persons who make them. This discrimination was considerably complicated since Ss often imitated E's verbalization, failing to discriminate between prompts and instructions. For example, E instructed S to "Point to *my* nose," and if S responded correctly (Discrimination 1), E asked for Discrimination 2 by saying "Whose nose?" If S did not respond correctly, E prompted "*your* nose." In Discrimination 1, S was trained to point to his own nose in response to that request, while in Discrimination 2 he had to be taught to inhibit the pointing response and to imitate E's verbalization ("*your* nose") in order to master the correct verbal label.

Some data on such "pronoun reversal" is presented in Figure 8. Michael was mute and Leslie echolalic when we began lan-guage training. Trials are in blocks of ten on the abscissa. The percentage correct within the block of ten trials is given on the ordinate. In the first set of trials, E gave the command "Point to *your* (body part)" (for example, "nose," intermixed among other body parts). In order to be correct, the child was required both to point to his own nose (Discrimination 1) and to verbalize *"my nose"* (Discrimination 2). This is called "Point to your, say my" in Figure 8. During the second set of trials, *E* gave the command "Point to *my* nose," which *S* had to do, and he had to learn to say *"your* nose" while he did so to *E*'s question "Whose nose?" The training to acquire this discrimination is called "Point to my, say your" in Figure 8. These two acquisitions were mastered within

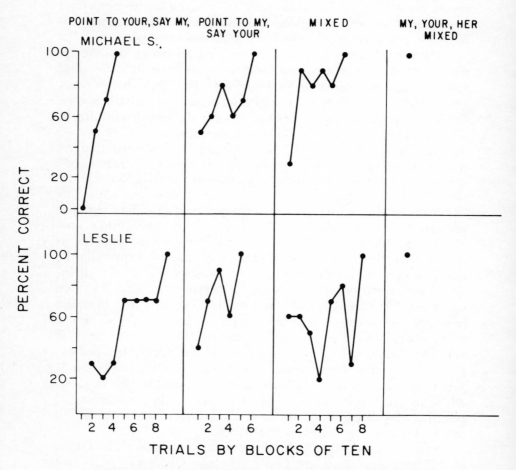

Figure 8. The acquisition of correct nonverbal response to certain possessive pronouns ("point to your," and so on) while the child was taught the concurrent verbal response denoting the appropriate pronoun ("say my," and so on).

60 trials. In the third set of trials, the two commands were rotated, which is called "mixed" in the figure. They learned this discrimination within 80 trials. The last point on the graph describes the performance of the children after they had been trained on the third pronoun ("Point to *her* nose.") when *E* gave all three commands, "Point to *your* (nose)," "Point to *my* (nose)," and "Point to *her* (nose)" in rotation. This is presented as "my, your, her mixed" in Figure 8. In order to be scored correct, the child now had not only to correctly point to a particular person's body part or possession, but also to label verbally the pronominal relation as well. By the time Michael and Leslie reached this last stage of the formal pronoun training, they performed without errors. They showed that they were well on the way to mastery of the basic and complex discriminations involving pronouns.

Time-related terms

The object of the next part of Program 3 was to introduce the child to terms which denote ways in which we order events in time. This is the first step in helping the child to relate his behavior to events in the past, present, and future and to begin to reconstruct what has happened to him and to plan for events to come.

The details of the laboratory training procedures are presented in Manual D in Chapter 6. We usually began with the term "first," although in retrospect we probably should have begun with "last," since for that term the spatial and temporal cues are more recent. We collected a large pool of thirty common objects, and randomly picked any five objects to form Set 1. These objects were then returned to the pool, and another set of five objects was then picked to become Set 2, and so on. To begin training, *E* placed Set 1 (key, cup, pencil, watch, ring) in front of *S* and told him to touch three of them in a certain order (touch watch, then cup, then ring). *E* asked *S* "What was the *first?*" The desired response (e.g., "watch") was prompted. After the child made the desired response, Set 1 remained, but it was physically rearranged, and a different selection of three objects was touched; the question was repeated, and the response prompted. After *S* reached criterion (five successive correct trials), Set 1 was replaced by Set 2 (five different objects), then Set 3 replaced Set 2. Once the child reached criterion on a new set, training was terminated on the concept "first," and the next concept, "last," was introduced. "What was last?" was taught in the same manner as "What was first?" After both were mastered, the two concepts were alternated (mixed). When they were intermixed, we used the same set of objects as training stimuli for both. That is, after *S* touched three objects in a certain order, he was asked which one was touched "first;" he responded; he was then asked which was touched "last," and so on.

"After" and "before" were taught next. Using the same material and stimulus presentations as in teaching "first" and "last," *E* asked "What came (*after, before*) the (object)?" Special supplementary techniques plus a complete example are described in Manual D in Chapter 6.

The data on the acquisition of the discrimination of "first" and "last" appear in Figure 9. Scott, a five-year-old echolalic, required 120 trials on Set 1 to identify correctly the object which was touched "first." (*S* had to verbalize the object and its temporal order: "car was *first.*") He arrived at mastery within 20 trials on Set 2 and was errorless from the beginning on Sets 3 and 4. Since he had not been exposed to the temporal ordering of these particular stimuli before (the ordering of Sets 3 and 4), it was their temporal ordering that he attended to. Temporal order acquired discriminative stimulus properties for him. We can also argue that since he had never been confronted with these particular stimuli before (the ordering of Sets 3 and 4) and had not been taught that particular response before ("boat was *first*"), his behavior is truly novel and "self-created." He was taught to "generate" (produce his own) correct phrases to stimulus situations he had previously not encountered.

This is another example of the "learning to learn" phenomenon, this time both over sets and over concepts. Moreover, we again encounter the heterogeneity of the children. For example, one can see how slow Kevin, a six-year-old mute, is in comparison to the others. Between the 10th and the 45th blocks on the concept "first," which corresponds to the 100th and the 450th trials, Kevin is apparently not learning anything. The data show how much more we have to know about this kind of acquisition before we become efficient in teaching it.

Miscellaneous concepts

We taught a vast array of abstractions. Some of these are presented in more detail in Manual E in Chapter 6. The children

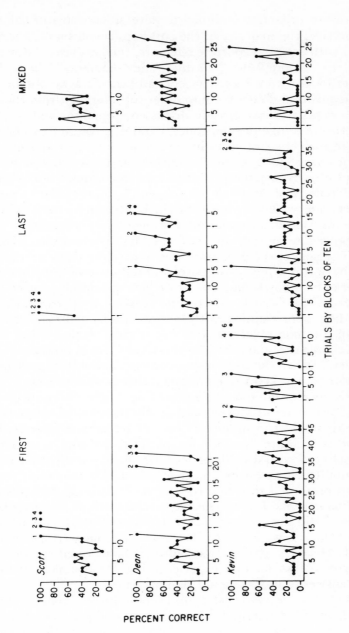

Figure 9. Acquisition of correct response to the concept "first" and "last" in three children. The figure shows the data in blocks of 10 trials. The numbers (1 through 6) above the acquisition curves refer to the various sets of objects used.

participated in programs designed to develop concepts of color, shape, and size; the majority of the children have been taught to use words with even less concrete referents, such as "fast," "slow," "down," "up," "more," "less," "same," and "different." The basic procedures for teaching these concepts and the data we obtained on their acquisition do not seem to differ substantially from those for the concepts we have already discussed, pronouns and time-related terms. *E*'s ingenuity in concept training to some extent is reflected in his choice of stimulus material. Such material must be made to vary along many dimensions and may consist of a number of objects (a large pile of blocks and a small one when teaching "more" and "less") or may depend upon the relative rate of occurrence of two events in time (which *E* began by instructing *S* to move his hand in a circular motion, first "fast," then "slow").

The procedure for training "yes" and "no" deserves some elaboration. The goal of the procedure was to give the child a simple verbal behavior to express his desires and tell us something about the extent of his knowledge. The procedure was divided into two parts, "yes-no" for factual matters, and "yes-no" for personal feelings. We began the training with "yes-no" for factual matters by employing common objects as training stimuli. *E* pointed to an object, such as a car, and asked "Is this a car?" *S* was prompted to answer "yes." When the child responded "yes" reliably on perhaps a dozen objects, *E* asked *S* to identify a different object, asking "Is this a car?" and prompted the answer "no." "No" is trained to criterion; "yes" is reintroduced, and finally the two are rotated.

Once the child had mastered "yes-no" for factual matters, *E* proceeded to training "yes-no" for personal feelings or preferences. *E* selected several foods or activities he was fairly certain *S* would enjoy (such as eating). *E* then asked "Do you want (result)?" and prompted the child to say "yes." Training proceeded as for factual matters. *E* then selected several foods or activities he was certain *S* did not like (such as a slap on the hand) and asked the child "Do you want me to slap you?" The answer "no" was prompted. Once the prompt was faded, if *S* answered the question incorrectly, we let him experience the consequences of his incorrect answer (e.g., we would slap his hand).

Whenever we decided that a child should know a concept, we spent from one to two hours a day of concentrated practice on that concept (with up to ten trials per minute, this practice could yield anywhere from 600 to 1200 trials per day). Without such massive and controlled exposure, the children seemed unable to make the necessary discriminations for subsequent training in their everyday environment.

Reference

Mansfield, J. T. *The operant conditioning of abstract motor response to prepositional speech in mongoloids.* Unpublished doctoral dissertation, University of California, Los Angeles, 1972.

Chapter IV
MAKING LANGUAGE SOCIAL AND SPONTANEOUS

Program 4: Conversation

T his program became part of almost all the other programs we have discussed. Conversation is a sophisticated matter; it can be defined as a verbal response whose form is some function both of another person's S^D. As the program progressed, more and more of the stimuli that controlled the child's verbal behavior became subtle, diffuse, and removed in time, as the manuals will indicate. Still, the reinforcement operations we performed sorted them out and established them as functional.

stimuli that controlled the child's verbal behavior became subtle, diffuse, and removed in time, as the manuals will indicate. Still, the reinforcement operations we performed sorted them out and established them as functional.

The child is initially taught to answer simple social questions like "How are you?" and "What's your name?" and so on. We tried to make the conversations easy by imbedding the child's answer within E's question ("How are you feeling, Ricky?" "Fine, and how are you feeling, Joan?"). In a sense, the question prompted the answer. Usually basic training in conversation was part of other programs and was taught concurrently once the early discriminations were established. It may be helpful to describe four "conversations" with Ricky at four different stages in his training. These examples trace Ricky's progress from a mere parroting of E's statements through learning to answer simple questions to more direct training for complex conversational speech. These conversations both give data and serve to illustrate our method.

The first "conversation" took place on the first day of treatment. Ricky was 8 years old, untestable, echolalic, tantrumous, and "classically autistic," with self-stimulation, no social attachment, apparent sensory deficits, and so on. S and E are sitting together facing a picture of children playing. E tries to interest Ricky in the book and asks Ricky to describe it. Ricky makes a grabbing reach at E's glasses.

> Ricky   Say please, I want your glasses (Ricky echoes E's earlier statement).
> E   Here, Ricky. All right, now it's my turn. Now give them back. Ricky, let go. What's this, Ricky?
> Ricky   What's this, boy?
> E   What's your name?
> Ricky   What's your name?
> E   How old are you? Ricky?
> Ricky   How are you? I want my glasses.
> E   Do you like my glasses?
> Ricky   Do you like my glasses?
> E   Say please, I want your glasses.
> Ricky   Say please, I want your glasses (E gives Ricky the glasses).
> E   All right, let me have the glasses, Ricky. Ricky, let go. I'll give them back. Attaboy. Good, good. Ricky, who's this?
> Ricky   Ricky, who's this?
> E   What's that, Ricky?
> Ricky   What's that, Ricky?
> E   Look, Ricky. Look where I'm pointing. Who's this, Ricky?
> Ricky   Say please, I want your glasses.

One month later we recorded the following conversation in a

similar situation, Ricky being taught to label objects and behaviors in a picture book. Although the focus of this training is on labeling (teaching S to discriminate between who the person is and what the person is doing), it is apparent that S is also learning to converse.

E   Ricky, *who* is this? Who is this, Ricky? Who is she?
Ricky   (unintelligible)
E   "No. Who is she? (pause) Betty? (pause) Betty?"
Ricky   "Betty."
E   "That's good. *What* is Betty doing?"
Ricky   Betty is dancing.
E   Good boy, Ricky. That's good, Ricky. Good boy, Rick. Good boy. Put your hand down, Ricky. Ricky, who is this?
Ricky   Betty.
E   That's good, Ricky. Who is this?
Ricky   Betty.
E   Who is this? (pause) Who is this? (pause) Ricky, who is this?
Ricky   (unintelligible)
E   No. Who is this, Ricky? (pause) Betty? (pause) Ricky, who is this? (pause) Betty?
Ricky   Betty.
E   That's right, Ricky. What is Betty doing? (pause) Betty is blowing.
Ricky   Betty is blowing.
E   That's good, Ricky, very good, Rick. Good boy. Good boy, Ricky. Who is this, Ricky?
Ricky   Betty.
E   That's good, and what is Betty doing?
Ricky   Betty is blowing.

A later recording (six months into training) shows us working within another context (training "expanded" descriptions) but simultaneously training conversation.

E   Ricky (pause), Ricky, what are you wearing?
Ricky   I'm wearing clothes.
E   What kind of clothes?
Ricky   Yellow shirt.
E   That's right. What else?
Ricky   (unintelligible)
E   That's right.
Ricky   Black tennis shoes.
E   That's right. What about your socks?
Ricky   Black socks.

> *E*   Very good. Very good. Ricky, what is that there on the dresser?
> *Ricky*   Book.
> *E*   What is a book for?
> *Ricky*   Book . . . book for reading.
> *E*   Very good, Ricky. Very good. That's good. Ricky, what's this, Ricky?
> *Ricky*   Nose.
> *E*   What's a nose for?
> *Ricky*   Nose for smelling.
> *E*   That's good, Ricky.

The film we produced on the language program (Lovaas, 1969) provides several good examples of training conversational speech. Much effort was spent in teaching the child to *initiate* conversations, for example, to ask questions about his immediate environment (Is this a table? Is this a chair?). Again, the film provides some good examples of this kind of training.

Some of the discriminations involved in conversational speech are very subtle and difficult to learn, as the following transcription indicates. Yet mastery of these discriminations is essential for subsequent progress. Note that Ricky and his therapist have nothing "concrete" to focus their conversation on (like a book of pictures), a situation which probably requires more difficult discriminations. Note that the "prompt" now is beginning to become imbedded in the conversation itself (Ricky's telling his name is his cue to ask the teacher what her name is); it's the beginning stage in the training of "connected discourse." This program had already begun during his third month of language training.

> *E*   Ricky, what's your name?
> *Ricky*   Ricky.
> *E*   That's right.
> *Ricky*   How are you feeling?
> *E*   No. Ask me what I asked you. Ricky! Say, what's your name?
> *Ricky*   Ricky.
> *E*   No. Say, what's. . . .
> *Ricky*   What's (pauses). . . .
> *E*   Your. . . .
> *Ricky*   Your (pauses). . . .
> *E*   Say, name.
> *Ricky*   Name.
> *E*   Now, say it all together.
> *Ricky*   What's your name?

E Joan. Good boy, Ricky. That's good. That's good. Come here, Ricky. Stand up, Ricky. Ricky, how are you feeling?

Ricky I am feeling fine.

E That's good. Ricky, come here. Ricky, come here. Now you ask me.

Ricky How are you feeling?

E I am feeling fine. That's good. That's good.

Ricky Lie down, please. Lie down. (Preceding this hour *S* had been taught how to order *E* to stand up, lie down, smile, etc.)

E Ricky, how old are you?

Ricky I'm 7 years old.

E That's right. Ask me, Ricky.

Ricky Ask me.

E No. That's not what I asked you. Ask me how old I am. Say, how. . . .

Ricky Are you feeling?

E No. That's not what I asked you either. I asked you how old you are. Now, you ask me. Say, how. . . .

Ricky How. . . .

E Say, old.

Ricky Old. . . .

E Say, are you.

Ricky Are you.

E That's right. Now say it all together. Say, how old are you?

Ricky I am 7 years old. How old are you?

E I'm 21 years old. That's good. That's very good. That's good.

Eighteen months into treatment Billy, another echolalic 8-year-old, was attending school and talked to the therapist about it (January 25, 1968).

E Tell me about school.

Billy The doors were locked and we couldn't get in.

E Then what happened?

Billy The doors opened.

E Who opened them?

Billy The cleaning man.

E What happened then?

Billy We said the pledge of allegiance. (Bill then repeated the pledge with his hand over his heart.)

E How is Rita this week?

Billy Rita had a seizure last week. Mrs. _____ helped her. She had to go home and rest. (Bill then imitated Rita having a seizure.)

Later in the conversation:

E What's for dinner, Billy?

Billy I don't know.

E Ask me. Say, what's for dinner, Ed?

Billy What's for dinner, Ed?

E Hamburgers.

Billy Oh, boy.

E What's for dinner, Billy?

Billy Hamburgers.

E Good, Bill. How did you find out you are having hamburgers?

Billy I don't know.

E You asked me.

Billy I asked you.

E Good, Billy.

Following this conversation, Billy was trained to ask questions of a third person as well as of the therapist. The following conversation ensued:

E What are you going to do at school tomorrow?

Billy I don't know. What?

E I don't know either, Billy. How can you find out?

Billy I can ask Mommie.

E She doesn't know either. How can you find out? (*S* was prompted to say he could ask Mrs. U., his teacher).

Billy O.K.

E How can you find out what you are going to do at school?

Billy I can ask Mrs. U.

E Good, Billy.

The last conversation we have from Billy was recorded:

E What happened at school today, Billy?

Billy Marty H. got in the cafeteria and started crying (pause). On the bus, Dale hit Cristy-Anne and Cristy-Anne started crying.

E What happened after that, Bill?

Billy Mr. B. changed Cristy-Anne (Mr. B. is the bus driver).

E Where did she change to?

Billy To the front window.

E Where, Billy?

Billy The front of the bus.

E Why did Dale hit Cristy-Anne?

Billy Christy-Anne hit Dale and Dale hit Cristy-Anne back.

E Why did Dale hit her?

Billy I don't know.

E Where were you sitting?

Billy Alone, and I changed seats with Susan.

E   Why did you change seats?

Billy   Susan asked me.

E   What does Susan look like?

Billy   Different.

E   'How does she look different?

Billy   She's blond.

E   Why else?

Billy   And she looks pretty.

E   Do you sit next to her?

Billy   Yeah, sometimes.

E   Who do you usually sit with?

Billy   Dale.

E   Dale who?

Billy   Dale R. (pause). This morning Jeannie got new shoes.

E   What kind of shoes, Billy?

Billy   Black and gold shoes.

E   Do you like them?

Billy   Yes.

E   What's Jeannie's last name?

Billy   I don't know. Lisa came on the bus. Susie said Bill hurt my feelings. (Bill mimicked their conversation at this point.)

E   What did Mr. B say about that, Bill?

Billy   Nothing, Ed.

It is important to remember that Billy was echolalic when we started his training, and although he could imitate sentences he could not generate correct ones. This is true of all the echolalic children we have trained.

Details of the training in Conversational Speech are presented in Manual F in Chapter 6.

Program 5: Giving and Seeking Information

It is apparent from the transcriptions above that the conversations we had with the children involved a great deal of "information exchange." In order to help such an exchange get started we developed a formal program in the lab which was intended to help the children learn how to request and transfer information and to discriminate between what they did or did not know. This program was to teach a format, then, that extended their behavioral repertoires and to provide a mechanism for facilitating conversations.

Essentially, *E* asks *S* a question from a large list of questions to which *S* sometimes knows the answer, sometimes does not (e.g., "What's your name?" which he knows; "What are you going to eat for dinner?" which he may not know). A third person is present in the room with the child and *E*. *E* asks *S* a question, and *S* is to ask the third person the answer to that question (seeking information) and then to relay that information back to *E* (giving information). In Figure 10 we show the acquisition of this behavior of seeking information, which is scored as correct if the child, without being prompted, addresses himself to an at-

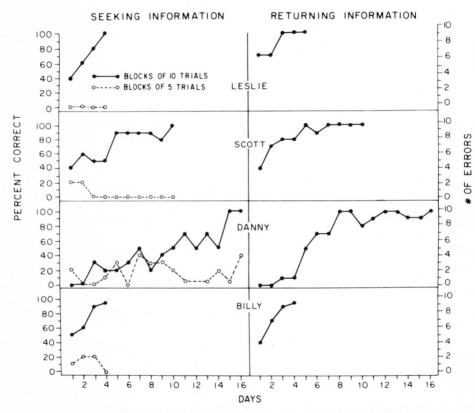

Figure 10. Acquisition curves for four children who were taught to ask various questions of one adult ("seeking information"), and then to relay that information to a second adult ("returning information"). The broken line shows errors, which means the child asked for answers to questions he already knew. The solid line gives the percentage of time the child sought or returned the correct information without being prompted.

tending adult after E has posed a question to him. The top of the figure shows (solid line) that Leslie learned to seek answers to E's questions by the fourth day of training (about a half-hour of training per day). Danny (6 years old, mute), on the other hand, required 16 days. The broken line shows errors, which means that the child would ask the attending adult the answer to a question for which he (the child) already knew the answer. As can be seen, Leslie made this discrimination (between answers she knew and did not know) from the beginning; Scott and Billy acquired it during training; while Danny did not learn the discrimination during these sessions. These data are of particular interest because Scott and Billy are acquiring a discrimination of a purely internal event, the difference between "knowing" and "not knowing." Having learned the correct answer, the child did not immediately "know" that he had to return this information to E; he had to be trained to do so in a separate step. The section labeled "Returning Information" shows how this behavior was acquired. It took 4 days for Leslie, 10 for Scott, 16 for Danny, and 4 for Billy to seek an answer to a question and to give that answer back to the person who had requested it.

Program 6: Grammatical Skills

In Program 2 we described procedures for building certain elementary phrases and sentences, using prompt, reinforcement, and stimulus rotation procedures much like the ones we have used in all the language programs. In terms the linguist might use, we have attempted to help the child make well-formed sentences, or grammatical sentences, by beginning with sentences composed almost entirely of "free" or "full" morphemes. For instance, "I want bread," "I want go," and "I want tickle" were all acceptable sentences at first. As training progressed, we began prompting and reinforcing the use of more complex surface structures. For instance, we began to demand the use of articles (the insertion of "to" in such sentences as "I want to go"), modification of nouns by adjectives, the use of prepositional phrases where appropriate, agreement between pronouns and subject-verb relationships in sentences, and the like. We can illustrate this training by giving excerpts from the "conversations" we had with some of the children. Let us first introduce Rick, at about one year into treatment, to illustrate the acquisition of grammar, particularly correct pronoun usage.

Ricky and *E* are looking at a picture of a lake with sailboats, people on the shore, and so on.

> *E*   Look at the picture. Who's this?
> *Ricky*   Mommy.
> *E*   Good. What is Mommy doing?
> *Ricky*   He is standing on the dock.
> *E*   No, she.
> *Ricky*   She is standing on the dock.
> *E*   Good. Look, what else is Mommy doing?
> *Ricky*   Mommy he is putting around his shoulders.
> *E*   No, she.
> *Ricky*   She is putting around his shoulders.
> *E*   Around her shoulders.
> *Ricky*   Her shoulders.
> *E*   Good, Ricky. Very good. What is Susan doing?
> *Ricky*   He is putting hands in the pocket.
> *E*   No, she.
> *Ricky*   She is putting hands in the pocket.
> *E*   That's very good. Her hands.
> *Ricky*   Her hands in the pocket.
> *E*   That's right. What's happening out here?

Most of the teaching of grammar was conducted informally without objective data recording. However, we also developed two specific programs for the teaching of grammar which dealt with the addition of inflectional affixes. These are simple lexical items, not complex syntactical rules. "S" for the plural and "ed" for the past tense are inflectional affixes. They do not change the grammatical class of the words (as is often the case with derivational affixes such as "ly") and, in general, the formation of words through the addition of inflectional morphemes is quite regular as compared to other kinds of affixes. Rules governing the addition of affixes are the simplest kinds of grammatical rules, and inflectional affixes are the simplest kinds of affixes. These may be some of the reasons we were able to develop a simple, successful, formal training program for teaching their use.

The acquisition of inflectional affixes allows the child to form some very common kinds of utterances about time and number. In particular, it seems that the transformation of verbs from present to past tense accounts for a large percentage of the descriptions people commonly make. This skill enables one to call upon one's past experience and that of others, to learn how the past relates to the present and, one hopes, to be in a position to evaluate the consequences of an act without performing it.

There are two stages to the program we have developed for teaching the transformation of verbs from present to past tense. We worked as follows. Using three Ss, Billy, Scott, and Leslie (5 to 8 years old, echolalic), we selected 10 common nonverbal behaviors (such as walking, dancing, closing, looking) which we already had taught S to label in the present tense ("I am walking across the room." "I am dancing." "I am closing the door." "I am looking outside.") The verbs describing these behaviors all required "ed" in the past tense. We then gave the children a performance pretest to assess whether they could use their verbs in the past tense. In this test, S was first told to perform the behavior and asked to label it in the present ("What are you doing?"). He was then told to stop and to label the behavior in the past tense ("What did you just do?"). None of the children could label their behaviors in the past tense, as can be seen in Figure 11.

Ss were then trained to transform the 10 sentences involved in the pretest to the past tense, but without the associated nonverbal performance. E merely asked S to repeat the present tense (E said: "Say, I am walking across the room."), then asked for the past tense by saying: "What did you just do?" and prompted the correct past tense. If we examine Billy's record on this task, which is labeled "verbal training" in Figure 11, we can see that he learned to criterion within the first block of 10 trials. Actually he erred and was prompted the correct transformation on the sentences numbered 1, 3, 4, and 7 on the first block of 10 trials; he made no mistakes when these sentences were repeated in the second 10-trial block. We then administered a performance post-test, identical to the performance pretest, in an attempt to determine whether the purely verbal training on transforming sentences had helped him to label his nonverbal behavior in the past tense. The children now performed considerably better. Billy, for example, raised his score from zero to 50 percent correct. He made mistakes in labeling the first behavior ("I am walking across the room"), which E corrected. He also made mistakes on numbers 3, 4, 7, and 8. The children were then trained specifically in correctly labeling behaviors in the past tense, which we trained as follows. They were told to perform the behavior, and while they were engaged in the behavior they were asked to label it in the present tense. This they already had mastered. They were then

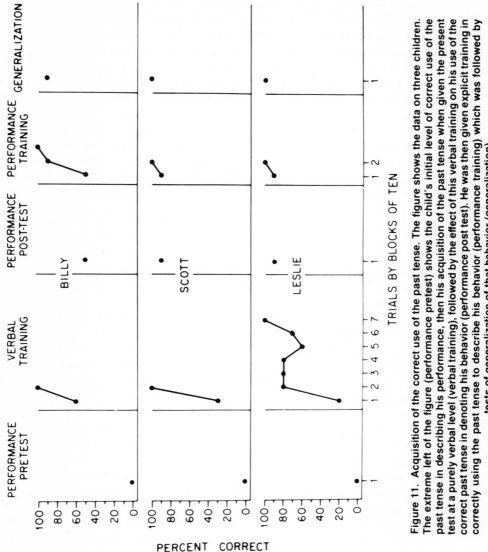

Figure 11. Acquisition of the correct use of the past tense. The figure shows the data on three children. The extreme left of the figure (performance pretest) shows the child's initial level of correct use of the past tense in describing his performance, then his acquisition of the past tense when given the present test at a purely verbal level (verbal training), followed by the effect of this verbal training on his use of the correct past tense in denoting his behavior (performance post test). He was then given explicit training in correctly using the past tense to describe his behavior (performance training) which was followed by tests of generalization of that behavior (generalization).

told to stop and asked (trained) to label the behavior in the past tense. They acquired this task of labeling 10 behaviors using the past tense within 20 trials, as can be seen in the *performance* training in Figure 11. Finally they were given a generalization test in which we selected 10 common but *new* behaviors (such as clapping hands, scratching head, pointing, touching). They could label these behaviors in the present tense, but they had not been trained to label them in the past tense. As the figure shows, their performance was errorless on the generalization test. The children made some minor (and understandable) errors, but these did not distract from the adequacy of their performance. For example, Billy transformed "touch" to "touched" ("I touched the window") and transformed "push" to "pushed" ("I pushed the car").

In summary, the data show that the children learned to transform simple verbs from the present to the past tense. During the generalization test, they both responded to new stimuli, and they also constructed new responses (grammatically correct sentences). Within our conceptual framework, one can state that verb transformation is a response created through differential reinforcement. In other terms, one might say that they had learned a grammatical "rule" by which they generated novel sentences.

The use of irregular verbs (run-ran, eat-ate) was taught as exceptions to the "ed" ending in the child's day-to-day activities. The acquisition seemed uneventful.

The program for pluralization also considered regular and irregular forms. *E* selected 10 common object labels which required the addition of "s" in the plural. He held up the appropriate number of objects and said, for example, "Here is one apple, here are two. . . ." The desired response was prompted, and so on. After *S* mastered the first 10 plurals, *E* trained pluralization to several more questions (S^Ds) (e.g., "Here are some . . ." "Here are many . . ."). *E* then tested for generalization using both new objects and new S^Ds. They learned to pluralize as they learned the verb transformations. Irregular plurals were taught in the same manner as irregular verbs, i.e., as they were encountered in the child's day-to-day functioning.

The procedures just offered, even with the more detailed accounts found in the manuals (see manual G and H), cannot possibly cover all the problems one encounters in teaching grammatical language behavior. Like any complex social behavior repertoire, it is too varied and extensive to be taught explicitly in the lab. However, it is hoped that the reader will be able to abstract (discriminate) the principles involved and generate his own programs for problems as he deals with children in everyday life. Now let us turn to some more elaborate programs.

Program 7: Recall

We have described programs for introducing the child to basic concepts of time. We have outlined manuals for teaching "first" and "last," "before" and "after," and verb transformations. Once the child had acquired some of these basic discriminations we then extended the time concept in many directions. One such direction involved teaching the child to describe his behavior, as it was increasingly removed from the present. We termed this training "recall." Recall is a behavior which can be said to "enrich the environment," both of the child and of the E. The programs on recall, therefore, as is the case with the remaining ones, relate quite directly to the terminal goals of the language project. Recall enriches the environment by enabling the child to transmit and record past events in a manner comprehensible to all. These records and transmissions may then become functional stimuli for persons not actually present when the event occurred. As such, they will control the behavior of both the speaker and the listener.

The recall program requires that the child have most, if not all, of the language skills discussed in the preceding programs. The manual involves 3 steps. The first step, which centers on recall of the immediate past, is taught much as were transformations. E and S engage in some behavior together, which S may be describing at that time. Five to 10 seconds may elapse, and then E asks, "What did you just do?" The child may answer or be prompted to answer, "I stood up, walked to the blackboard, wrote on it, looked out the window, sat down." Gradually E decreases his instructional involvement until S is performing and then recalling as many as six to eight different activities per trial. This practice serves to gradually increase the delay between the stimulus input and S's verbal reconstruction of that input. Recall training serves, in a sense, to "build" the child's memory.

The second step in the program involves the verbal reproduction of events with a somewhat longer delay and of activities which are more complex and provide less specific cues for recall.

When the child has completed this step, he should be able to recall a sequence like "We got a drink, went downstairs, saw a dog, bought some candy, and came back." We are now talking about delays of up to 15 minutes.

The final step involves recall of events anywhere which have occurred hours or days in the child's past. When the child masters this phase, he should be answering questions like "What did you do last weekend?" *E* must know what has happened to the child in order to prompt him to give a correct response when necessary. Detailed description of the procedures is given in Manual S in Chapter 6.

Data from the recall training on two children, Leslie and Scott, are presented in Figure 12. The abscissa denotes from one to two hours of training per day. The figure shows the acquisition (the increase in recalled events with decreased prompting) of recall from the three stages in which the children were taught to verbally reproduce events in their past. At first these events involved simple acts in the immediate past (such as drinking or eating) and later in training became more elaborate (were recalled with adjectives, and so on) and more removed in time. The training of recall is presented in more detail in Manual I in Chapter 6.

As training progressed and the child acquired the basic discriminations involved in recall, reinforcement became less contingent on spontaneous, perhaps not always accurate, descriptions of his behavior and environment. We wanted to build the beginning of fantasy, and we called this new program "story-telling."

Before we describe the "story-telling" program, it is important to point out that the principal disadvantage of our training program centered on its failure to produce the kinds of spontaneous, cross-situational, generalized speech that normal children display. We have no objectively recorded comparisons, but it soon became apparent that many of our children did not "use" language as normal children do, often giving the parent the problem of trying to "shut the kid up" once he learns to speak. Most of the children seemed not to want to speak, except in a situation where there was a powerful reinforcer available such as food. Whenever one uses experimental (artificial) reinforcers for speech, that speech probably becomes highly discriminated. The amount of spontaneous speech seemed to be some function of the range of reinforcing stimuli functional for a particular child. The more developed children gave more spontaneity. However, in the ab-

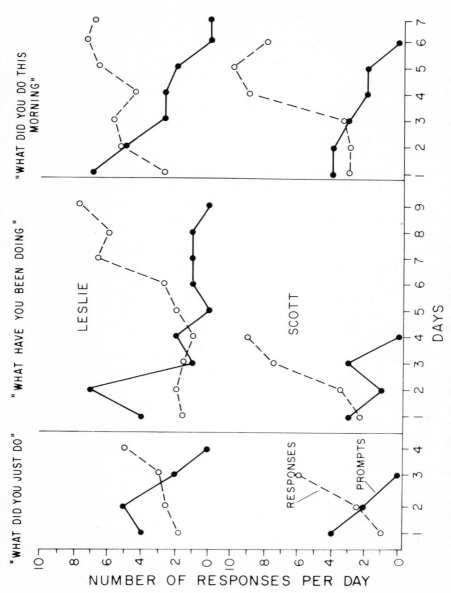

Figure 12. Recall training on two children in three different situations. The solid line shows the use of prompts, and the dotted lines show correct unprompted responses as training progressed.

sence of independent measures of a child's motivation, these are clinical impressions only. We shall return to a discussion of such motivational variables later.

Program 8: Spontaneity

Details of the spontaneity training program are presented in Manual J in Chapter 6. Strange as this may seem to some, we actually built a program to help the child become more spontaneous. We began such spontaneity training by holding up a "poster" on which was pasted a picture of *one* object that the child could label. *E* asked, "What do you see?" and prompted the answer. The number of pictures on the poster were then increased in gradual steps, to two or three to a dozen or so; and reinforcement was given contingent on larger and larger responses. The child was said to have mastered a poster when he had labeled all the components of the poster without requests (prompts and the like) to do so. After the child had been reinforced for such "extended" responses using the kind of controlled stimulus presentations allowed by the posters, we moved on to material and questions like "What do you see on the table?" and "What do you see in this room"? and "Tell me about yourself."

In "Tell me about yourself," *E* started *S* labeling his body parts and clothes. If an unusual response occurred, it was immediately and generously rewarded, wherever it occurred in the chain. Let's look at some data. Figure 13 shows the chaining of an increasing number of body parts (on the ordinate), over training days (about half an hour of training per day) for three children— Scott, Leslie, and Danny. By the 12th day, Leslie would, without additional cues from *E,* produce: "eyes, nose, hair, shirt, arm," and so on, pointing to each part as she labeled it. Although we trained Danny for 50 days, his performance was still quite variable, sometimes being very good (up to 18 "items" without intervening prompts) and sometimes producing very little.

It seemed a relatively small step, once the child could describe his own behavior and body, to teach him to describe his surrounding environment. We have some data to describe how such learning occurs in the record of Scott, whom we taught to describe his breakfast, at one year into his language training. He

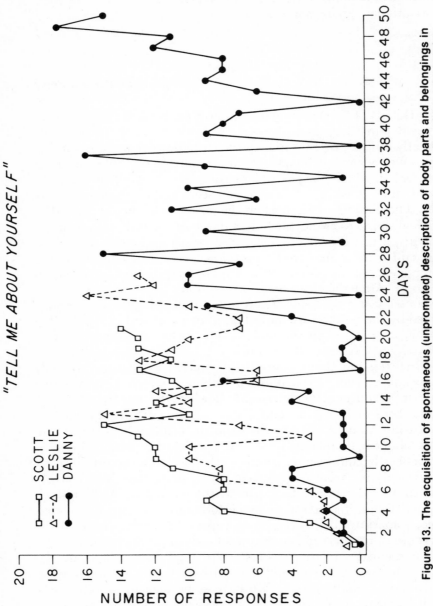

"TELL ME ABOUT YOURSELF"

Figure 13. The acquisition of spontaneous (unprompted) descriptions of body parts and belongings in three children. The ordinate gives number of separate parts that the child would offer without the teacher prompting him over training days.

was 5 years old and echolalic when he came to us. Data on "Tell me about breakfast" is given in Figure 14. He received 15 to 30 minutes training on this task per day, over 16 days (on the abscissa). The ordinate gives the number of responses per trial and the number of prompts for a particular response. The data given in Figure 14 show that he learned to describe his experience around breakfast so that eventually he used rather extensive verbalizations, unaided by *E*. On the 16th day of training Scott gave the following account, which reflects the amount of detail we required:

> *E*   What did you have for breakfast?
> *Scott*   Bacon and eggs, orange juice, and milk. Eggs are yellow, eggs are good. I like the eggs. The bacon is red and white, the bacon is good, and oh, I had scrambled eggs, and I like the bacon. Milk is liquid, milk is good, and I like the milk. Orange juice is good, O.J. is soft—no! I had grapefruit. Grapefruit is good. I eat it with a grapefruit spoon, and that's all.

Program 9: Storytelling

Program 9 on storytelling became a direct extension of Program 8 on spontaneity training. What Program 9 attempts to do is to move the child's language from control by concrete and experimentally manipulated S^Ds to less observable stimuli. We wanted the child to use language as in fantasy for his personal gratification. We began to reinforce extensive idiosyncratic description whenever possible. Our purpose was to increasingly free the child's verbal behavior from the control of immediate and concrete stimuli, to bring it under the control of the child's feelings and experiences, and yet to keep it sufficiently public so that we could "share his expressions" and agree that his descriptions were "sensible." As it is possible to reinforce "psychotic" verbal behavior as well (Lovaas, 1967), the shaper has to keep some kind of criterion of "comprehensibity" or "sensibility" in mind.

It seemed that we should build extended verbal repertoires to supply a range of reinforcers for fantasy behavior. This presupposes that the child is reinforced by controlling large aspects of his personal environment, beyond the necessary operations for eating and sleeping. Many autistic children do not find their en-

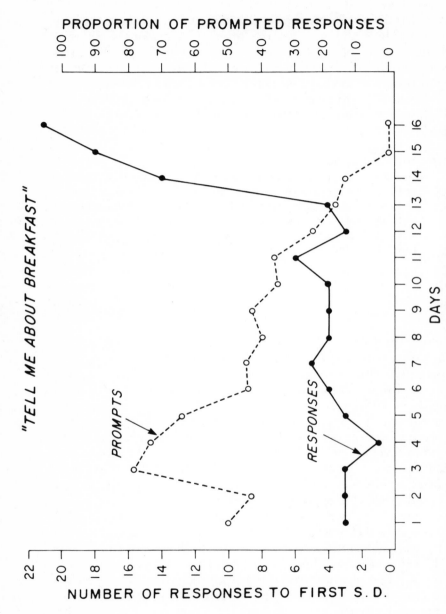

Figure 14. The decrease in the teacher's use of prompts and the increase in unprompted responses in a child's description of his breakfast with increasing training days.

vironment to be that reinforcing, and with such children we failed to produce verbal fantasies. But for those children whose environment contained more varied reinforcers, language became rich and appropriate. Let us illustrate this point. Ricky always enjoyed himself at Disneyland, and when he was taught to describe and order his experiences, a question like "What do you want to talk about?" could bring about a large repertoire of verbalized experiences ("I went to the Matterhorn, and we went through the water.") with quite appropriate affect. Another child, or Ricky himself, when we first began treatment with him, might have spent the entire day at Disneyland without being able to enjoy talking about it later.

The mute children did not reach this level, but many of the echolalic children became quite elaborate in their descriptions. The transcribed tape recordings from two such children serve to illustrate the degree of sophisticated expressions some of the children attained toward the end of their training. Eric was 12 years old and was echolalic upon admission. Like the other children (like Rick, who was also echolalic) at intake he lacked a labeling vocabulary and was unable to answer even a simple question like "What is your name?" He was treated for one year for three hours per week. His parents served as co-therapists, which extended his training on a daily basis.

The following conversation was recorded on audio tape and then transcribed verbatim. Eric and his therapist are seated at a table discussing a book filled with pictures of many common household items. The items on the first page included an electric mixer, a toaster, a fan, and a radio. It is obvious that Eric goes beyond the immediate stimulus situation given by the book. He is, in fact, using his imagination and "telling a story."

> *Eric* I want to talk about the egg beater, makes eggs and the fan turns on and blows the wind off. Turn on with a switches. It blows. I put toast in the toaster and make toasted cheese sandwiches. I make . . . I put . . . I make . . . turn on the music and I listen . . . I listen . . . I listen to the music and it sings lots of things.

Quite interesting in this sequence is Eric's apparent search for the correct verb with which to describe how to operate the radio ("I make . . . I put . . . I make . . . turn on. . . ."). Later in the same session, Eric turns to a page in the book with pictures of the sun, the moon, a rainbow, and stars. The rainbow is depicted behind a group of pine trees (note Eric's reference to "Christmas trees"). Eric's father is present during the session:

> *Eric*   Talk about the sun coming up in the west. Talk about the sun . . . sun sun . . . rises . . . rises comes up in the west clouds . . . west clouds.
>
> *Father*   Does the sun rise in the west?
>
> *Eric*   Sun . . . Where's the sun come up? Comes up in the west. Goes down in the west.
>
> *Father*   Where does it come up from?
>
> *Eric*   The east.
>
> *Father*   Right.
>
> *Eric*   The crescent moon's up in the sky and see those colors of the rainbow. Reds and yellows, green and blue and purple and Christmas trees in the Christmas mountains. Stars up in the sky. Talk about these enough.

Eric's speech may be judged to be creative, it goes beyond the immediate concrete stimulus situation, and it entertained us as it seemingly entertained him.

Billy was another child to illustrate such elaborate speech. He was echolalic and 6 years old at the beginning of treatment. This conversation, which takes place without any discrete stimuli, was recorded after Billy had been in treatment for two years.

> *E*   What's new, Billy?
>
> *Billy*   We're going to have a carnival on Friday. Can I pull Susie dog's tail?
>
> *E*   No, Bill.
>
> *Billy*   Why?
>
> *E*   Because it would hurt her.
>
> *Billy*   Hey, you remember the monster on Voyage to the Bottom of the Sea?
>
> *E*   Yes, Bill. Does he walk like this? (*E* pretends to be monster.)
>
> *Billy*   No! Ed (therapist's name), like this. (He demonstrates.)
>
> *E*   Like this, Bill? (*E* imitates Billy.)
>
> *Billy*   Yea, that's right . . . (pause) . . . I got a joke for you, Ed.
>
> *E*   What is it?
>
> *Billy*   Al the gorilla was reading a newspaper. (*E* and Billy both laughed. Billy thought the joke was very funny.)

More detail on how we shaped this kind of "fantasy-behavior" is presented in Manual K in Chapter 6. Note that the child is

now verbalizing events that do not have an explicit external referent, but which are more correctly called an expression of private
"ideas" and "images." It can now be said that *E* has taught the
child to create and respond to fantasy material. *E* created, and in-
directly controls, through the manipulation of *S*'s history, these
ideas and images. Incidentally, this process of responding to
"ideas" and "images" (stimuli which have no explicit and concurrent external, physical referent) is called *displacement* in linguistics, and is considered to be a most unique achievement of man.

Informal Training

The language skills the child needs to effectively communi-
cate with his environment are so comprehensive and varied that it
was simply impossible to formalize the procedure and record data
on all of them. Once the teachers or parents had mastered the
essential principles involved in the early programs, they could
generate their own with considerable ease. The data did not seem
to reveal any new insights into the child's learning process.

We tried to teach the children about interpersonal relationships and questions of motive, matters of feelings and attitudes.
We constructed situations which could bring their feelings out,
and then we labeled them. For example, we would place a child
in front of a swimming pool, where he was very frightened, and
teach him to label that state ("I am frightened") and to discriminate that from how he felt when he was given a swing, which he
loved ("I am happy").

We experienced much success in extending language relating
to sports and games, apparently because these behaviors became
reinforcing. We taught the children baseball, basketball, board-
type games (like checkers), and nursery games (like London
Bridge and ring-around-the-rosey). We taught them how to take
turns, about the thrill of winning and how to be a "good sport,"
about the importance of setting and adhering to rules, and about
verbalizing your own performance. It would have been impossible to accomplish such training without language, and of course
language became enriched through this training.

As a person's language is perhaps only as rich as his experience, we emphasized experience and "doing things." We tried to
help the children understand natural phenomena of all kinds. We

Picture G. Before a child is sent off to school we "practice school" at home. We will go to the child's prospective school, and assess exactly what it is that the teacher has her children doing. Then we will practice and master these behaviors in detail in the child's home before he goes to school. Early parts of school, then, consist merely of shifting stimulus control where the teacher and the other children acquire control over those behaviors which the parents and therapists already can control. In this picture the child's therapist plays the teacher, while Mark's mother and the other therapists play students. In these sessions we try to teach Mark to listen while he is in a group of other people, to take turns in asking questions, to listen to what the group is saying, etc.

helped them to plant and care for small gardens. Such teachings
were closely and complexly related to a large variety of behaviors
which we had already taught. Plants, of course, lead to the concept of growth. For example, the children had learned about size,
about small plants and big plants, about small boys and big men.
The concept of growth refers to the change of small to big. We
taught that plants grow by giving them water. One child de-
duced, "Put some water on my head." We took the children to
zoos and pet stores and discussed the animals. We taught them to
label the weather and its consequences ("It's raining, so I can't go
outside to play."). We took them for walks and trips and had
them label and describe the things around them.

We began to explore the actual teaching of logical thought
and reasoning about everyday events, which many would consider
a basic pay-off behind language. One is referring here to behaviors like inference, deduction, and the understanding of causation. We explored the teaching of these processes in the context
of other programs. Some of these processes may be simpler than
we thought. For example, in working out a program for causation, mere correlation in time of the two (cause-effect) events
sufficed to get the children on the way. The following conversation illustrates an attempt to teach "about causes." Ricky is presented with blocks of different colors and different shapes which
we use as beginning material for the teaching of the concepts *same*
and *different*. He had just been slapped for "acting crazy" (whining and self-stimulatory psychotic behavior). The therapist is trying to reestablish his good relationship with Ricky and to tell
him *why* he was slapped. Notice the repetitions which we
thought were important.

Ricky   (tearful from *E*'s reprimand) I want to go the bathroom. (At that
         time this was Ricky's favorite "out" from unpleasant experiences.)
E   In a minute.
Ricky   In about four minutes.
E   Now come on. Give me a hug. Come on. That's a good boy. Good
         boy. Why did I hit you, Ricky?
Ricky   Because I was crying.
E   Yes. It's all right now. Do you cry a lot?
Ricky   Yes.
E   Want to sit down there? (Points to chair)
Ricky   No. Want to go to the bathroom.
E   Sit down first (Ricky sits). Why did I hit you, Ricky?
Richy   Because I was crying.

E   That's right.
Ricky   I want to go to the bathroom.
E   Okay. In a little bit. Why did I hit you?
Ricky   Because there was . . . (unintelligible).
E   No.
Ricky   Because I cried.
E   That's right. Feel better now, Ricky?
Ricky   Yes.
E   Good.
Ricky   I want to go swimming.
E   You want to do a lot of things, don't you?
Ricky   I want to go swimming.
E   Later, Ricky, we'll go swimming. Do you want to look at the blocks
        here?
Ricky   No. I don't look at the blocks.
E   Why are they all the same, Ricky?
Ricky   Because they're blue.
E   Good.

After two or three years of language teaching (with the echolalic children) the program became so complex that we were unable to disentangle the antecedents. For example, the child whom we described earlier as requesting "some water on my head" to facilitate his growth illustrates this complexity. One does not just reinforce such behavior, one wants to do something else as well. Therefore, we terminated our formal efforts at that point.

Recordings of Spontaneous Verbalizations

The final data which we shall present consists of excerpts taken from the recordings of spontaneous verbal behavior of two of the patients during different stages of treatment. Rather complete behavioral descriptions were kept of the first seven patients (who were all hospitalized during our treatment). The staff (*E*s who were students, teachers, nurses) were also instructed to immediately write down, when possible, the child's spontaneous *normal* verbal behavior. While this was very easy in the first four or five months of treatment, when the child produced no such behavior, some children eventually became so spontaneous that the recordings had to be limited to examples or excerpts.

We shall present the data on two of these children, Ricky and

Billy W. They are representative of the other children we have
seen. Rick was echolalic and Billy W. was mute at the beginning
of treatment. The records were taken over the 14 months of their
treatment. In addition to recording the child's verbalizations, the
staff were also told to write a description of the context in which
the child's speech occurred. Over the 14 months, some 20 staff
members wrote in the patient logs, producing several staff recordings on any one day. These recordings were usually not independent since S was attended to by more than one staff member and
usually several of the staff would take notice of the child's speech.
These recordings were entered along with other notes about the
patient (everyday nonverbal behavior, eating, sleeping, play, vis-
its, and so on) into a patient log.

   These handwritten logs were subsequently typed and rated
for spontaneous speech by a rater, an undergraduate psychology
student, and one of the Es. The undergraduate rater was unfamiliar with the children and the events of the study. She was told
that we were attempting to devise a system that would describe
the appropriate, spontaneous verbal behavior of our children,
both quantitatively and qualitatively. We then told her that we
were trying to ascertain which of several possible systems was the
simplest to teach a new person. She was instructed that she would
be asked to read through three months of notes written about the
children. She was told that we were looking for instances of spontaneous verbal behavior, that is, verbal behavior which occurred
without being asked for, which was not being specifically trained
at the time or prompted by E, but for which the determining
cues could only be inferred from the behavior itself.

   The rater was then given a list of common examples and was
read the recordings made by E for Rick during August. She then
read through Rick's log for January, March, and October, and
wrote down any instances of spontaneous verbal behavior. These
months were selected by E as being typical of a sparse, a medium,
and a full month of spontaneity. They were presented in the order
March, January, October.

   When the rater had finished this task, she was presented with
a new set of instructions that served to clarify the assignment of
points. The rater was given her own notes and asked to assign 1
point for use of single words and phrases, 1 point for comments
written by the therapist without specific reference to the patient's
own words (for example, "Ricky carried on quite a spontaneous

conversation with some members of the staff."), and 2 points for instances of the child's speech which exemplified the use of complete sentences. Once again August was used as a source of examples. The rater then assigned points to her own notes on January, March, and October.

Both the rater and E chose approximately the same number of instances and assigned the same number of points in each month tested. The data are summarized in Table 2. Both readers saw the same progress in the patient's behavior. Since the statements were chosen more or less as samples from a pool and the rater did not have comparable experience with the children, the same statements were not always chosen by both; however, in almost every

Reliability Data

Month	Datum	Experimenter's	Rater's
January	Number of examples chosen	3	5
	Number of points assigned to statements chosen	5	6
March	Number of examples chosen	21	23
	Number of points assigned to statements chosen	32	40
October	Number of examples chosen	28	32
	Number of points assigned to statements chosen	49	52

case, the quality of the statements were similar. *E* had read all of the logs, while the rater had read only samples from different months. With the broader picture, *E* tended to disregard some of the simpler examples. Perhaps this was the reson why *E* differed consistently with the rater in the direction of underestimation. The data show that instances of spontaneous verbal behavior can be reliably identified from such written logs, but, because of our failure to record (or assess) reliability in the original (log) recordings, these data ought to be viewed with reservations. However, a description of what the children spontaneously talked about as they gradually acquired mastery of language would perhaps be the most important data in a language program. We shall attempt to illustrate such language for Ricky (8-year-old echolalic) and Billy (5-year-old mute). We shall first provide a numerical score ("points") which is intended to quantify the frequency and complexity of spontaneous, appropriate verbal behavior. Scores were assigned in the same manner as for the reliability check. For each month, we will also give examples of the most typical type of behavior for that month and attempt to illustrate the most complex.

Ricky's spontaneous verbal behavior (*S* initially echolalic)

July (1st year): 0
August: 0
November: 0
December: 0
    Median: Spontaneously labeling objects.
    Complex: Requesting to draw a rocket ship and a merry-go-round.

January (2nd year): 5
    Median: Saying "hi" and interacting with therapists.
    Complex: Using phrases like "kiss it and make it better." Rick hit his therapist, seemed concerned, said "How are you feeling, Joan?"

February: 17
    Median: Requesting songs, paper for drawing, to go home. Asking questions about his mother, TV programs.
    Complex: Working with other children, prompting them, telling them to "pay attention," and reinforcing them when correct without prompting by therapist.

March: 20
> Median: Labeling actions of others in complete sentences, recalling past events without prompting. Ricky now teases a lot and is able to label his own behavior as teasing.
>
> Complex: Ricky has generalized the use of "I don't want to" (in new situations without formal training). He makes analogies about new experiences, such as saying the dark room is "like the dark sky." He is able to answer riddles about familiar activities. For instance, *E* says "I am at the amusement park. I go up and down. What am I?" Ricky answers, "Ferris wheel."

April: 30
> Median: Ricky is using "I don't want to" regularly, commenting on pictures in books and coming events. Commenting on things he is being trained to do.
>
> Complex: Ricky is able to use "supposed" properly and spontaneously, e.g., "I am supposed to use my napkin." He is able to discuss events in the future using time concepts, e.g., "I am going home Thursday, three more days, no, two more days." (Two days is correct in this case.) He is also beginning to control his own behavior verbally; he says, "I am not going to gag (whine, etc.) any more."

May: 27
> Median: Ricky is asking and answering questions and making requests of peers spontaneously. He is noticing and asking questions of strangers and verbalizing his feelings to some extent.
>
> Complex: *E* allows Ricky to go on short walks by himself occasionally. After one such walk Ricky returned and told me that it was "amazing" that he had gone by himself. *E* told him that flowers grow up and so do people; he said, "Pour some water on my head." He understands part of the concept of growing up.

June: 21
> Median: Joan, Ricky's original therapist, left the project at the beginning of June. Throughout the month, Ricky makes comments about her: "I miss Joan." "I want to go to Joan's house." "Two more months and I go to Joan's house." (He was told Joan would return for a visit in two months.)
>
> Complex: Ricky was very upset about Joan's having to leave. The

rest of the staff tried to tell him he would still have fun. He would reply, "I don't want to have fun at the beach. I want to go to Joan's house." Rick is also beginning to verbalize the reasons for events on his own, "I can't go to La Cienega because I am sick." He is able to verbalize some very abstract feelings, "I want to get better."

July: 30

Median: Verbalizing reasons, "I like Mrs. Dumont because she is a nice friend." "The fly is too hard to catch. He goes real fast." Talking about being a big boy and using, "I want to do it myself."

Complex: Ricky has the concept of difficulty. Says "I don't know" or "That is hard" when he can't answer a question. Points out that the hands on the clock are "sneaking" and that a picture in a book looks like Chuckie, another patient. It does. Is beginning to make fine descriminations about his environment.

August: 39

Median: Ricky is constantly analogizing new experiences with familiar ones: "Sprinkler is like a little shower," blowing bubbles in the bathtub water is "just like the swimming pool," "Canteloupe is just like watermelon," spinning on the swings is "just like an elevator."

Complex: Ricky is able to verbalize reinforcement contingencies: "You give me an airplane spin because I do such good recall." He is verbalizing his fears and talks about those he has overcome: "I am not afraid to swing fast."

September: 20

Median: Pamela, one of the girls on the project, is sent back to State Hospital this month. Ricky is talking about her constantly: "Where is Pam?" Hears a sing-song voice and says, "Just like Pamela." Labels toy figures Ricky and Pam.

Complex: He is able to verbalize delayed reinforcement contingencies: "Ed, give me an airplane spin when I finish working." He recognizes the quality of his own behavior: "I did very well on the cards." "I shouldn't get so upsetted."

Billy's spontaneous verbal behavior (S initially mute)

July (1st year): 0

August: 0

September: 3

Billy is using "go" at the door and "bread" to request bread at meals.

October: 41

Median: He is using "I want" followed by one word to express desires for food.

Complex: Recognizes and asks for his father: "I want Daddy." Billy is able to use the word "more" correctly in order to get a second helping at meals.

November: 19

Median: Bill is using "I want" plus one word to designate reinforcements other than food: "I want push" and "I want swing."

Complex: He uses "Go away" when he wants to have someone leave him alone. He greets his peers with "Hi."

December: 22

Median: He is requesting reinforcement in many ways: backrides, pushes, being picked up.

Complex: Billy uses "the" correctly as in "Open the door." He also uses the pronoun "me" correctly in some requests, as in "Push me."

January (2nd year): 23

Median: Simple requests for reinforcement. He spontaneously greets his therapist with "Hi" in the morning.

Complex: Billy is labeling objects he sees. He is using "1, 2, 3, go" to initiate racing games with others.

February: 35

Median: Billy is labeling many objects and things he sees like sky, truck, car, contents of the doll house.

Complex: Using verbs in his requests. He commands the therapist to "come," uses infinitives such as "I want to eat," "I want to eat candy."

March: 32

Median: Billy is using the names of the people he knows in greetings, as in "Hi, Mary," or simply naming people around him.

Complex: He is using verbs in his requests and requesting things other than simple reinforcements. He now asks for help buttoning his jacket and to go "potty." He is beginning to develop some sense of time, e.g., he greets *E* one morning with, "Hi. Sleep, wake up."

April: 55

Median: Using "all done" correctly to indicate when he has finished an activity. Spontaneously counts numbers he sees, as on elevator buttons and TV channels. He is greeting therapists, peers, and strangers with "Hi." He is using "the" for more objects, "I want the ball."

Complex: Billy is using some fairly complex sentences with several pronouns: "I want you to tickle me," "I want to tie my shoes."

May: 55

Median: Billy is using more complex sentences for more requests, e.g., "I want you to chase me." He is consistently including names in greetings: "Hi, Ricky," "Goodbye, Daddy."

Complex: Billy is using "Yes" and "No" spontaneously both to answer questions and to express desires or respond to commands. Giving some commands to therapists, using prepositions such as "come over" and "sit down."

June: 63

Median: Billy is using complex sentences composed of pronouns, articles, and prepositions, as in "I want a drink of water."

Complex: He is labeling actions he sees in pictures or performs himself, such as "dancing" and "jumping." Becoming interested in books, asking for them, labeling what he sees in them. Naming the colors of familiar objects and letters.

July: 84

Median: Billy is now very spontaneous when looking at books, labeling objects, people, picking out letters he knows, using "turn the page." He often labels the colors of things he sees.

Complex: He begins to use the word "outside," asking to go outside, labeling it when he is outside. He sometimes goes through long strings of labels of things he sees, e.g., "letters," "ball," "swimming," "trike," "sky blue," "window," and "red," "green," "tether ball," "outside," "sky," "fence."

August: 89

Median: Billy is using "outside" quite frequently in complex sentences: "I want to go outside." He is labeling familiar objects seen in magazines and books, through windows, and on TV.

Complex: Sometimes he will label his own actions in complete sentences, as in "I am reading a book." He is using some generalization in labeling, calling a helicopter a "big fan" and labeling the blue tiles in a design he made as "sky."

September: 77
Median: Same level as August.
Complex: Quite concerned about going home. Asks for Mommy and Daddy, labels people in magazines as Mommy and Daddy, starts asking for brother, "Pat." He is able to follow instructions of a stranger, a janitor, and help him clean some windows. He is using "no" to express denied requests: "No money, no coke, no candy."

Reinforcement and the Maintenance of the Language Behavior

We felt that one of the most important variables in the study was the administration of the experimental reinforcement (stroking, exaggerated social approval, goodies to eat, slaps, loud "no," attention withdrawal, and so on). But the large amount of interaction (we literally lived with some of the children) could well have produced language through some hypothetical mechanism such as "exposure" or "stimulation," quite independently of its role as reinforcing stimulus. Therefore, one year into training, we ran a separate study on Ricky and Pam in which we temporarily disconnected the relationship between these reinforcing stimuli and the child's behavior. We did this by shifting the experimental reinforcers from a response-contingent to a time-contingent delivery. During the time-contingent delivery the child received as much social stimulation as before, we talked to him just as often, and we showed him as much affection and concern; but we acted contingent on the time elapsed since the last interaction, rather than contingent on the child's response. This procedure should tell us whether our use of reinforcers was necessary in maintaining appropriate language.

The data from this intervention are presented in Figure 15. Days (Ss received about 6 hours of training, distributed throughout the day) are plotted on the abscissa. Correct responding, which is plotted on the ordinate, means correct answers to the abstract terms Ss had been taught up to this time, such as prepositional and pronominal terms. We obtained two days of baseline data (days 1 and 2), followed by six days (days 3 through 8) of

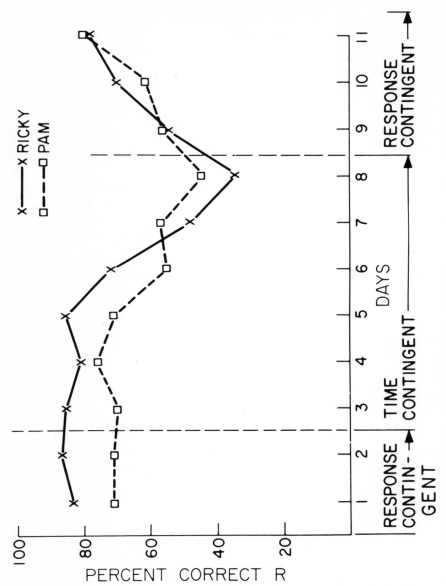

Figure 15. The loss of correct abstract terms in Ricky and Pam when reinforcement was given contingent on time (time contingent) versus correct use of the abstract terms (response contingent).

reinforcement delivered contingent on time elapsed since last delivery, rather than on the child's correct behavior. Finally, the reinforcement is reinstated contingent on correct responses (days 9, 10, and 11). Obviously, the children did not maintain correct behavior independently of the experimental reinforcement. For these effects to be maintained, then, appropriate reinforcing conditions have to be arranged.

References

Lovaas, O. I. A behavior therapy approach to the treatment of childhood schizophrenia. In John P. Hill (Ed.), *Minnesota symposia on child psychology.* Minneapolis: University of Minnesota Press, 1967.

———. *Behavior modification: Teaching language to psychotic children,* instructional film, 45 min., 16 mm.-sound, Appleton-Century-Crofts, New York, 1969.

Chapter V
IMPLICATIONS
AND SPECULATIONS

Relationship to Other Data on Language

Let us now consider how our method and data relate to other similar (behavioristic) work in language. We will also relate our procedures to data on normal language development and to theoretical orientations within linguistics. Finally, we will offer some speculations about directions for future research on language.

Although we have conceptualized language development as the acquisition of responses and stimulus functions, one usually talks about language development in terms of three aspects: the semantic, the syntactic, and the phonetic. It might be helpful to relate our data and others' data to these three divisions, beginning with semantics.

Semantics. A major area in language development, the field of semantics, concerns the acquisition of meaning. How do verbal utterances become associated to the appropriate context? One usually speaks of two dimensions to this context: One can focus on the environmental stimulus input that triggers the verbal behavior, or one can focus on the verbal behavior as input, triggering further behaviors in either the speaker or the listener.

We have gone to some length to show how, through differential reinforcement, verbal behavior may come under the control of a large range of environmental stimuli, external or internal. We showed how we could bring verbal behavior under the control of stimuli which were both subtle and dynamic, such as the temporal and spatial relations between objects and behaviors, differences between purely internal events such as known and unknown material and minute differences between statements like "Ricky is a bad boy," "Is Ricky a bad boy?" and "Ricky is a big boy." Skinner (1957) has speculated extensively on the power of reinforcement in bringing verbal behavior under appropriate stimulus control, and our data support his speculations. Our data on semantics are perhaps our strongest point and relate to a small body of similar investigations that have been published over the last few years.

One of the more detailed accounts of operant procedures for language acquisition, including semantics, is contained in the work of "the Kansas group"—Baer, Risley, Sherman, Wolf, and so on. These studies describe prompting, fading, timing of reinforcement, stimulus rotation, and a myriad of special procedures very similar to those employed in our studies. In their first study, Wolf, Risley, and Mees (1965) were able to establish a 10-word labeling vocabulary in a 3½-year-old psychotic and echolalic boy. Detailed procedures and results were not given in the 1964 report for the labeling program, but they were reviewed in a later article (Risley & Wolf, 1967). The 1967 study is particularly interesting since it involved four psychotic children with echolalic speech and attempted to establish broader classes of functional speech. The procedures employed are strikingly similar to those we have outlined, even though the two programs were developed independently. Their data also reflect the positive acceleration (savings over tasks) that characterizes our results. The authors also comment on many of the learning difficulties we have encountered, such as the loss of previously mastered material as new stimuli are introduced and the difficulty of shifting behavior from the prompt to the training stimuli.

Hewett's (1965) study is one of the earliest reports of a behavioral approach to the acquisition of beginning language repertoire. He worked with a 4½-year-old mute autistic boy, building both a basic labeling vocabulary and some basic components of conversational speech. His procedures have extensive overlap with those we have described. Prompting, fading, and stimulus rotation are all mentioned by Hewett as part of his training procedures. He employed a comprehensive reinforcement environment, underscoring the importance of an "artificial" motivational system in working with psychotic children. Hewett's child was reported to have acquired a 32-word vocabulary within a six-month period; the list included 105 words one year later.

Another group of related studies are concerned with teaching "comprehension" as in the work of Stark, Giddan, and Meisel (1968), who describe the acquisition of beginning comprehension in a five-year-old autistic boy. Their data show the acceleration of the child's acquisition in the decreasing number of trials required for mastery over successive responses.

There are several less detailed accounts of programs attempting to establish labeling behavior, such as that reported by Cook and Adams (1966); Salzinger *et al.* (1965); Sloane, Johnston, and Harris (1968); and MacAuley (1968).

Literature on the acquisition of abstractions (pronouns, prepositions, and the like) is more scarce than that for simple labeling. There are some references (Risley and Wolf, 1967) to selected children who eventually acquired such abstractions; however, these references are usually offered as informal data only.

Historically most writers in the field of language have not debated the importance of differential reinforcement in the establishment of meaning, which may explain why there are so few investigators researching this area. Yet obviously we have not resolved a number of issues on how to teach semantics. Some quite surprising findings may be ahead on what defines a stimulus, which seemingly is the critical issue in teaching semantics. Certainly we were surprised at the relative ease (Figure 10) with which we brought the child's verbal behavior under the appropriate control of "knowing" (versus "not knowing") certain factual events about his environment—a purely "internal" event. We hope we will see much more work in this area: what the child is learning about his environment when he is reinforced, how subtle a difference he can respond to, how broad a range of events may constitute a stimulus, and so on.

If we turn our attention to the acquisition of grammatical skills, on the other hand, we see the beginnings of a significant literature. This work is now reviewed as "syntax."

Syntax. While many investigators think that differential reinforcement and modeling play some role in the acquisition of semantics, they feel that syntax (grammar) is too complex to be understood in terms of learning processes as we now know them. Early attempts, such as those by Guthrie (1935) and Hull (1943), to define responses in topographical terms (as patterning of muscle or effector activity, like a physiological reflex) severely limited the ability of learning theory formulations to account for complex behavior, and virtually excluded grammatical behavior as being learned. The expression of grammatically correct responses (sentences) required not just one fixed output, but sets of responses with different and interchangeable topographical features (different "responses" in the Hull-Guthrie sense). The problem is complicated by the fact that people will speak in grammatically correct sentences even though they may never have been reinforced for (or "practiced") these specific sentences in the past. Brown and Fraser (1964) point out that children are able to understand and construct sentences (and grammatical forms) they have never heard but which are nonetheless, well formed, i.e., well formed in terms of the general rules that are implicit in the sentences the child has heard. Because it is very difficult to account for this apparent fact within the Hull-Guthrie formulations, many linguists have postulated certain theoretical concepts such as the concept of "generative" grammar or "rule-generated" language and have endowed these concepts with many neurologically-based (innate) determinants.

The argument that language has a strong innate determinant is of course not new. For centuries the psychologists and philosophers who have given thought to the origins of human behavior and who have wondered how complex behaviors like language come about either describe language as determined by innate, organic structures or describe language as learned or determined by environmental or experimental variables. The first position, the nativistic one, is currently most closely associated with Chomsky (1965) and Lenneberg (1964). The environmentalist position has been most closely associated with Skinner (1957) and Mowrer (1960), and to some extent with Berko (1958), Brown and Fraser (1964), and Ervin (1964). We hope our findings will lend more credence to some of those conceptions rather than others.

The reader will remember that we presented considerable data to show that, by certain reinforcement operations, our children came to understand and correctly express novel and grammatically correct sentences. How can we conceptualize such flexibility within learning theory? We find the concept of *response class* directly useful, as the response class concept allows for the expression of behavior which has not been specifically reinforced in the past, provided other responses within the same class have been reinforced. Although most critiques of learning approaches to language appear not to be fully cognizant of it, the notion of response classes is not new. Skinner (1953) defined a response (an operant) not in terms of its topography, but as a generalized or functional *class* of responses which one can identify by showing how, when one changes the strength of one response, one is simultaneously altering the strength of several other responses without directly intervening on them. A very "simple" illustration of this concept can be found in shaping the barpress of a rat. If a rat has been reinforced for pressing the bar with its left foot, then (under certain circumstances) it is now more probable that in the future the rat will press the bar with his right foot or his head and "express" a similar wide range of new appropriate behaviors which had not been specifically reinforced on the bar. All these different responses, whose expression has been altered because of the change in the strength of one response, are said to constitute a response class.

To illustrate the notion of response classes from language development, suppose one reinforced an infant for emitting the phoneme "ah." One may observe an increase in the emission of range of other phonemes as well as facial expressions (mouth and eye movements), even though these additional responses have not been directly reinforced. We would say that we had isolated a response class. The interesting part of this concept (of response classes) is that they cannot be know *a priori;* what does or does not constitute a class is an empirical question. One knows that one has isolated a class when the members of that class interact in a *lawful* manner to reinforcement operations (or some other environmental intervention). This is exactly Skinner's (1953) definition of the term "response."

How does this notion of response classes help us understand

the acquisition of grammatical forms? One of the earliest reports relating the concept of a response class to grammatical forms comes from the study by Salzinger, Feldman, Cowan, and Salzinger (1965). Salzinger observed the language development in one child who was reinforced for the response "gimme candy." After the response "gimme candy" was reinforced, he observed an increase in the use of the "gimme" response with a whole series of new words and even strings of words without the additional "specific reinforcement of these combinations." Examples include, "gimme tape," "gimme office," "gimme wait," "gimme no more cloudy again," and several others, including a perfectly logical, although ungrammatical request for assistance, "gimme pick it up." The concurrent appearance of these similar responses illustrates the concept of the response class.

Several other investigators have presented data relating response classes to the acquisition of grammatical forms. Guess, Sailor, Rutherford, and Baer (1968) did so in the case of pluralization. These authors present data on the acquisition of plurals by a 10-year-old retarded girl (cf. their Figure 1, p. 301). The child was taught the plural forms of three object labels she had previously mastered in singular form. After this relatively short training period, this child correctly generalized the plural form to other objects. That is, after she had learned the plural response to some objects she would now use the correct plural label on *new* objects even though she had not been specifically trained to pluralize these. It was this observation that led the authors to argue that the plural morpheme may be conceptualized as a (generalized) response class, thus explaining the appearance of behavior that has not been directly taught.

Baer and Guess (1971) report on a study that further serves to illustrate the usefulness of differential reinforcement procedures in speech training. They taught three institutionalized retarded children to correctly identify quantitative relationships between stimuli, as described by comparative and superlative relationships (concepts such as "big-bigger," "small-smallest"). The result of this training shows clearly that once the child had been trained to master these concepts on some stimuli, the child generalized the understanding of these concepts to new stimuli without further training. Baer and Guess relate the response class concept to their data in a particularly succinct manner:

> . . . the response class concept . . . describes a significant fact of response development: that there often emerges from the organism more

behavior exemplifying the dimensions of his experience than that experience has taught directly to him. In this conceptual approach, language and speech may be conceived to be a large number of highly generalized response classes, at both the receptive and productive levels, exemplifying the same dimensions or rules that characterized the persons training or experience. Thus, teaching a child to identify correctly the quantitative relationships between stimuli, as indexed by comparative and superlative objectives, could result in an organized set of responses that the child then can apply correctly to new stimuli, thereby generating response to new words within his old grammar, without further training. (p. 130)

Schumaker and Sherman (1970) used similar imitation and reinforcement procedures to teach three retarded children to use verbs in past and present tense. Their results show:

. . . that, as past and present tense forms of verbs within an inflectional class were trained, the children correctly produced past and present tense forms of untrained verbs within this class. When verbs from two or more classes were trained, the children correctly produced the verb tenses from each of these classes. Thus, the imitation and reinforcement procedures were effective in teaching generative use of verb inflections. (p. 273)

The work of Hart and Risley (1968) on establishing the use of descriptive adjectives in the spontaneous speech of disadvantaged pre-school children provides further illustration of the applicability of the response class model in language learning. Disadvantaged pre-school children were observed to display very low rates of adjective—noun combinations in everyday spontaneous language use. During experimental intervention pre-school materials were dispensed to the children in free-play periods contingent upon spontaneous requests for those materials when the child referred to the color as well as the label of the desired item. The procedure resulted in an increase in the use of previously observed color—noun combinations. The authors of this study argue from the data that word classes form functional response classes.

Our own data replicates and serves to extend the studies we have just reviewed. For example, our work on the inflectional affix "ed" (as given in Figure 11) directly supports Schumaker and Sherman's (1970) work as well as the work of Guess, Sailor, Rutherford, and Baer (1968) on the plural affix. The children were indeed acquiring very broad and appropriate classes of linguistic behaviors. Consider again our data on the acquisition of pronouns, prepositions, or our data on the temporal terms, and the like. It is apparent in these data that the children both learned to respond correctly to stimuli that were novel to them (for example, they would eventually correctly respond to the command "put A on B," even though they had never heard that particular sentence before), as well as to verbally respond with correct terminology (sentences) even though that particular sentence, in its physiological topography, had never been taught to the child or previously expressed by him. For example, the child may say "I touched (an object like 'X') *before* (the object 'Y')," which was the correct thing to say, yet he had not previously emitted and therefore not been trained on that particular response.

In the latter example the child is not simply using word classes, he is constructing a sentence. If one accepts the notion that word classes and morphemes function as response classes, then this provides strong argument that children can learn what positions individual words may occupy in a given sentence. This is a rather complex matter, since it is also true that a particular word class may occupy a number of positions, depending upon the type of sentence employed. It is this complexity which has led some investigators to propose that one must know the "rules" which govern sentence structure in order to properly combine word classes. Our question now becomes whether such "rules" can be considered response classes, whether the reinforcement of the permissable *orders* of words (and the nonreinforcement of nonpermissible orders) can become response classes and account for the acquisition of the complex "rules" governing syntax and sentence structure. As Salzinger (1965) puts it, "A second kind of complexity is introudced by response classes of a somewhat larger size (than, say, word classes). To the outside observer these response classes appear to be quite obviously based upon rules. Thus the 'rule' for sentence type is a grammatical one or a series of these having to do with the arrangement of words and phrases." We may speak of words as forming the response unit of interest when we discuss the discrimination of word classes, and sentences as forming the response when we speak of the acquisition of sentence structure.

Our own data give ample demonstration that one can prompt and differentially reinforce a child for arranging words into sentences and that, as a function of this training, he will then combine words into new and correct sentences. All our echolalic children, and most of the mutes, acquired such behavior. The tran-

scriptions we presented in the result section illustrate this kind of
learning, as do Salzinger's data (1965). The Wheeler and Sulzer
(1970) study provides us with a very direct illustration. They
worked with an eight-year-old boy, variously diagnosed as brain
damaged, retarded, and autistic, who spoke in what the authors
refer to as "telegraphic" English, leaving out most of the articles
and auxillary verbs. Through a combination of chaining, imitative prompting, and differential reinforcement, the child was
trained to use a particular kind of sentence structure which included articles and verbs to describe a standardized set of pictures. The sentences were of the form "The (noun) is (present par-
ticiple of the verb) the (noun)." (E.g., "The man is smoking the
pipe.") Since the use of this form generalized to sets of untrained
and novel stimuli, the authors argued that a functional response
class had been established.

Risley, Reynolds, and Hart (1970) have also presented procedures and data which support the feasibility of using prompts and
differential reinforcement to build and extend sentence structure.
Working with culturally disadvantaged and linguistically impoverished children in a program they refer to as "Narration
Training" (which is very similar to our "Spontaneity Training"),
they give the following account of their method:

> If the child had responded to the question, "What did you see on the way
> to school?" with, "A doggie," the teacher nodded and said, "What kind
> of doggie?" The child answered, "A German Shepherd." The teacher
> praised, gave him an M&M and then asked again, "What did you see on
> the way to school?" He answered, "A doggie"; the teacher looked expec-
> tantly, raised her eyebrows and waited. The child then said, "A German
> Shepherd doggie," and was praised and given an M&M. The next time
> that the child responded to the question with, "A German Shepherd
> doggie," the teacher nodded, smiled, and asked what the doggie was do-
> ing; to which the child responded "Fighting." This was reinforced and
> the child again was asked, "What did you see on the way to school?" The
> child responded, "A German Shepherd doggie,"; the teacher raised her
> eyebrows and waited and the child said, "A German Shepherd doggie was
> fighting."

They present data on how the effects of this training
generalized to new situations that had not been specifically
trained.

Similar success at building sentences has been reported by
Stevens-Long and Rasmussen (1974). They worked with an autis-

tic boy and, by using imitative prompts and reinforcement, built both simple and compound sentences. They also present data that this behavior was under reinforcement control and generalized to new stimulus situations in which the child had received no direct training.

Finally, working with animals (chimpanzees), Gardner and Gardner (1971) and Premack (1970) provide very strong support for the concept of response classes and the power of discrimination learning in building sentence structure. Neither Premack nor the Gardners have presented their method (training protocols) in sufficient detail as yet, but one is struck by the large amount of initial apparent similarity between their procedures and the ones we have reported with the autistic and retarded children. Consider, for example, Premack's report on training programs for the acquisition of prepositions (1970, p. 113 and 114). Here he speaks of choosing and rotating stimuli in such a fashion as to allow S to discriminate the correct dimensions of the training stimulus ("to assure that our subject uses syntactic definitions from the beginning . . .," p. 114), the use of prompts to facilitate the desired response ("to bring about the desired behavior by limiting the probability of other kinds of behavior . . .," p. 114), tests of generalization to new (untrained) stimuli, cautions that S's correct response to prepositions may not extend beyond certain stimulus dimensions (the color chips used in training) without additional learning, and tests of simultaneous acquisition of productive language as receptive language is trained and mastered. Exactly how the chimps' rate of acquisitions compare to that of autistic and retarded children is not known. There is a tendency by those who work with chimps not to report detail of the acquisition process, but one may guess that chimps acquire language with more ease than most of the autistic and retarded children we have reported on here. In any case, both Premack and the Gardners report positive acceleration as a characteristic feature of the acquisition they observe, and both studies note a substantial amount of stimulus generalization.

It is apparent from our data and similar research on semantics and syntax that the concept of response classes and discrimination training procedures can yield behaviors that far exceed any simple-minded notion of what one should consider as *learned* behavior. It is also the case, of course, that we would have been unable to remediate as well as we did had our procedures merely taught topographic-specific responses. The response class notion does imply that, from a set of instructional procedures, it is possible for a child to make major steps ahead. Most objections to behavior change interventions based on learning models fail to recognize the response class concept and base their objections on outmoded conceptions of the terms *stimulus* and *response*. To the extent that these key terms are misunderstood, critics of learning interventions do not come to grip with the issue of "what is learned," or "what can be learned."

The reader who wants to familiarize himself more extensively with the conceptual basis of the response class model and its relationship to the acquisition of complex behavior may want to read excellent discussions on this topic by Wiest (1967) and MacCorquadale (1970). Exactly how far one will be able to extend this notion of a response class is hard to say. Beyond certain points the process would break down, and reinforcement would no longer act to strengthen a unit. Both the person's history and his genetic make-up will determine these boundaries. Research such as we have reported here does help to define what is a stimulus and what is a response and what can be learned by people. Conceivably, the child will be able to learn as complex verbal stimuli and verbal responses as those of the investigator who is describing him, since the latter probably also learned his verbal behavior.

Phonetics. It would seem a simple matter to engineer programs for phonological development once we already had some knowledge of how to teach a child semantics and grammar. But this is not necessarily so. Let us introduce the problems involved.

We began our efforts to accelerate phonological development in the mute autistics through a straightforward shaping procedure. We attempted to reinforce their spontaneous vocalizations through successive approximations toward recognizable words. Rhinegold *et al.* (1959) had already shown such reinforcement control over the vocalizations of three-month-old infants and suggested the feasibility of a reinforcement model to account for phonological development.

After several months of shaping vocalizations through approximations we succeeded in increasing the rate of the reinforced sound (e.g., "ma"). However, we seemed at the same time to restrict the output of other sounds, and the first target word ("ma") extinguished as soon as we began to reinforce approximations to the second target word ("dee"). Obviously, we weren't getting anywhere, and we made no particular progress on phonological development until we developed procedures for the acquisition of verbal imitative behavior (Lovaas *et al.,* 1966). In this study, which we reviewed in Chapter 2, we built verbal imitative behavior through a set of discriminations where the child's verbal response had to resemble its stimulus (the adult's vocalization). Several developments preceded our study. The Baer and Sherman (1964) model of "generalized imitation" formed the most important base. Briefly, Baer and Sherman viewed the acquisition of imitation as the acquisition of a discrimination in which the topological similarity between the adult's behavior and the child's behavior came to be discriminative for reinforcement.

The use of discrimination training procedures to build verbal imitative behavior does obviously assure one of some progress in phonological development for the mute child. Our date (*cf.* Figure 1) confirm that. But casual observations also showed large differences between the "imitation-trained" child and the echolalic child who already imitated the adult's speech. It was striking to observe how clearly, richly, and "effortlessly" the echolalic child imitated the adult's speech. They "spoke" a lot and "played" with speech. The imitative behavior of the previously mute children, on the other hand, stayed closely dependent on the experimental reinforcers, frequently deteriorated and "drifted" away from criterion, and sounded stilted. In general, our language program was not as successful for the mutes as for the echolalics. If the child was already echolalic, even though he did not know the meaning of his vocal expressions or how to arrange them in appropriate sentences, then it seemed easy for us to rearrange behavior (syntax) and bring it under appropriate stimulus control (semantics). The fact that we were less successful in creating and maintaining new behavioral topographies seems to point to problems in our understanding of phonological development.

There were some interesting exceptions to our failure at phonological training. A few of the mute children became echolalic, and by that we mean that their word production suddenly became extensive and took on the qualities of the echolalic child's imitations. We don't know why these children became so verbally expressive. Perhaps some principle other than, or in addition to, discrimination training does underlie phonological development. In any case, there remain several interesting problems to be answered in this area. Let us discuss some of these problems in the section that follows.

Psycholinguistics and Some Speculations

So far we have attempted to relate our discussion of phonology, semantics, and syntax to rather objective data. Let us conclude the discussion by presenting some speculations based on more informal observations. We shall introduce these speculations through some observations on psycholinguistics.

There was no question that the child learned, through the language we had taught him, to interact more extensively and effectively with us. This alone would have been a sufficient reason to teach language. An interesting question, though, can be phrased like this: Granted that the child's language came to control us and granted that our language came to control him, did his own language ever control his own behavior? There are many ways to phrase this question of "internal" control, and the kinds of questions one asks depends on one's conceptual framework. For example, one may ask, did the language acquisition facilitate the child's awareness of himself as a person? Did he now achieve a better hold on reality? What innate cognitive structures did his language activate? Did he become intellectually curious? If one considers language to be the tool of the mind or the vehicle for thought, then we were in a rather favorable and unique position to throw light on these basic questions in psycholinguistics. We will offer some of our thoughts on this problem of "internal" control.

We were disappointed. We hoped again and again that we would stumble upon a construct which, once the child mastered it, would lead to a sudden step forward (such an "aha" experience as Helen Keller supposedly underwent when she learned the label for water as shown in "The Miracle Worker.") There were no sudden awakenings. There seemed to be no large internal reorganizations. Would it not have been nice if the child had said: "Now that I can speak well, I see how I have been very sick, but now I am well." No one said that.

One can imagine that we failed to activate these internal states or central constructs for a number of reasons. Perhaps we did not teach them right. There are no known rules for how to build language, and we may have ended up with the wrong procedures. It may have been that the language structures we taught went in through the wrong "channels" and therefore did not trigger the appropriate central processes.

On the other hand, suppose we did it right, but we were looking for something that does not exist. We may have been given the wrong problem to solve. Perhaps there are not central processes in the first place, no minds to be awakened, no cognitions to fire, and no egos to be repaired. Perhaps such internal control does not exist. Ultimately, this is the most disturbing element in the behavioristic philosophy of man, that the "mind" as we now know it may not be a source of his direction.

Possible mechanisms in internal control. Let us illustrate by an empirical example what a behaviorist may mean when he talks of language producing internal control. The illustration is taken from some work the author did some years ago trying to shape language in normal speaking children. A normal child enters a room where an attending adult seats him in front of a box. The adult tells the child that he will get candy and other goodies for talking to the box, and she then withdraws to a corner on the opposite side of the room and seats herself behind a screen. Various children say different things like "Hello, Mr. Box," "How are you, Mr. Box?" When the children were reinforced for these statements, they tended to be repeated. Not much interesting was happening until one child said, "What shall I say?" He was reinforced for this utterance by a reward emptying in a tray near the box. He then repeated the statement, was again reinforced, *rose from the chair and walked across the room to the attending adult,* and directed his question to her. That was unusual behavior since the children usually did as they were told, namely sat in the chair and did not walk around. Why did he rise from the chair and walk across the room? Let us try to answer this way. Walking across the room is operant behavior and can be controlled in two ways—through reinforcers and through S^Ds. We did not reinforce him for walking across the room; we only reinforced him for talking to the box. So we may conceivably rule out reinforcement control. What about S^D control? Instructions are good examples of S^Ds. What had we told him? We did not tell him to walk across the room; in fact, we had told him to sit down, so the S^D was probably not given by us. If it was an instance of S^D control, then the child must have produced the S^Ds himself. How did he produce these S^Ds? One might suspect that the statement, "What shall I say?" generated or otherwise "gave him" the S^Ds which triggered his walking across the room. There seems no other immediate cause for his behavior, and walking across the room, as trivial as it may seem, should have a cause—some variable acting at the time the behavior took place.

This is an admittedly simplified example of internal control, but it serves to illustrate the problem. Behavioristic attempts to understand internal control are probably not radically different from many other conceptions; in a general sense, internal control is said to exist when one behavior system controls another and both systems reside within the same person. The behavioristic conception of internal control may have an advantage over other conceptions since it suggests certain explicit *mechanisms* of internal control and the conditions under which such control becomes established. What are these mechanisms?

Let us consider potential mechanisms behind internal control by first examining instances of social or external control. We have tried to illustrate this control in Figure 16. Consider first the upper half of the figure which gives a simple form of this control. Restricting ourselves to control over operant behavior, the figure

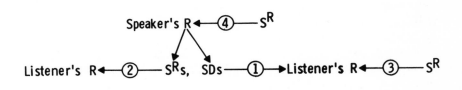

Figure 16. The upper half of the Figure shows a simple form of social control, where the Speaker's R generates discriminative stimuli (S^Ds, arrow 1) and reinforcing stimuli (S^Rs, arrow 2) for the Listener's R. Note the presence of reinforcement as necessary to maintain both these relationships (arrow 3 and 4). The lower half of the Figure shows a more complex form of control, where the Listener's R provides reinforcers and S^Ds for the Speaker (arrow 5 and 6, respectively).

shows how one person (the speaker) can control another person (the listener), by presenting S^Ds and reinforcers for that person's behavior. This control is given by arrow 1 and 2 respectively. Notice also that in order for the listener to come under the control of the speaker's S^Ds, the listener has to be reinforced for responding to that S^D (as given in arrow 3). Finally, the speaker has to be reinforced for giving these S^Ds and S^Rs, as shown by arrow 4, otherwise he would cease to do so.

Now consider our experience with the autistic children. Imagine that the autistic child is the speaker, and that the therapist is the listener. When the autistic children spoke, they controlled us both in terms of the S^D properties of their speech (as we would carry out almost any of their requests), and their speech of course reinforced us extensively. Also notice that we were reinforced for responding to their S^Ds (arrow 3), and that we reinforced them for speaking (arrow 4). Since differential reinforcement was available (as given by arrow 3 and 4) it seems that conditions were ideal for social control to be established.

The upper half of Figure 16 presents probably the simplest instance of social control, and it is easy to engineer a more complex system using the same constructs. Consider that we were willing agents in this control, which produces two additional points of interaction as given in the lower half of Figure 16. This diagram is extended to show how our behavior as listeners produced the reinforcers for the speaker's behavior (arrow 5), and that we did also strengthen his efforts at controlling us by arranging for the S^Ds which allowed his behavior to occur (arrow 6).

Now let us try to describe *internal* control, by considering that the speaker and the listener are the same person. According to this analysis, it would be possible for a person to control himself if one of his behaviors generated S^Ds and reinforcers for his other behaviors. In order for such control to exist a person must have experienced a specific history with regard to such control, because both the S^D and the reinforcement functions are acquired functions. For example, the S^D properties of the child's verbal behavior (e.g., the sentence in the earlier example, "What shall I say?") must have been acquired through differential reinforcement. We may guess that the child had been reinforced for asking this question in the presence of adults (the adults answered his inquiry), and he had not been reinforced for asking the question when no one was there. But this is also important: Unless adults continued to reinforce him for seeking them out when he asked questions, his question would no longer generate the S^Ds which made him turn to adults for answers. Internal control as a set of stimulus functions requires extrinsic differential reinforcement, both for its initiation and maintenance.

Keeping this analysis of self-control in mind, let us return to certain observations on the autistic children. We noted that despite the fact that they acquired much language which increased their social control, they did not simultaneously give evidence of internally organized control. If our conception of internal control is in fact correct, then we can see how it was unrealistic of us to have expected any reorganization of other behaviors concurrent with their newly acquired verbal behavior because control by internally organized (response generated) stimuli is a function of a specific kind of reinforcement history. The verbal behavior we taught these children had no public existence for the children before we began to teach, and therefore contained no stimulus functions which would modify their other behaviors, operant or otherwise. Whatever public life their verbal behavior had enjoyed, we had provided. In the same sense, whatever private life they would possess, we would give them. This analysis of internal control, whether correct or not, is certainly consistent with behavioristic notions of personality: Whatever is now private was once public. Skinner has argued this point nicely in his book on *Verbal Behavior* (1957).

Some data on internal control. So far we have argued that language serves internal control by providing certain stimulus functions that determine the occurrence of other behaviors within the person who speaks. Now the question is: Does it work that way? Certainly many social practices are based on the premise that internal control does work. Social systems, like education, organized religion, psychotherapy, and so on, intend to effect changes in a person's non-verbal behavior by changing that person's verbals. Loosely speaking, we say that they attempt to control our feelings and loyalties and so on by controlling the way we "think." When the Bible says, "Thou shall not covet thy neighbor's wife," it means to control certain non-verbals (adultery) by removing certain stimuli ("thought") which help control those non-verbals. It attempts to prevent the occurrence of a terminal response in a chain of responses by *suppressing* early members of that chain. When a therapist helps a patient speak more favorably about himself, then the therapist intends the new forms of verbal behavior to generate stimuli that control a more pleasant

form of interpersonal behavior as well as an increased feeling of
well being. He attempts to initiate a chain by *strengthening* the
early member of such a chain. Recently a whole new area of
treatment techniques have been initiated which is referred to as
"cognitive behavior modification." It is beyond the scope of this
book to evaluate that field, but it would seem that many of the
techniques within that area rest heavily on the principles and as-
sumptions we have discussed here.

Unfortunately, important as this area of research is, there
exist very little explicit data on this problem of verbal control
over non-verbal behavior. Some data are reported by Luria
(1961), who presented the first systematic work in this area. His
studies sought to demonstrate various levels of nervous system
control, and were only secondarily concerned with internal control the way we have discussed it here. In more recent work,
Lovaas (1961), Risley and Hart (1968), and Sherman (1964)
manipulated a person's verbal behaviors and then observed for
changes in that person's concurrent nonverbal behavior. Essentially, these investigators arranged for a situation in which a child
may give himself various instructions or instruction-like commands, and then observed to see if the child in fact acted on his
own instructions or commands. In general, one could observe instances of such internal control, but it appeared to be a rather
weak form of control and it was short lived, extinguishing
quickly. The only exception to this took place when Risley,
Reynolds, and Hart (1970) made special efforts to maintain the
control through external differential reinforcement of the
verbal—non-verbal relationship. Risley had pre-school children
describe a certain part of their day's behaviors, like whether they
had painted or not that morning. Merely reinforcing the child for
describing his painting did not produce a noticeable effect on the
painting unless the child had, in fact, painted and was differentially reinforced for correctly verbalizing this non-verbal behavior. Under such efforts to maintain control in the verbal—
non-verbal relationship, Risley could effect changes in the child
by merely manipulating the child's verbal behavior. Risley's
work suggests, and casual observation lends some support to this,
that the critical variable in internal control is the presence of differential reinforcement for such control (arrow 3 in Figure 16).
Without some external monitoring of the conditions under which
such reinforcement is given and withdrawn, it seems unlikely
that a person would subject himself to the unpleasant task of

withdrawing positive or presenting negative reinforcers for himself, as well as the equally important task of keeping track of the
exact conditions under which he should experience these
reinforcers.

One may ask, if such internal control is weak, why do people
persist in trying to direct themselves? Why does a person persist
in making decisions about his life, when he does not follow
through with those decisions? If he does not act on his decisions
he is receiving no extrinsic reinforcement for making decisions.
In fact each time a person makes a decision without acting on it
he is losing reinforcement, and his verbalizations are extinguishing whatever S^D properties they once possessed. In the absence of
extrinsic pay-off, how can we justify such extensive performances?
Psychology has yet to demonstrate that a person, by taking
"thought," can change the course of his own behavior. Others
usually have to provide such assistance. One can help others but
it seems that one cannot help oneself.

Even if we were to grant the existence of some forms of internally generated control, most (private) dialogues are not problem
(or direction) oriented to start with. They seem essentially neutral
in content. Thus one is always describing one's experiences. We
continuously code what we see and hear, we exclaim to ourselves,
sooth, attack others in private duels, and so on. It is virtually
impossible to "pull a blank," something is always going on "up
there."

If these private behaviors are operants, and if they have no
extrinsic merit, what are the reinforcers that maintain them? To
pose an explicit question: why do people pray? Millions have
prayed for thousands of years, and still do. For some, it is their
main behavioral repertoire. If God does not listen, who does? Or
consider dreams. In our dreams we talk to others night after
night, but surely there is no one there to reinforce such behavior.

Self-stimulatory behavior. To answer the question of why certain forms of private language occur at a high rate without apparent extrinsic reinforcement, it may be helpful to turn to an
examination of other behaviors that occur at a high rate even
though these behaviors are not maintained by social consequences
or other extrinsic reinforcers; that is, they do not appear "goal-
directed," and seem to be void of any "problem-solving" properties. The main consequence of the behavior is more of the same
kind of behavior. We can quite clearly see this phenomenon in
autistic children who exert great effort to rhythmically and

monotonously rock, hand flap, spin, gaze, twirl, jump, pace, etc. They are in continuous motion, never still. And this behavior persists for months and years, without signs of extinction. We called this behavior "self-stimulatory" since the child seems to engage in this behavior primarily to "stimulate" himself from the kinesthetic, proprioceptive and vestibular feedback involved in these activities. Rimland (1964) and Ornitz (1974) have both made similar comments. We speculated on the "need" of the nervous system to be stimulated in this manner, when socially more appropriate behaviors could not serve the same function. In this way self-stimulatory behavior would be as primary as eating and drinking. If we consider self-stimulatory behavior as operant behavior, then it is the child rather than society who programs or controls the reinforcers that maintain it. We have discussed self-stimulatory behavior in autistic children in some detail in an earlier publication (Lovaas, Litrownik, & Mann, 1971).

Self-stimulatory behavior occurs not only in autistic children but can be observed in a number of other persons as well. Berkson (1967) has reported on such behaviors, which he labels "stereotyped motor acts," in retarded children and describes its persistent and high rate. Casual observation suggests that infants self-stimulate extensively, as when they babble, gaze at their hands, nonnutritively suck their fingers, touch blanket to face, etc. Perfectly normal children self-stimulate when they are alone with nothing else to do. At such time they show a striking similarity to autistic children. Adults also show rather obvious examples of self-stimulation when they are not otherwise engaged (for example, as when they are "waiting" by themselves, they pick their ears and noses, stroke their faces, grimace, groom, etc.). The impression one gets from observing people at such time is that they are "full" of self-stimulatory behaviors.

Perhaps the clearest area of research relevant to self-stimulatory behavior has been summarized by Kish (1966) on sensory reinforcement with animals. Research on sensory reinforcement deals with the conditions under which animals will respond for sensory input of moderate intensity, such as changes in light intensity, incidental sound productions like the clicking of relays, etc. The implication of this work, of course, is that animals have a "need" for sensory stimulation, are controlled by such consequences, and that self-stimulatory behavior is an example of behavior which is maintained by such reinforcers.

Two kinds of operants. Apparently, then, organisms respond to

obtain reinforcing stimuli which appear unrelated to social reinforcement or the reduction of biological reinforcers as we now
know them (appetitive reinforcers, sex, pain reduction, etc.).
This set of reinforcing stimuli may be labeled *sensory reinforcers*
(Kish, 1966) and we may call operant behavior which is maintained by sensory reinforcers *self-stimulatory operants*. Self-
stimulatory operants differ from *extrinsic* or *social operants* in terms
of *who* controls the reinforcer. In the case of self-stimulatory operants, the organism himself controls the reinforcers, hence shapes
and/ or maintains his own behavior. In the case of extrinsic or
social operants, it is others (i.e., society) who control the reinforcers and others, then, control the form and maintenance of the behavior.

    Language and thought as self-stimulatory behavior. Language and
thought may have a social etiology, but once initiated, any
number of reinforcers could maintain it. If sensory reinforcers can
maintain nonverbal behavior, they can equally well maintain verbals. With this in mind let us return to the problem of the mute
children who failed to maintain a high rate of verbal behavior.
We suggest that the mutes never learned to self-stimulate with
language. The echolalics, on the other hand, gave every evidence
of self-stimulating with language even before we began training.

    In recent research (Lovaas, Koegel, Varni and Lorsch, 1975)
we report that children engage in verbal behavior which satisfies
some of the criteria of self-stimulatory behavior. For example,
certain autistic children emit verbal behavior that echoes, either
immediately or with delays of hours or days, the speech of others.
Their speech productions are often loud and clear, allowing for
easy recording. We observed no systematic change in these children's verbal behavior, even though they spoke alone for as many
as 30 sessions, with some sessions lasting up to 90 minutes in
length. There was no reason to believe that the children even
knew what they were talking about. We found similar data with
the normal children we ran. With no apparent extrinsic reinforcement for this verbal behavior one would expect, if the behavior is dependent on extrinsic reinforcement, that the rate
would fall off a bit, extinguish so to speak: But it did not.

    The proposition that private language is maintained by sen-
sory reinforcers is difficult to test. First, one has to rule out more
parsimonious sources of reinforcement such as the conditioned social reinforcement generated by speech. Skinner (1957) has argued very persuasively for the conditioned reinforcement support

of private verbal events. Also, psychodynamic notions have been advanced to the effect that language may "bind anxiety"; that is, be based on escape or avoidance schedules. Secondly, not all private language is self-stimulatory; some forms of private language facilitate changes in the external world. Apparently, language directed toward the rearrangement of one's extrinsic environment is functional in that aspect. That is, up to a point one's language moves others about, and participates in the manipulation of one's physical environment. But verbal behavior directed towards the rearrangement of one's own behavior may not be functional for that purpose.

This analysis of language and thought as self-stimulatory behavior is similar to Freud's primary process thinking (1970) and Piaget's egocentric thought (1955). Freud and Piaget introduced these constructs to allow for the essentially nonsocial, non-reality-oriented, non-problem-solving basis of thought and language. Our view of language as self-stimulatory behavior appears less tied to instinctual gratification (Freud) and less controlled by maturational, age-related variables (Freud and Piaget). In our analysis, self-stimulatory language and thought function to preserve the nervous system; it is behavior necessary for biological survival.

Returning now to our efforts at building language in non-linguistic psychotic children, the most immediate problems for us concern the discovery of the conditions for maintaining high rates of output. This probably entails changing inappropriate self-stimulatory motor behavior (such as rocking) to socially appropriate self-stimulation, such as language and thought. How to do this is not known.

Let us finish our discussion on language by turning to more data-based issues concerning certain leads on how to build a more efficient training program. We will first look at suggestions for improving the program by examining data from language acquisition in normals, and then by considering certain peculiarities which developmentally retarded autistic children show during discrimination learning.

Suggestions for Program Changes from Language Development in Normal Children

When we designed our program we proceeded with total disregard for what others considered important to know about nervous system determinants of language. This seemed a desirable point of departure for us since the organically-based theories of language acquisition virtually rule out any hope of building language through environmental interventions. Now that we have succeeded in building complex language by manipulating environmental variables, it may be appropriate to turn to some investigations that suggest the contributions of certain potentially *neurological* variables in the hope of strengthening a language program such as we have outlined. If those behaviors that possess strong organic determinants require minimal environmental instigation, then it would seem that one could speed up the acquisition process by incorporating such supposedly organically controlled features. In particular, one may want to capitalize on what many investigators consider to be maturational determinants in language learning.

Suggestions about these genetically (maturationally) determined behaviors typically emerge from observations on language development in normal children. One of the most intriguing and probably most well-documented observations to come out of this work on language development in children is their use of certain grammatical forms, different from those of adults, which generate utterances that appear not to have been directly imitated, probably not directly shaped, at least on the basis of their grammatical correctness.

The form most often discussed governs utterances which are typically two to three words long. This form has been carefully outlined by Braine (1963) and Bellugi and Brown (1964), among others. Basically, the form can be described as a two-word utterance involving the use of an "operator" or "pivot" word plus one member of an "open class" of words. This form has been referred to as the "P-X" form (P for pivot and X for the open class). Pivots are high frequency words which tend to be restricted to a given position in a sentence, most frequently to the first position in a two-word utterance. Pivots are usually few in number and are generally nonsuffixed, unmarked forms (Miller and Ervin, 1964). Brown and Bellugi report that pivots are typically modifiers, while open-class words tend to be nouns.

When the child begins to combine words, it is generally observed that he uses a pivot and one member of the open class to form a two-word utterance. The open class is the only other class in the child's repertoire at first, and thus contains all the words except pivots. One of the interesting features of the utterances generated by this form is that they are not always grammatically correct by adult standards. For instance, "two" is frequently a member of the child's pivot class. Use of this word in the first position results in the generation of such utterances as "Two water," and "Two mommy." It is argued that imitation and reinforcement cannot account for the production of such "errors" because the child has certainly not imitated these utterances, and it is possible that he will not be explicitly reinforced for making blatant errors.

The frequency and relative stable positional relationship of modifier and noun in adult English also makes this form one of the most salient ones. As Brown and Bellugi point out, the P-X form is the forerunner of the noun phrase. The noun phrase may be used in isolation to name or request something; it may be used in the subject, object, or predicate nominative position in a sentence. It is a "subwhole of a sentence," as Brown and Bellugi suggest. "It has a kind of psychological utility." Certainly all of these features contribute to a kind of "natural" salience for the noun phrase and the P-X form. It may be appropriate to begin training the child to combine words by selecting a small class of "pivot" words and a larger open class. If the P-X (or noun phrase) forms are as genetically determined as many writers suggest, then it should be acquired quicker than any other two-word combinations. This would be relatively easy to test.

Another possible advantage of applying normal developmental sequences to language training for deviant children is that normal development seems more economical than the step-at-a-time program we propose. Let us examine this suggestion briefly. Several studies indicate that simple abstractions are often acquired by normal children in the context of the P-X form. Brown and Fraser (1964) outline the emergence of possessive pronouns. At first, proper nouns are combined with common nouns to produce such utterances as "Daddy hair." Only later is the possessive affix "s" added by the child. Klima and Bellugi (1966) indicate that negation is first expressed by adding "no" or "not" to the P-X utterance to produce phrases like "not Evie chair." Later "don't" and "can't" are added. A final example also comes from Klima and Bellugi and describes the acquisition of interrogatives. At first the child merely uses the P-X phrase, changing only intonation to produce questions like "That car?" Later "wh" words are added to the basic phrase, e.g., "Where that cat?"

Another interesting observation pertains to the very regular pattern in which certain language forms develop across children. Such data have been used to infer genetic determinants. An early review by McCarthy (1954) showed that the first vocalizations, followed by cooing and then vocal play, emerge between 0 and 6 months. Children begin to imitate sounds between 6 and 10 months, to vocalize recognition at about 8 or 9 months, and to say their first word between 9 and 13 months. They are following simple commands and imitating words by 14 months. Labeling emerges between 18 and 22 months. The child comprehends simple questions by 20 months, combines two words by 24 months, first uses pronouns, phrases, and sentences at 24 months, and begins to understand prepositions by 26 months.

There are other interesting observations on normal language development, some of which are already part of our procedures. Jakobson and Halle (1956) proposed, for instance, that the child learns to produce phonemes in a particular sequence which reflects the differentiation of successive contrasting distinctive features. The vowel-consonant distinction is the first to be acquired because it affords maximum differences of these features. Distinctive features are based on differences in the place and manner of articulation and acoustic characteristics. Each new phoneme emerges in an order dependent upon the ease of distinguishing and reproducing its distinctive features relative to other phonemes. Jakobson predicted that the first utterance a child makes will be "pa," which consists of two sound elements that are polar opposites in terms of distinctive features. In English, the acquisition of the "l" and "r" sounds involve the finest discrimination of such features. We did incorporate some of these considerations when we developed our program (to facilitate the discriminations), but we did not investigate these suggestions systematically.

Normative descriptions of language development usually report that comprehension precedes production by some margin. We have not yet assessed, in a systematic way, how comprehension (Discrimination 1) affects the acquisition of expression (Discrimination 2).

Whether reinforcement procedures do or do not produce the kinds of developmental data we have described remains an open question. Little would be gained if we tried to show, on a purely conceptual level, how we could accommodate these data within a reinforcement framework. On the other hand, it seems easy to check empirically whether these behavioral sequences, which supposedly have a heavy biological determination, are easier to teach than those which are more arbitrarily arranged.

Suggestions for Program Changes from Discrimination Learning with Autistic Children

Not a great deal is known as yet about discrimination learning among special groups of children, such as psychotic or retarded children. Such children may pose special difficulties, such as attentional deficits to certain kinds of stimulus inputs or deficiency in response to commonly employed reinforcement stimuli. Let us first illustrate some potential problems from certain studies which have used exceptional children as Ss.

Wasserman (1969), working in our laboratory, examined discrimination learning in autistic children. She employed 12 Ss, four who were echolalic and seven who were essentially mute. Her children, with perhaps two exceptions, were representative of the more regressed half of the psychotic continuum and similar to the ones we have employed in our language acquisition programs. The problem the child had to solve in her experiment seemed rather simple. He was presented with two colors and was rewarded for consistently denoting (e.g., pointing to, or otherwise identifying) one or the other (e.g., the red and not the blue). The position of the colors were intermixed to avoid the acquisition of position cues. Alternatively he was presented with two geometric forms; one was correct, and he was rewarded for pointing to it. Wasserman's first attempt to teach the discrimination problem used a noncorrection procedure, which is the procedure most typical of the way in which discriminations are taught in laboratory studies and perhaps learned in everyday life. In the noncorrection procedure the child is rewarded for making a correct response, and if he makes an incorrect response he is not punished and loses nothing, except that he must wait until the next trial to try again. It is remarkable that under these conditions, only four of the 12 Ss learned the solution (consistently identified a color or shape) within 1000 trials. Rhesus monkeys do a lot better. Monkeys learn to criterion (e.g., 10 successive correct choices) within the first 25 trials (Harlow, 1945). Moreover, Wasserman reports that the eight Ss who did not reach criterion showed no improvement; they responded at the chance level throughout. Some of her Ss were presented with more than 2000 trials and still did not learn. The eight who did not learn were mute and (with one exception) engaged in considerable self-stimulation. The four Ss who did learn within the first 1000 trials were characterized by echolalia (rather than mutism), and they did not engage in self-stimulatory behavior during the study.

The Wasserman Ss who failed apparently did not attend to the visual cues in the experimental display. They appeared to perseverate on position cues (e.g., consistently picking the left stimulus), behaving so as to minimize effort and seemed relatively unresponsive to the E's reinforcement contingencies. Similar position perseveration strategy, a "stay side" pattern, has been seen as the most primitive response method in the discrimination learning of very young children (below 2.5 years of age; White, 1963).

Eventually Wasserman was able to teach seven of the eight failing Ss by running through a variety of procedures. For example, she tried correcting the child when he was wrong, by prompting (showing him) the correct response. She tried increasing the power of her reinforcers through food deprivation and the use of punishment (E slapped S's hand and said "no") when the child made an error. Less successful procedures included decreasing the number of extraneous cues and making relevant ones more salient (e.g., by using a black-white discrimination instead of color). It is notable that no one procedure appeared to be a "key" procedure for all the children. She did conclude, however, that the *differential reinforcement* that accompanies a correction procedure may be instrumental in evoking attending (or discriminated) behavior. Given these observations, we may speculate that one reason that autistic children seem so inattentive to their surroundings is that they are indifferent to the reinforces those surroundings provide.

One may also turn to studies of the mentally retarded in the hope of gaining further information about discrimination behavior in psychotics. Within this body of literature the work of Zeaman and House (1963) with retarded Ss may throw some light on the difficulties autistic children experience in discrimination learning situations. Zeaman and House (1963) offer a two-factor theory of discrimination learning. They suggest that S first learns to attend to the relevant stimulus dimension and then learns to respond to the positive element of that dimension. This model has been tested in other experiments (Shepp & Zeaman, 1966). The results of these experiments indicate that the learning curves of retardates may be composed of two portions. The first portion is characterized by a flat, steady, chance level of responding followed by a second portion in which a rapid and positively accelerated curve appears. Zeaman and House observe that the major difference between the curves of normals and those of retardates is the increased length of the initial flat portion of the curve for retardates. They suggest that the primary difficulty of retarded children centers on the longer time they require before they attend to relevant cues. They have found that increasing the number of relevant dimensions (increasing the magnitude of the physical differences between stimuli and/or increasing the number of intradimensional shifts in a series of problems) serves to increase the rate at which Ss learn a discrimination (i.e., decreases the length of the initial flat portion of the curve). A primary difference between retarded and autistics may be that the retarded children are more responsive to experimental reinforcements than are autistics, and hence are more quickly brought under the control of all cues, both relevant and irrelevant ones.

Certain recent studies in our laboratory on perceptual deviations in autistics may provide some clues as to why autistic children encounter such great difficulty in discrimination learning. The main focus of this research centers on our finding (Lovaas *et al.*, 1971) of what we referred to as "stimulus overselectivity" or "overselective attention." In that study three groups of children (autistic, retarded, and normal) were reinforced for responding to a complex stimulus involving the simultaneous presentation of auditory, visual, and tactile cues. Once this discrimination was established, elements of the complex were presented separately to assess which aspects of the complex stimulus had acquired control over the child's behavior. We found that: (a) The autistics responded primarily to only one of the cues, the normals responded uniformly to all three cues, and the retardates functioned between these two extremes. (b) Conditions could be arranged such that a cue which had remained nonfunctional when presented in association with other cues could be established as functional when trained separately. The data failed to support notions that any one sense modality is impaired in autistic children. Rather, when presented with a stimulus complex, their attention was overselective.

Shortly thereafter, we replicated this finding in a two-stimulus situation (Lovaas & Schreibman, 1971) in which autistic

*S*s again showed overselective attention by responding to only one of the two stimulus components, while normal *S*s tended to respond to both.

We also found (Schreibman & Lovaas, 1973) that when autistic children were taught to discriminate between two life-like boy and girl figures, they made this discrimination on the basis of only one or a peculiar combination of components of these figures. For example, one child discriminated the figures on the basis of their shoes; when the shoes were removed, he could no longer tell the boy and girl figures apart.

We hypothesized from these findings that autistic children would encounter difficulties in learning situations requiring *shifts in stimulus* control over behavior. There are at least three such shifts (substitutions) which are basic to normal functioning. In each of the following three situations the organism receives two stimulus inputs, roughly simultaneously: (1) In classical conditioning, behavior elicited by a particular stimulus (the US) comes under the control of contiguously presented, previously neutral (the CS) stimuli. Many consider that classical conditioning underlies the acquisition of appropriate *affect* and the acquisition of *secondary* (symbolic) *reinforcers*. The autistic child appears to have problems in both kinds of acquisitions. (2) Stimulus overselectivity should lead to problems in the acquisition of environmental contexts that underlie meaningful speech. One can argue that speech exists without meaning to the extent that it has an impoverished context. The acquisition of a context for speech probably involves shifts and extensions in stimulus control to simultaneous presentations of auditory, visual, tactile, and other cues. Much autistic speech (e.g., "echolalia") appears to be contextually impoverished. (3) Stimulus overselectivity should also seriously interfere with learning when prompt and prompt fading procedures are employed. In most teaching situations, the teacher "helps" the child to the correct response by some form of "guidance," "aid," or "suggestion," as in prompt fading techniques. This, of course, involves added cues which should interfere with the autistics' learning.

The first study to investigate problems with shifts in stimulus control was conducted by Koegel (1971), who raised the question of whether autistic children would learn a discrimination more easily if there were *no prompts* available and also whether between-modality or within-modality transfers affected learning.

Briefly, this is what he did. Two groups of children (autistic and normal) were pretrained in a color discrimination task. The intent was to use the color cues as prompts subsequently for more difficult training stimuli. Once the children had mastered the color discriminations the colors were presented simultaneously with training stimuli in a prompt-fading procedure which was used to train four different discriminations. The results were as follows: First, autistic Ss failed to transfer from the color prompt to the training stimuli more often than normal Ss. Second, gradually fading the prompt generally produced a transfer for normal Ss but not for autistic Ss. Third, those autistic and normal Ss who did not transfer to the training stimuli continued to respond correctly to the faded color cue, and autistic Ss discriminated differences in the color (prompt) discrimination that were as small as those the normal Ss discriminated. In other words, they were capable of making extremely fine discriminations, but they had particular difficulty in shifting from one cue to another.

Shortly after Koegel's study was completed, Schreibman (1975) asked whether situations could be arranged so that prompts would work to the child's advantage. The purpose of Schreibman's research was to develop a prompting procedure that would be effective in teaching discriminations to autistic children. Two prompting procedures were used, (a) the provision of an added stimulus as an *extra-stimulus prompt*. This prompt requires that the child attend to both the prompt and the training stimuli and was systematically faded to determine if transfer could be accomplished. (b) Provision of a *within-stimulus prompt* that emphasized the relevant component of the training stimulus. This prompt was also faded by gradually reducing the emphasis. It was hypothesized that the within-stimulus prompt would be effective since it does not require the child to transfer from one stimulus dimension to another.

Six autistic children were each trained on four difficult discrimination tasks. Two of the tasks involved visual stimuli (forms on cards), and two involved auditory stimuli (two-syllable nonsense words). For the visual tasks, the extra-stimulus prompt consisted of E pointing to the correct card and gradually withdrawing the pointing prompt. The within-stimulus prompt involved exaggerating the relevant component of the form discrimination and gradually reducing this emphasis. For the auditory discriminations the extra-stimulus prompt consisted of the sound of a buzzer presented contiguously with the correct stimulus. This buzzer was faded by decreasing its intensity. The within-stimulus prompt involved emphasizing the relevant component (syllable) and gradually reducing this emphasis.

The results indicated that the autistic children failed to learn the discriminations without a prompt. The Ss always failed to learn when the extra-stimulus prompt was employed, while they usually did learn when the within-stimulus prompt was employed. These findings were independent of which modality (auditory or visual) was required for the discrimination.

Schreibman's study opens up an important area for us: to begin to tailor educational procedures, as represented in our language training program, in an attempt to "work around" the children's problem. It is also important to note that, as we learn more about autistic children, their potentially "basic deviance" seems less severe and less absolute and hypotheses concerning damage to "language learning centers" become less tenable.

References

Baer, D. M., & Guess, D. Receptive training of adjectival inflections in mental retardates. *Journal of Applied Behavior Analysis,* 1971, *4,* 129–139.

Baer, D. M., & Sherman, J. A. Reinforcement control of generalized imitation in young children. *Journal of Experimental Child Psychology,* 1964, *1* (1), 37–49.

Berko, J. The child's learning of English morphology. *Word,* 1958, *14,* 150–177.

Berkson, G. Abnormal stereotyped motor acts. In J. Tubin and H. F. Hunt (Eds.), *Comparative Psychopathology: Animal and Human.* New York: Grune and Stratton, 1967.

Braine, M. D. S. The ontogeny of English phrase structure: The first phase. *Language,* 1963, *39,* 1–13.

Bellugi, U., & Brown, R. (Eds.) *The acquisition of language.* Yellow Springs, Ohio: The Antioch Press, 1964.

Brown, R., & Fraser, C. The acquisition of syntax. *Child Development Monographs,* 1964, 229, 43—79.

Chomsky, N. *Aspects of the theory of syntax.* Cambridge: M. I. T. Press, 1965.

Cook, C., & Adams, H. E. Modification of verbal behavior in speech deficient children. *Behaviour Research and Therapy,* 1966, *4,* 265–271.

Ervin, S. M. Imitation and structural change in children's language. In E. H. Lenneberg (Ed.), *New directions in the study of language.* Cambridge: M. I. T. Press, 1964.

Freud, S. *Beyond the pleasure principle.* New York: Liveright, 1970.

Gardner, B. T., & Gardner, R. A. Two-way communication with an infant chimpanzee. In A. Schrier & F. Stollnitz (Eds.), *Behavior of nonhuman primates*. New York: Academic Press, 1971.

Guess, D., Sailor, W., Rutherford, G., & Baer, D. An experimental analysis of linguistic development: The productive use of the plural morpheme. *Journal of Applied Behavior Analysis*, 1968, *1* (4), 292–307.

Guthrie, E. R. *The psychology of learning*. New York: Harper, 1935.

Harlow, H. F. Studies in discrimination learning in monkeys: V. Initial performance by experimentally naive monkeys on stimulus-object and pattern discriminations. *Journal of General Psychology*, 1945, *33*, 3–10.

Hart, B., & Risley, T. Establishing use of descriptive objectives in the spontaneous speech of disadvantaged preschool children. *Journal of Applied Behavior Analysis*, 1968, *1*, 109–120.

Hewett, F. M. Teaching speech to an autistic child through operant conditioning. *American Journal of Orthopsychiatry*, 1965, *35*, 927–936.

Hull, C. *Principles of behavior*. New York: Appleton-Century-Crofts, 1943.

Jakobson, R., & Halle, M. *Fundamentals of language*. The Hague, Netherlands: Mouton & Co., 1956.

Kish, G. B. Studies of sensory reinforcement. In W. K. Honig (Ed.), *Operant behavior: Areas of research and application*. New York: Appleton-Century-Crofts, 1966.

Klima, E., & Bellugi, U. Syntactic regularities in speech of children. In J. Lyons and R. Wales (Eds.), *Psycholinguistic papers*. Edinburgh: Edinburgh University Press, 1966.

Koegel, R. *Selective attention to prompt stimuli by autistic and normal children*. Unpublished doctoral dissertation, University of California, Los Angeles, 1971.

Lenneberg, E. H. Language disorders in childhood. *Harvard Educational Review*, 1964, *34* (2), 152–177.

Lovaas, O. I. Interaction between verbal and nonverbal behavior. *Child Development*, 1961, *32*, 329–336.

Lovaas, O. I., Berberich, J. P., Perloff, B. F., & Schaeffer, B. Acquisition of imitative speech by schizophrenic children. *Science*, 1966, *151*, 705–707.

Lovaas, O. I., Litrownik, A., & Mann, R. Response latencies to auditory stimuli in autistic children engaged in self-stimulatory behavior. *Behaviour Research and Therapy*, 1971, *9*, 39–49.

Lovaas, O. I., and Schreibman, L. Stimulus overselectivity of autistic children in a two-stimulus situation. *Behaviour Research and Therapy*, 1971, *9*, 305–310.

Lovaas, O. I., Schreibman, L., Koegel, R., & Rehm, R. Selective responding by autistic children to multiple sensory input. *Journal of Abnormal Psychology*, 1971, *77* (3), 211–222.

Lovaas, O. I., Koegel, R., Varni, J., & Lorsch, N. Some observations of the nonextinguishability of children's speech. In preparation, 1975.

Luria, A. R. *The role of speech in the regulation of normal and abnormal behavior.* New York: Liveright, 1961.

MacAuley, B. D. A program for teaching speech and beginning reading to non-verbal retardates. In H. N. Sloane, Jr., and B. D. MacAuley (Eds.), *Operant procedures in remedial speech and language training.* Boston: Houghton Mifflin Co., 1968.

MacCorquadale, K. On Chomsky's review of Skinner's "Verbal behavior." *Journal of the Experimental Analysis of Behavior,* 1970, *13* (1), 83—99.

McCarthy, D. Language development in children. In L. Carmichael (Ed.), *Manual of child psychology, 2nd ed.* New York: Wiley, 1954.

Miller, W., & Ervin, S. The development of grammar in child language. *Monographs of the Society for Research in Child Development,* 1964, *29* (1), 9—34.

Mowrer, O. H. *Learning theory and the symbolic processes.* New York: Wiley, 1960.

Ornitz, E. The modulation of sensory input and motor output in autistic children. *Journal of Autism and Childhood Schizophrenia,* 1974, *4* (3), 197—215.

Piaget, J. *The language and thought of the child.* New York: World Publishing Co., 1955.

Premack, D. A functional analysis of language. *Journal of the Experimental Analysis of Behavior,* 1970, *14* (1), 1—19.

Rheingold, H. L., Gewirtz, J. L., & Ross, H. W. Social conditioning of vocalizations. *Journal of Comparative and Physiological Psychology,* 1959, *225*, 68—73.

Rimland, B. *Infantile autism.* New York: Appleton-Century-Crofts, 1964.

Risley, T. R., & Hart, B. M. Developing correspondence between the non-verbal and verbal behavior of pre-school children. *Journal of Applied Behavior Analysis,* 1968, *1* (4), 267—281.

Risley, T. R., Reynolds, N., & Hart, B. The disadvantaged: Behavior modification with disadvantaged preschool children. In R. H. Bradfield (Ed.), *Behavior modification, the human effort.* San Rafael, California: Dimensions Publishing Co., 1970.

Risley, T. R., & Wolf, M. Establishing functional speech in echolalic children. *Behavior Research and Therapy,* 1967, *5,* 73—88.

Salzinger, K., Feldman, R., Cowan, J., & Salzinger, S. Operant conditioning of verbal behavior of two young speech-deficient boys. In Krasner and Ullman (Eds.), *Research in behavior modification.* New York: Holt, Rinehart and Winston, 1965.

Schreibman, L. Within-stimulus versus extra-stimulus prompting procedures on discrimination learning with autistic children. *Journal of Applied Behavioral Analysis,* 1975, in press.

Schreibman, L., & Lovaas, O. I. Overselective response to social stimuli by autistic children. *Journal of Abnormal Child Psychology,* 1973, *1* (2), 152—168.

Schumaker, J., & Sherman, J. A. Training generative verb usage by imitation and reinforcement procedures. *Journal of Applied Behavior Analysis,* 1970, *3,* 273–287.

Shepp, B., & Zeaman, D. Discrimination learning of size and brightness by retardates. *Journal of Comparative and Physiological Psychology,* 1966, *62* (1), 55–59.

Sherman, J. Modification of non-verbal behavior through reinforcement of related verbal behavior. *Child Development,* 1964, *35,* 717–723.

Skinner, B. F. *Science and human behavior.* New York: MacMillan, 1953.

Skinner, B. F. *Verbal behavior.* New York: Appleton-Century-Crofts, 1957.

Sloane, H. N., Johnston, M. K., & Harris, F. R. Remedial procedures for teaching verbal behavior to speech deficient or defective young children. In Sloane and MacAuley (Eds.), *Operant procedures in remedial speech and language training.* (Boston: Houghton Mifflin Co., 1968.

Stark, J., Giddan, J. J., & Meisel, J. Increasing verbal behavior in an autistic child. *Journal of Speech and Hearing Disorders,* 1968, *33,* 42–48.

Stevens-Long, J., & Rasmussen, M. The acquisition of simple and compound sentence structure in an autistic child. *Journal of Applied Behavior Analysis,* 1974, *7,* 473–479.

Wasserman, L. M. *Discrimination learning in autistic children.* Unpublished doctoral dissertation, University of California, Los Angeles, 1969.

Wheeler, A. J., & Sulzer, B. Operant training and generalization of a verbal response form in a speech-deficient child. *Journal of Applied Behavior Analysis,* 1970, *3,* 139–147.

White, S. H. *Learning in child psychology: The 62nd yearbook of the National Society for the Study of Education.* In H. W. Stevenson (Ed.). Chicago: University of Chicago, 1963.

Wiest, W. M. Some recent criticisms of behaviorism and learning theory: With special reference to Breger and McGaugh and to Chomsky. *Psychological Bulletin,* 1967, *67* (3), 214–225.

Wolf, M. M., Risley, T., & Mees, H. Application of operant conditioning procedures to the behavior problems of an autistic child. *Behavior Research and Therapy,* 1965, *3,* 113–124.

Zeaman, D., & House, B. J. The role of attention in retardate discrimination learning. In N. R. Ellis (Ed.), *Handbook of mental deficiency.* New York: McGraw-Hill, 1963.

Chapter VI
LANGUAGE TRAINING MANUALS

The following manuals were prepared with the help of Meredith Gibbs and Judith Stevens-Long. The manuals are illustrative of the way we taught the language behaviors we have reviewed in this book. They should be viewed as preliminary drafts only, in need of revision. Specifically, the manuals do not incorporate suggestions from recent findings on transfer within versus transfer across stimulus dimensions in prompting. Similarly, many recent findings in discrimination learning, such as pretraining S to withhold responding in the presence of S-, have not been incorporated in these manuals. Future revisions should benefit from these findings.

Before the teacher reads these manuals he should familiarize himself with the section on "basic training principles," and the various special teaching problems we have presented throughout this book. As these manuals are procedurally incomplete, they are intended only to give concrete examples and further extension of the basic training procedures.

Note that the abbreviation E in these manuals refer to any adult working with the child in the position of a teacher. This could be a parent, a psychologist, a student, or a teacher. E is likely to mean a professional person for the laboratory training, and the child's parent for generalization training in the child's everyday environment.

Note also that we have related our work to similar work on language teaching, and we have presented references to studies which describe methodologies for teaching labelling, use of correct grammar, and so on. The reader may want to familiarize himself with those procedures as well.

When one reads these manuals, it is important to keep in mind how little we know about certain important areas of language learning. We have tried to identify some of these areas in the main body of this text. The more important areas deal with the effect of the child's mood on language learning, how much receptive language one should build before beginning training on expressive language, optimal sequencing of learning steps, and the like. We have avoided incorporating these areas in the manuals because no data exist on how to cope with these problems.

Manual A: Labeling Discrete Events

Labelling is the first and most basic manual in the language program. The object is to teach the child to answer common questions like "What is this?" and "What are you doing?" A large number of common objects and normal, everyday behaviors serve as training stimuli. The training procedure typically begins with a type 1 discrimination procedure. In the preliminary stages of training, it may be particularly advantageous to use food items as training stimuli, as the child is likely to attend to these stimuli.

Receptive Speech. E and S sit facing each other across a table. Receptive training begins when E places TS1, such as a piece of toast, on the table in front of S. E waits for the child to visually fixate on the object before beginning the training trial. Since the onset of the trial may become a reinforcer, one must insure that it is not presented just after tantrum behavior or too much activity. It may be helpful to restrain the child at first (keeping his hands on his lap or teaching him to hold his hands on his lap when told to do so) so that he will make a discrete response, rather than reaching part of the way to several objects before making a complete response. Once *E* has *S*'s attention, he gives a command such as "Touch the toast," or initially perhaps only the command "Toast." *E* waits for a few seconds to see if the child will make the desired response. Three possible response alternatives now exist. (1) *S* may respond correctly, at which point he is reinforced (fed). (2) *S* may not respond, at which point *E* repeats the command and concurrently prompts the desired response by taking the child's hand and placing it on the correct object. The child is initially reinforced for responding to the prompt. (3) *S* responds incorrectly, like reaching for *E*'s hand or leaving the chair, at which point *E* turns his head away so as to ignore *S* (places *S* on a 5-second time out or, if the incorrect behavior persists, on a longer duration of TO). If TO does not work *E* presents a loud aversive "No," and if this also fails to suppress the wrong response, *E* may give *S* a sharp slap on the hand. Once *E* has presented the child with the appropriate consequence, the training stimulus is removed (e.g., placed beside or under the table), and *E* remains passive for at least 5 seconds. The second trial is then started by *E* first placing the toast on the table, and shortly thereafter (e.g., within 3 seconds) presenting the command. In a way, the presentation of the visual stimulus should alert the child to the fact that the verbal stimulus is about to appear. It is important that the stimuli are presented succinctly; the discrete onset should help make them discriminable. *E* gradually gives less and less of a complete prompt until the child is responding on his own to the command alone. For instance, on the second trial *E* may take the child's hand and move it only three fourths of the way toward TS1. After several more trials of diminishing prompts, *E* may merely touch *S*'s arm after giving the command. Eventually *E* may present the training stimulus with no prompt stimulus. If *S* does not respond, *E* may reinstate a partial prompt for one or two trials and then again attempt to remove the prompt entirely. It is appropriate to expect considerable difficulty in shifting from the prompt to the training stimulus. *S* will respond to the barest remnants of the prompt, and cease responding altogether when the prompt is totally removed. We have discussed this problem at some length earlier in the book. If *S* does not shift from the prompt to the training stimulus, *E* may simply have to wait for the child to make the correct response on his own. *E* gives the command, and if *S* does not respond within a specified time limit, for example, 5 seconds, *E* removes the train-

ing stimulus and presents the child with a period of time out
(TO), for instance, E turns away for 10 seconds. The training
stimulus is then re-presented, and E again waits for the child to
respond. We discussed alternate tactics in the section on basic
training procedures in the main part of the book.

E repeats this procedure until S is giving the desired response
at the criterion level (for example, S gives correct responses (R1)
on 9 out of 10 presentations of TS1). TS2 is then introduced.
That is, a new object is presented, for instance, a glass of milk,
and E gives the command "Point to the milk," or just simply
"Milk." TS2 is then presented until the child reaches criterion on
TS2.

Once the child has reached criterion on TS2, TS1 ("Toast") is
reintroduced and R1 recovered. The two training stimuli are then
presented together, and rotation between them is initiated.
When the child can identify TS1 and 'TS2 when they are presented in nonsystematic order, TS3 may be introduced. For instance, E may select "bacon" as 3, which is first trained in isolation. That is, E gives the command "Show me the bacon" (again,
a differently worded command), and the desired response is
prompted. TS3 is repeatedly presented until S is pointing to the
bacon on 9 out of 10 trials. E may then reintroduce TS1 and TS2.
Depending on the level of the child, E may train TS2 or TS1 and
TS3 alternately or he may proceed directly to stimulus rotation.
When the child can correctly discriminate perhaps a dozen objects, E may begin training expressive speech.

Expressive Speech. E presents the training stimulus, for example, the original TS1 (toast). As soon as S visually fixates the
stimulus, the adult prompts the label "Toast." When the child
responds to the prompt, he is reinforced (e.g., he is given a bite
of toast). The training stimulus is then removed (for 3—5 seconds)
and represented on the next trial.Training proceeds along the same
lines as for receptive speech introducing TS2, training alternately
with TS1, etc. After the child has mastered perhaps a half dozen
labels using this paradigm, E will want to begin asking the question "What is it?" This question is not asked in the preliminary
stages of training, since it may block a good response to the
prompt and, conceivably, may also block S's perception of the
training stimulus. In general, the less E says at first, the better.

Verb labels, e.g., running, jumping, laughing, are taught in
much the same manner as object labels. E may begin by performing some activity, such as jumping. E simultaneously presents

the question "What am I doing?" *E* waits 5 seconds and if no response or an incorrect response is forthcoming, repeats the question and immediately gives the prompt "jumping." New training stimuli are introduced as for object labels. Once the child has mastered a dozen or so labels, *E* may change the training situation by having *S* perform the activity and asking the question "What are you doing?"

Once *S* has mastered approximately 10 labels, it becomes cumbersome to try to review all of the labels, both new and old, equally in every session. At this point, one may begin to intersperse previously mastered stimuli with new stimuli in some ratio which must be determined for each child, depending upon how much review seems necessary. Usually, a trial for review every 5 or 6 training trials will suffice. However, for a particular child, one may need to increase the ratio so that all previously mastered labels may be reviewed 2 or 3 times each session.

Training Stimuli

The objects and activities which are selected for label training should meet two criteria, particularly at the onset of training. They should be common, everyday things, objects and activities the children use frequently and often see others use. This criterion is important because it should make the labels more immediately useful for the children. Second, the labels should be maximally different. The child will have less difficulty learning to discriminate between "cup" and "ball" than "cup" and "car," or between "walking" and "jumping" than "walking" and "talking." As a corollary to this rule, the objects and activities themselves should be maximally different. "Cup" and "ball" are easier to discriminate than "cup" and "glass," similarly "walking" and "sitting" make an easier problem than "walking" and "running."

Special procedures. This manual and the teacher's understanding of the learning principles we described earlier should help the child get started on his first step into language acquisition. But many special problems will arise, requiring the exploration of certain special procedures. Let us mention some of these.

Some children will acquire labels very quickly, while others will be experiencing considerable difficulty. If the child has particular difficulty in mastering labels, certain special procedures we have developed may be of use. Several children will experience considerable difficulty in prompt use, which probably points to our ignorance of effective procedures in this area. Therefore, we have begun to explore new steps in this training that consider some of our recent findings on the autistic's use of prompts. Specifically, we now try to exaggerate (and thereby prompt) relevant parts of the training stimuli, in this manner. When TS1 and TS2 are presented simultaneously (and it is in this step that S will have the most problems) E may initially make TS1 many times its original ("natural") size. For example, if TS1 is toast and TS2 is milk, E may employ a small glass of milk while TS1 (the toast) is a large, visually very dominant, 2×2 foot piece of bread. This may allow S to make the discrimination on the basis of size cues (which minimizes S's reliance on E's pointing prompts, which seem so prepotent and difficult for S to relinquish). In subsequent steps TS1 is gradually reduced in size to approximate TS2. Later E may want to use several different sizes of TS1, just to extinguish S's use of size cues in this discrimination.

One may want to explore different kinds of prompt cues, and a position discrimination is particularly useful for some children. Three objects are placed on the table and the correct object or the training stimulus is placed slightly in front of the others; alternatively, the training stimulus may be consistently presented on the right or on the left. Most children will develop a position discrimination rapidly. When the child is discriminating position reliably, the training stimulus is gradually moved into line with the other objects. If it has been to the left, for instance, it is moved closer to, then partially in front of, then completely in front of, and then to the right of the others. The position of the training stimulus is then switched in nonsystematic order.

A matching procedure is more appropriate for the child who is readily imitating and is carried out as follows: E selects three objects for the child and a matching set of three objects for himself. E tells S to "Touch the ————" (preferably using the command which will later be used for regular receptive speech training). Simultaneously with the presentation of the command, E touches the object in his own set that matches the training stimulus in S's set. E's set of objects should be placed on the table in the same order as those of S. The procedure may be modified for teaching verb labels. E performs the activity to be labelled, has S imitate him, and gives the command, "jump," (or the appropriate label).

Gradually, matching is faded. E comes less and less close to actually touching the object in his set, or performs the activity less completely on successive trials. Eventually, E is giving a mere suggestion of the activity or the act of touching. *E* may then remove his set of objects completely or discontinue performing the prompting activity altogether.

Otherwise we are exploring ways of teaching *S* not to respond to a particular stimulus. Consider this problem: If TS1 and TS2 are displayed, and *E* asks for R1, then *S* has to learn not to respond to TS2. Therefore, we have explored a variation on the training procedure which can be illustrated as follows: *S* is taught to give R1 to TS1, and once R1 is reliably established, instead of presenting TS2 "at full intensity," TS2 is gradually introduced into the situation. For example, *E* has taught *S* to point to TS1 (a piece of toast placed on a table in front of *S*) when *E* asks "toast." Now *E* places TS2 (milk) on the same table when TS1 is presented, but some distance (say four feet) away from TS1, and therefore only in *S*'s peripheral field of vision. That is, TS2 would initially be a "low strength" stimulus, which helps *S* not to respond to it. Gradually, then, TS2 is moved more into *S*'s visual field and is eventually presented ("full strength") right next to TS1. If *E* had presented TS2 (at full strength) initially, without such pretraining, *S* very likely would have responded to TS2 as often as to TS1.

Here is an example of another variation in the training procedure which is being explored by the staff at the University of California at Santa Barbara Autism Project (under Dr. Robert Koegel). Although the example describes the training of abstract terms (color), it serves to illustrate the problems involved. The project had initially tried to teach the labels "red" and "white," using different-colored chips, and failed to make much progress with several of the children, apparently because the children were not attending to the training stimuli (the chips). They therefore used familiar objects such as a glass of red punch and a cup of white ice cream, and reinforced the child with the appropriate food if he pointed to the correct object when asked to do so. As these children already knew to reach for ice cream and punch when asked to do so, these labels were then used as prompts in teaching the child to respond to color. The prompts were gradually faded, until the child responded correctly to the color label (e.g., *E* continued to present "red" quite loudly and clearly, while "punch" was gradually faded in intensity until it became inaudible). The training procedure is of interest since it maximizes *S*'s attention to the training stimuli. Obviously, *S* may still not respond to the color of the stimuli, since the stimuli differ on a number of other dimensions, such as size and texture.

These extra cues would have to be faded out in order to insure that S was in fact responding on the basis of color. Note that this variation in the training procedure resembles the manner in which normal children acquire certain labels. For example, normal children seem to learn certain adjectives first in conjunction with certain specific objects, such as "big Daddy," "red car," "cold snow." (Perhaps when we know more about the manner in which normal children learn, we will also be in a position to better help the deviant child. That is, we really don't know the extent to which the procedures we have outlined for the psychotic child are "special" or unique, until we know what the procedures are which help normal children learn. Conceivably, the final procedures may have extensive overlap. We are required to undertake considerable revision and exploration since we don't know how language is acquired).

In any case, exploration of various pretraining steps and the use of certain kinds of prompts and training stimuli rather than some others should lead to major revisions of these manuals.

Generalization

When the child has mastered perhaps a dozen labels, E will want to begin generalization training. Numerous examples of an object are introduced (e.g., many cups, many chairs, many tables). Examples outside the original training situation are now emphasized. Training now becomes part of the child's everyday life. It is just not possible to present the child with sufficient instances of a label in the laboratory situation. But the outside world is replete with appropriate stimuli. Maximal differences are of course, no longer our concern; on the contrary, minimal differences are important in the beginning. One begins by extending training to examples of the label which are similar to the original stimulus, and gradually one uses instances which are more diverse. The child may be said to have developed a "concept" when he is able to correctly label members of a class upon first presentation.

Manual B: Prepositions

The object of this manual is to teach the child to label spatial relationships between objects. Later, one will attempt to teach the child about his own position in space and the relationships between major objects. The manual for prepositions is an example of a program which always begins with receptive speech training.

Receptive Speech

E and S are seated at a table and on top of the table is a small container, such as a cup, and a small object, like a penny. E instructs S to place the object in the container ("Put the penny *in* the cup," or E may simply say "in.") If the complete command is used, E should vocally stress the word "in." The correct response is prompted if necessary by taking S's hand, placing the penny in it, and putting the penny in the cup. The prompt is then faded in the usual manner, by E gradually diminishing his participation in S's response, until he barely touches S's arm, and so on. When the child is reliably responding to the preposition "in" (e.g., making 9 out of 10 correct responses without prompts), E begins to train a second preposition, usually "under." The same object may be utilized (the penny), but a different container (e.g., a small box) is used. E may say "Put the penny under the box," or simply "under." The response is prompted, and the prompt faded. When S has mastered "under," "in" is reintroduced and $R1$ retrained, then "under" is retrained, and so on, until S is making no more than one error each time E switches the training stimuli. During the entire procedure thus far, one container has been used for "in" and another for "under." In all probability, S is now learning that when one container is present he is supposed to place an object *under* it, and when another container is present he should place an object *in* it. That is, S is probably not learning anything about prepositions, but we employed two different containers to facilitate S's discriminations, and "get him on the way." In order to bring S under the control of (allow him to attend to) the verbalized prepositions, E begins to fade one of the containers, for example by gradually removing it so far away from S that it is simpler for S to use the same container for both "in" and "under."

When S can respond correctly to "in" and "under," using the same container and with rotated trials, generalization training may be instituted using new containers and placing objects one at a time or simultaneously. New prepositions such as "beside," "on top of," "behind," and "in front of" may be taught using the same procedures, omitting any steps which seem unnecessary for a particular child. Thus, for one child it may be necessary to train a new preposition in isolation, then alternately to train the new preposition and a previously mastered preposition and finally to present the new preposition in nonsystematic order with a previously mastered one. For another child, it may be sufficient to simply train the new preposition in isolation without concern for nonsystematic presentation.

Expressive Speech

When the child has mastered 5 or 6 prepositions for receptive speech, E may begin expressive speech training. The procedure is exactly the same as that for receptive speech except that now E places the object in or under the container (or E may instruct S to do so) and then asks S "Where is it?" The desired response, e.g., "in" (or "in the cup"), "under," (or "under the box,") are prompted, etc. It will probably not be necessary to use different containers in the initial stages of expressive speech training if the child has a good beginning on receptive speech. To test for this possibility, E should try to introduce TS2 using the same container as that for TS1. Once "in" and "under" have been trained, E should begin using many different objects and containers, as for receptive speech. New prepositions may be introduced at this stage.

Generalization

As with most of the other programs we will present, once the child has completed the laboratory training phase of the program, generalization training is carried out in the child's everyday life. The object now becomes to teach the child about his own position in space and the relationships between major everyday objects— to stand "on top of" the table, to hide "behind" the dresser, to sit "inside" the closet, to put the books "on top of" the bed, place his slippers "under" the bed. The rule is, teach the child the correct response to the most common prepositional relationships in the lab to facilitate later the day-to-day interaction you have with him.

Once S can carry out the most common demands involving prepositional relationships, E may begin generalization training on expressive speech, by first instructing S to sit on a chair, for example, and then present the question "What are you doing?"

The child is then prompted to reply "I am sitting on the chair." *E* may then ask "Where is the record player?" and prompt the answer "on the table." *E* may then ask *S* to "sit on the bed," to stand "on top of the chair," and so on, and prompt *S*'s correct verbalization of these behaviors. The language training film which we produced gives certain examples both of the laboratory training of prepositions and of their extension into everyday life. Obviously, the opportunities for the training and testing of generalization are infinite once we take the child's training into the real world.

Manual C: Pronouns

This program includes the training of genitive pronouns (my, your, his, her) and personal pronouns (I, you, he, she). We have not systematically evaluated the question of which to teach first. However, we have generally taught the genitive first.

Genitive Case Pronouns

Receptive speech training for "your." Training in the receptive use of the genitive case for the pronouns my, your, mine, yours, his, and hers proceeds as follows: A large number of common personal possessions (such as clothing, or jewelry) and body parts (nose, eye, ear, arm) are used as training stimuli. The child should already know how to label these possessions and body parts. Training for the genitive case of receptive speech means that the child must now learn to correctly identify the personal referent of *E*'s statements, i.e., the child must discriminate the pronoun used in *E*'s sentence. *E* begins with the sentence, "Point to your nose" (or some similar body part) or *E* may simply state "your nose." At the same time *E* prompts the correct response by touching *S*'s nose (and *S* has been previously taught to respond to this prompt). Once this response is established, *E* introduces, and eventually rotates, the second stimulus, "Point to my nose" (or just "my nose"). The introduction and rotation of these stimuli proceeds in the same manner as we described for TS1 and TS2. Once this discrimination is established, and *S* points to his own or *E*'s nose when asked to, the discrimination is "broadened" by introducing other body parts. The training stimuli may now go as follows: "Point to my nose," "Point to your ear," "Point to my eye," and so on. We argue that *S* has mastered this phase of pro-

noun training when he can correctly point to a particular possession or body part which has not been used in training (for example, when he can correctly point to his own or *E*'s hair, even
though he has not been specifically trained to do so).

  Expressive speech training for "your" and "my." In this discrimination the child will be required to verbalize a particular pronominal relationship. Confusion over pronoun reversal is the problem
most characteristic of this stage. The child has just been taught to
"Point to your ————," and the desired response was to point to
one of his own body parts. When *E* said "Point to my ————"
the desired response was to point to one of *E*'s body parts. Now
when *E* says "Point to your ————" the child must now point to
his own body part and must say "My ————." Of course, "my" is
the label the child has heard applied to *E*'s body parts. In order to
abate some of the confusion, the S^D is changed from "Point to
————" to "Whose ———— is this?" *E* says "Whose ———— is
this?" and simultaneously points to the appropriate object, e.g.,
points to *S*'s nose. *S* is then prompted to say "My nose." Once *S*
has completed this step and can discriminate reliably between the
two pronouns on one body part, new body parts may be introduced as described.

  Another procedure, which we have not systematically
explored, but which may constitute a useful pretraining step by
diminishing the confusion in pronoun reversal, starts out pronoun training with proper nouns, like "Mommy," "Daddy"
and/or the child's name. During this part of training, the child
may be taught to point to "Mommy's nose" as distinct from
"Stephen's nose," or any other part. This may help in the sense
that the child is taught to attend to, not just the body part, but
the appropriate referent.

  Expressive speech training for "his" and "her." Once the child has
mastered the possessive pronouns "my" and "your" for several
body parts and possessions, *E* may introduce the training on the
expression of "his" and "her." A third person (or a picture of a
person) is introduced into the training situation. *E* points to that
person's nose, for instance, and asks "Whose nose is this?" The
child is prompted to say "his nose." The prompts are faded, and
the child drilled to criterion as usual. At this point, *E* may alternate training on "his" with training "my" or "your" in a systematic stimulus rotation with "my" and "your." This will, of course,
depend on *E*'s experience with the child in similar programs. It
may be possible for some children to immediately begin training

on such systematic rotation of pronouns and body parts. Other children will require training in isolation on each change in the training stimulus.

Nominal Case Pronouns

Step 1. Expressive speech training for "I." It is difficult to say whether it is best to teach the child personal or possessive pronouns first. We have merely presented these in an order we generally use. Personal pronouns are taught using a large number of common activities. *E* performs such an activity or prompts *S* to perform it and then asks, "What are you doing?" *S* is then prompted to say "I am ————" (for example, "I am jumping.") It may be useful for *E* to point to *S* as he asks the question "What are you doing?" during the initial stages of training. Both of the prompts will then have to be faded, as was the case for the possessive pronouns. *E* chooses one activity (such as standing, pointing, jumping, smiling, or laughing) for use in Steps 1, 2, and 3. Again, only one activity is used in the first steps. Once *S* has mastered the desired response, *E* may proceed to Step 2.

Step 2. Expressive speech training for "you." *E* performs the activity selected for use in Step 1 himself and asks the child "What am I doing?" He may, of course, simultaneously point to himself. The child is prompted to say *"You're—."* Prompts are faded, and training is continued to criterion.

Step 3. Rotation of "you" and "I." Steps 1 and 2 are repeated until *S* is making no more than one error per shift. "What are *you* doing," and "What am *I* doing?" are then rotated in nonsystematic fashion as usual. Again, only one activity, the same as that employed in Steps 1 and 2, is used. When the child is responding at criterion level for nonsystematic stimulus rotation, *E* may begin to change the activity (behaviors) from one trial to the next using the same procedures as those outlined for the switching of body parts in training possessive pronouns. Again, if the child has difficulty switching activities, the new activities may be introduced and trained one at a time while *E* continues to switch the pronouns nonsystematically.

Step 4. Expressive speech training for "he" and "she." Once the child is able to respond to questions about "you" and "I" presented in nonsystematic fashion, for several activities, *E* may begin training "he" and "she." A third person is introduced into the training situation as in training for the genitive case. The third person performs some activity, and *E* asks "What is *he (she)* doing?" The correct response is prompted, the prompt faded, and drill continued to criterion. At this point, *E* may either systematically alternate training on "he" with training on "you" and "I" or he may proceed directly to nonsystematic stimulus rotation, depending on *E*'s judgement of how successful *S* will be. This judgement is based on *E*'s experience with the particular *S* involved.

Step 5. Expressive speech training for combined use of genitive and nominal pronouns. When the child has mastered both personal pronouns and possessive pronouns, one can proceed to train their combined use. One begins by rotation of questions about possessive pronouns in a nonsystematic fashion with questions about personal pronouns. When *S* has mastered such rotation, *E* may engage in some simple activity which involves a body part or possession. For example, *E* may touch *S*'s nose and ask "What am I doing?" *S* will then be prompted to say, "You are touching my nose." Training on this stimulus may be continued until *S* reaches criterion, or, if *E* feels the child can handle it, he may change the training stimulus on the next trial to "What are you doing," and have *S* touch *E*'s nose ("I am touching your nose.") Training proceeds as for individual pronouns, skipping any step which *E* may feel is unnecessary for a particular child. A third person may be introduced once *S* has mastered several such combinations for both "you" and "I." For example, "He is touching your eye" may be trained.

Manual D: Time Concepts

The object of this manual is to teach the child to use the words "first" and "last" and "before" and "after" to describe simple temporal relationships. We usually have begun with "first," although, in retrospect, one may be better off beginning with "last," as the spatial and temporal cues for that concept are most recent.

Expressive speech training for "last." *E* places five objects (Set 1, e.g., key, boat, pencil, ball, and watch) on the table in front of the child. It is advisable, as in the first stages of training for labels, to select objects within a set for maximal stimulus differences. Both the label for the object and the physical appearance of the object should be considered for differences. We have used five objects to reduce the probability that S will be reinforced by merely labelling one of the objects by chance without discriminating its temporal relation to the others. E tells S to touch three of the five objects in a certain order (e.g., "Touch the key, touch the pencil, touch the boat."). E then asks the question "What came last?" or "What did you touch last?" and prompts S to make the desired response, e.g., "boat." Prompting may include both the verbal prompt "boat" and a nonverbal prompt (taking S's hand and placing it on the boat.) Of course, both prompts must be faded. After the child makes the desired response, set 1 remains, but a new selection of three objects within the set is touched (e.g., pencil, boat, key), and the question is repeated ("What did you touch last"). S is prompted ("the key"), and so on. This procedure is repeated, using the same set of five objects and a new selection of three on each trial until S reaches criterion (e.g., 9 out of 10 correct responses). Now a new set of objects is introduced (e.g., cup, book, spoon, dish, paper). S is trained to criterion on Set 2, and then it is replaced by Set 3. When S can make 10 consecutive correct responses on a new set, we assume he understands the concept "last" and proceed to training "first." The use of new sets, and the use of new object selections within these sets, "forces" S away from a particular object (or other irrelevant cues) and "enables" S to "abstract" (or "attend" to) the relevant stimulus in this discrimination, which is the temporal arrangement (time).

Expressive speech training for "first." The sets are used over again, but the question "What came last?" is replaced by the question "What came first?" He is prompted and trained as before. When S is able to make 10 correct responses in a row upon presentation of a new set, "What came last?" may be reintroduced, and so on.

Rotation of "first" and "last." Nonsystematic stimulus rotation is carried out using a new set of objects (objects not employed in training "first" and "last"), and a new selection of objects within this set is made on each trial, rotating the question "What came first?" with "What came last?" Prompting and fading may be employed as usual if necessary. When S is able to make 10 consecutive correct responses upon presentation of a new set of objects, mastery is assumed. E may then begin training "after" and "before."

Expressive speech training for "before" and "after." The same

materials and stimulus presentation may be employed as for
"first" and "last." However as usual, special care must be taken to
make sure that each object serves equally as the object for one
stimulus ("before") as for the other ("after"). *E* instructs *S* to
touch 3 of the objects and then asks "What came *after* the
————" (the first object touched). For example, if the key was
touched first, *E* asks "What came after the key?" During the initial stages of training, it is probably advisable always to make the
desired response correspond to the second object touched. Once
the child has proceeded through nonsystematic stimulus rotation
using this procedure, *E* may repeat the procedure, requiring the
child to give responses corresponding to the first and third objects
touched as well as the second. Once the child has mastered "after," *E* begins training on "before."

Special procedures. For children who seem to have special
difficulty in mastering these concepts, a supplemental procedure
similar to the position discrimination for labelling may be
employed. In this case, *E* will place the objects on the table so
that the desired response corresponds to the label for the object
which appears consistently on the left. Once the child has developed a position discrimination (i.e., makes 10 consecutive correct responses on a new set of objects), *E* will gradually place this
object slightly in front of, then completely in front of, then to the
right of the other objects. When the child completes this phase,
E may begin switching the position of the objects corresponding
to the desired response in a nonsystematic fashion. It may be
necessary to develop a position discrimination both for "first" and
for "last." In any case, the position discrimination must be faded
before training on a new concept is begun.

Generalization. Introduction of a new set of objects serves as
one test of stimulus generalization. Many possibilities present
themselves as training is moved from the laboratory to everyday
life. For example, *E* might wish to train and test generalization,
using a sequence of activities. Here training merges closely with
the procedure for recall presented in Manual H. So far as we could
tell, the children got a lot out of this program on "time," particularly when they began to understand concepts like "later." Like
normal children, autistic children want immediate gratification,
and their understanding of postponing but not relinquishing
gratifications seems critical in helping them suppress their frus-
trations and concurrent whining and fussing. The time concepts
generalized nicely to outside activities, as when we taught "la-

ter," beginning with 3-second delays of food consumption. S would be shown a food, which he wanted to eat immediately, while E would give "later" as an S^D for an increasingly longer delay in reaching for the food. Such generalization training was instigated for most of the child's preferred behaviors, like "going swimming later," "first we finish class," and "Joan comes back tomorrow."

Manual E: Other Simple Abstractions

In this manual, we shall present training procedures for two more types of simple abstractions, illustrative of the many we have taught. They are a procedure for teaching color and a procedure for teaching the use of "yes" and "no." The procedure for color follows closely the program for teaching simple labels and should serve as an example of how this procedure may be adapted for the teaching of many kinds of simple abstractions. For example, if the teacher substitutes objects with different forms (like blocks of different forms), the child will be learning about forms. The procedure for "yes-no" training is slightly more complex and may serve as an example of the ways in which the program can be modified for the teaching of concepts which do not fit easily into the usual procedure.

Color and form

Receptive speech. The object of this procedure is to teach the child to discriminate among colors and to label them appropriately. As in teaching labels, receptive speech training is generally useful as a pretraining procedure. E places, on the table in front of S, three objects (blocks, plastic chips or the like) which differ only in color, and not on any other dimension (like size or shape). E then presents TS1, that is, he asks S to point to or give him a color. He may say "red" (or "Give me red"), which means that S has to give E the red object. E prompts and fades, as he has in other kinds of training. Once S reliably responds with R1 (gives E the red object), even though this colored object is changing position among the other colors on the table, then E introduces TS2 and trains as per basic training steps. Some children acquire color recognition very early, others are slower. For the fast learner, relatively few colors (say three or four) are trained in the lab before the color recognition is brought "outside." If the child has too many difficulties at this level of receptive speech, the matching and position discriminations outlined in Manual A may be easily modified for use in this manual. E simply uses colored blocks or blocks of different shapes in place of the objects described in Manual A and teaches the child to match colors as a pretraining step in receptive training.

Expressive Speech. To begin expressive speech training, E selects several of the colored blocks used in receptive speech training. E presents one of the blocks to S, waits for S to visually attend to the block, and asks "What color is this?" (Again, for the first few trials, E may simply give the color label and omit the question.) The desired response is prompted, the prompt faded, a new stimulus introduced, and so on. When the child is labeling several colors correctly, the color discriminations may be used to facilitate the acquisition of shape.

We have usually taught form labels after the color labels, but we know of no reason that should be necessary. In the initial stages of form discrimination, that is, while E is teaching receptive speech, E may assemble, for example, a blue block (square), a red circle, and a yellow triangle. E says "Hand me the *blue square*," "Hand me the *red circle*," and so on. When S is able to correctly respond to these commands for three or four different shapes, E may begin asking simply for the square, e.g., "Hand me the square," dropping the color label from the S^D, which essentially means that E is removing the prompt. Once the child is responding well to commands containing no color labels, E may begin fading color as a cue altogether by using different-colored examples of the same shapes or same-colored examples of different shapes. Expressive speech training is carried out exactly as for color and object labels.

Generalization training. As in all the other programs, E may take the child's training outside the experimental situation in order to train and test for generalization. The color of eyes and hair, clothing, or furniture may be used. The shapes of tables and containers and toys may be included. Color and form discrimination, once mastered, are often quite useful in facilitating new learning. For example, one will find many kinds of programmed learning materials for teaching reading in which color is initially used to help the child form the correct discriminations between words. Keep in mind that once more we are going into the child's everyday life to extend the child's understanding (discrimination) of color only after we have helped him attend to (discriminate) colors in the controlled lab environment.

Yes-No training

Yes-no training involves the teaching of two procedures; one is labeled "yes-no for factual matters" and the other "yes-no for matters of personal feelings." One generally begins with "yes-no for factual matters," as such training allows one to use more concrete training stimuli.

Expressive speech training of "yes-no for factual matters." The object of this procedure is to give the child a simple tool for expressing his knowledge about the environment, so that he can begin to affirm or deny the truth of statements about the real objects and events around him.

E selects a number of real common objects. He places them in front of S, picks up one of them, waits for S to visually fixate the object, and asks, "Is this a ———?" E begins by asking only questions which can be answered in the affirmative. For example, E may pick up a cup and ask S, "Is this a cup?" The desired response, "yes," is prompted. E presents a different object on the next trial, e.g., "Is this a boat?" and prompts the answer "yes." Over successive trials the prompt is faded until S is answering "yes" reliably. E may then begin training "no." E picks up an object, like a cup, and asks, "Is this a boat?" S will almost certainly say "yes." E corrects S and prompts the desired response, "no." Again, E picks up a different object on the next trial, such as a boat, and asks "Is this a cup?" The desired response, "no," is prompted. Over successive trials, the prompt is faded. When the child is reliably answering "no," training for "yes" is repeated, then "no" is reintroduced, and so on. When the child is making no more than one error in ten tries when E switches the questions from ones that require "no" to "yes" and vice-versa, the questions are presented in nonsystematic order.

Special procedures. Different sets of objects may be used to teach "yes" and "no" and a new set introduced in rotation if this procedure seems to facilitate S's performance. If the child has difficulty in the initial stages of training, E may institute a procedure analogous to the matching procedure for simple labels. E holds up the object in question and asks S, "What is this?" S labels the object and E asks, "Is this a ———?" prompts the correct response, and so on. One may consider that S's answer ("yes" or "no") to the last question is helped to the extent that he can match his own and *E*'s label (the basic discrimination for a "yes-no" answer) when his own label has been made more available. Eventually this extra cue (*S*'s initial labelling of the object) may be faded.

Expressive speech training of "yes-no" for personal feelings. The object of this procedure is to give *S* the words to answer questions about his own personal feelings and desires and thus to help him acquire some control over what he wants people to do, and not to do, with him.

In the first stages of this training, we have found it useful to concentrate on teaching *S* to answer questions about the foods and activities he appears to strongly like and dislike. In the first step, *E* selects a number of foods and activities he is fairly certain *S* enjoys (e.g., candy, ice cream, swinging, tickling). *E* then asks *S* if he would like to eat one of these foods or engage in one of these activities, e.g., "Do you want some candy?" *S* is prompted to answer "Yes." A correct response is followed by giving *S* the food or activity involved. *E* may switch the food or activity on the next trial, providing it is another that *S* enjoys, and in this way avoid stimulus satiation.

When *S* is reliably answering "yes," *E* selects several foods or activities he is fairly certain *S* does not enjoy (e.g., spinach, being pinched, staying inside instead of playing). *E* then asks *S* (for example), "Do you want me to pinch you?" *S* is prompted to answer "No." It is important that if *S* gives an incorrect response, i.e., answers "yes," this response is followed by the appropriate consequences, e.g., *E* pinches *S*. *E* then repeats the question, prompts the correct R, and helps *S* avoid the aversions. We consider it important to "consequate" definitely and succinctly, because if there are no consequences for an incorrect transmission, part of the meaning of "yes" and "no" is obscured. Once the child is reliably answering "no," training for "yes" is reintroduced, and so on.

Generalization. For factual matters, generalization may be tested and/or trained for colors, shapes, body parts, pronouns (e.g., "Is this my nose?"), or almost any of the other basic skills which *S* has mastered. For personal feelings, the S^D may be changed and generalization taught for a number of questions generally requiring "yes-no" answers. For example, *E* may ask *S* "Do you like ————?" (e.g., "to go swimming"). Another approach involves the feelings and desires of a third person, e.g., "Does

Billy want to be tickled?" The use of a third person, of course, is best carried out when S sees another person engaged in some activity like eating and displaying obvious visual cues to his feelings on the subject or talking about how much he does or does not like it.

Manual F: Conversational Speech

This program is tied to almost all of the other programs described in these manuals. Basic training in conversation is embedded in other programs as well. In the first stages of this particular procedure, the child is taught to answer simple "social questions" like "How are you?" and "What's your name?" in a manner which encourages further conversational exchange between S and E. These answers require largely one-word statements, and in that sense the program resembles labelling (program 2). As training progresses, all of the material from programs such as recall, describing, and storytelling (to be outlined next) become material for conversational speech. In the second stage of the procedure, the training of conversational speech centers on teaching the child to discriminate between what he does and does not know, to request and transfer information, and the like.

Part 1. Social Questions

The object in this phase is to teach S to answer simple social questions in a manner that provides further stimuli to which a second person may respond in turn.

One begins by teaching S to answer a question asked by E with both an answer to the direct question and a further question or comment to which E can respond. To facilitate such training, S must be able to take a command directly, that is, when E says, "Say I am fine, how are you?" S should be able to say, "I am fine, how are you?" In order to do this, the child must first be able to imitate a long sequence of verbal responses. Second, he must be able to discriminate between words he is supposed to imitate and those he is not (i.e., he must be able to respond correctly to the command "say"). This discrimination may be built in a number of ways. E may pause after "say," never reinforcing any response that occurs in the pause. E may repeat "say" in a very soft voice, and the rest of the sentence much louder. Time out may be made contingent upon S's repeating the word "say." Further instructions may be found in Manual M, "breaking echolalia." Once the child is able to respond to direct commands for verbal responses, the central procedure may begin.

E asks S a social question such as "How are you?" or "How old are you?" If S answers correctly, he is reinforced and then prompted to ask E, "How old are you?" or "How are you?" At first it may be necessary to reward both parts of the response, i.e., the answer and the further question. E then responds to S's question. On the next trial, E may repeat the original question (i.e., "How are you?"). Over successive trials, the prompts are faded and reinforcement for the answer alone is dropped. Eventually, only the response "I am fine, how are you?" will be reinforced, and only when it occurs without prompts. When the child is performing at criterion level for the first question, a new question is introduced, e.g., "What's your name?"

When S has mastered this form of response to several such questions E should begin requiring S to give longer chains of responses before delivering reinforcement. The target response might be an interchange such as $E:$ "How are you?" $S:$ "I am fine, how are you?" $E:$ "I am fine. What is your name?" $S:$ "Ricky. What is your name?" $E:$ "Joan. How old are you?" $S:$ "Eight. How old are you?" and so on. At first, E will reinforce each correct response S makes. Gradually, E requires more and more interchange before rewarding the child.

As S masters other programs, such as recall and describing-accounting, the material may be brought into the context of conversational speech, e.g., E asks, "What did you do this morning?" S then describes his morning and asks E, "What did you do this morning?" Generalization may be trained and tested, using material from other programs. Another approach to generalization training is to involve a third person in the conversation, having him ask the child the training questions.

Part 2. Requesting and transferring information

The object of this procedure is to teach the child to discriminate between what he knows and what he does not, to request information from another person when he needs such information and then to transfer that information as appropriate.

E compiles a list of questions, some of which S will be able to answer and some of which he will not, but will have to ask someone else for the requisite information (e.g., "What is your mother cooking for dinner?" "How old is your brother?" "What did she do this morning?"). A third person, e.g., the mother, is present during the training sessions. *E* presents one of the questions to *S*. If the child cannot answer the question (and *E* should be fairly certain that *S* has the appropriate information), the child is prompted to say, "I don't know," and to repeat the question to the third person. The third person answers the child's question, and *S* is then prompted to repeat the answer to *E*.

Questions to which *S* does not know the answer may be trained first, and then one may want to pose him questions that he can answer to teach him the difference between the two situations. Typically, however, when the child reaches this stage of the program, it is possible from the earliest stages to present questions he can answer intermixed in nonsystematic order with those he can not answer. On the other hand, it is usually necessary, at least at first, to reinforce *S* at several points in the chain of responses required to complete this interaction, i.e., to reinforce him for asking questions as well as for giving answers to *E*. It is sometimes useful to have the third person deliver reinforcement where appropriate to direct *S*'s attention away from *E*. For instance, a typical training trial may go like this in the beginning:

E What are you having for dinner tonight?
S No response.
E Say "I don't know."
S I don't know.
E Good boy! (Delivers reinforcement.) Now ask your mother. Say "What are we having for dinner?"
S What are we having for dinner?
E No. Look at your mother. Good. Now say "What are we having for dinner?"
S What are we having for dinner? (Mother may deliver reinforcement for the child's asking her.)
Mother Stew.
E Look at me. Good. What are you having for dinner? (*S* makes no *R*.) Say "Stew."
S Stew.
E Good. (Delivers reinforcement.)
      Eventually, *E* will fade each of the prompts (e.g., "Say ———," "Look at ———,") and the final repetition of the question will be dropped. *E* will also discontinue all intermediate reinforcement, delivering reinforcement only at the end of the interchange. An ideal trial at criterion level may go like this:

E   What are you having for dinner?
S   I don't know. (Looks at mother.) Mother, what are we having for dinner?
Mother   Stew.
S   (Looks at *E*) Stew.
(*E* delivers reinforcement.)

Manual G: Verb Transformations

The object of this manual is to teach *S* to transform verbs from the present to the past tense. The manual is an example of the specific and concrete manner in which we taught grammatically correct speech. Specifically, we had hoped that the child might acquire behavior with which to call upon his past experience and that of others, to learn how the past relates to the present, and then to be in a position to evaluate the consequences of an act without performing it.

The manual involves two steps; the first teaches the child to make the correct verbal response (i.e., the verbal transformation), and the second helps the child attach the correct verbal response to his own behavior. The regular inflectional affix "ed" is taught first, and irregular forms are taught later.

Expressive speech training for regular verbs. E selects 12 to 15 verbs which label common activities and require the "ed" affix in the past tense (e.g., walked, jumped, closed). E may begin this training at a purely verbal level, by giving S the present tense of a sentence (e.g., "I am walking") and teaching S to respond with the past tense of that sentence ("I walked") when asked to do so. In a subsequent step, E may perform an action and simultaneously label it, e.g., "I am closing the door." E then asks "What did I just do?" and prompts S to say "You closed the door." E repeats this procedure using the same verb until S can correctly answer the question "What did I just do?" The response is prompted, the prompt faded, the first verb is then reintroduced, and so on.

Once the child is able to properly transform perhaps a dozen verbs in response to *E*'s question, *E* moves on to the next step and begins giving S commands, having S label the activity while he performs it ("What are you doing?") and then answer the question "What did you just do?" For example, E tells S to "close the door." While S is performing this activity, E asks "What are you doing?" *S* should be able to answer this question "I am closing the door," since he already has completed the program for simple labels. When *S* has completed the activity, *S* returns to *E* and *E* asks "What did you just do?" The desired response is prompted, e.g., "I closed the door." After *S* shows mastery of the first set of verbs, *E* selects a new set of regular verbs and tests for generalization. If *S* transforms most of these verbs correctly upon first presentation, *E* may move on to irregular verbs.

During the initial stages of training transformations, it is recommended that one choose verbs which require a rather extended period of time to perform. If the response can be performed very quickly, it is possible that *S* will use the past tense to answer the question "What are you doing?" If *E* uses a verb like walking or jumping or closing, *E* will have time to have *S* make several discrete responses such as correctly labeling the activity while he is performing it, stopping the behavior and returning to *E* before labeling the action in the past tense.

Expressive speech training for irregular verbs. The procedure is the same as for regular verbs, that is, *E* performs an activity, asks *S* "What did I just do?" and so on. It is to be expected that the child will require longer to learn a number of these forms than the regular forms. Drill is continued on regular verbs while the irregular ones are being taught. A regular verb may be included every five or six trials during this phase once *S* has mastered several irregular forms. Of course, since there are no rules governing the irregular forms, it will not be possible to test for generalization of form. *E* must teach the proper form for each new example until *S* has mastered most of the forms which will be useful to him. Generalization may be tested in the individual by using a third person. The third person is instructed to perform some activity, and *S* is asked "What did he just do?" Needless to say, we moved slowly on the acquisition of irregular verbs, since it is difficult to master. Also, it is possible to understand a child who does not know the irregular form.

Manual H: Plural and Singular

The object of this manual is to enable *S* to pluralize noun labels using the proper endings and to discriminate between referents of the singular and plural cases.

Expressive speech training for the regular case. As in training transformations, one begins with the regular case. *E* selects 10 common object labels which require the addition of "s" in the plural form (e.g., "apples," "flowers," "blocks"). These should be objects for which *S* has already mastered the labels. *E* selects one of these objects and places two examples of the item in front of *S*, for example, two apples. *E* picks up one of the apples and says, "Here is one apple." Holding the first apple in one hand, *E* then picks up the other apple and says "Here are two . . ." (waiting for *S* to supply the missing word, "apples"). If *S* does not respond, *E* prompts the desired response, in this case, "apples." Training on one item (e.g., the apples) is continued until *S* gives the differential response (apple or apples) reliably, without prompting. *E* then selects a new set of objects (e.g., pencil, pencils) and trains a second regular form, returns to the first, and so on. After *S* has mastered perhaps 10 regular plurals, *E* changes the nature of the training stimulus. Several examples of an object are placed in front of *S*, for example, three or four apples. *E* says "Here are three (or four) . . . ," or "Here are some . . . ," or "Here are many . . . ," and so on.

Expressive speech training for irregular forms. Irregular forms are taught using the same procedure as that for regular forms. Again, as is the case for transformations, irregular forms take more time and require more extensive specific training. Regular forms are reviewed occasionally; perhaps in every five or six trials one regular form may be presented, once *S* has mastered several irregular forms.

Generalization. Generalization for regular forms may be tested by the introduction of new training stimuli, the labels of which are pluralized by the addition of "s." For irregular forms, new examples of the same objects may be used, provided the child has shown generalization of simple object labels. For both regular and irregular forms, generalization may be tested by using different numbers of objects as the training stimuli and new questions, such as "Here are several . . . ," "Here are a couple of . . . ," and so on. This is a particularly useful way to test generalization for irregular forms where the new S^Ds have been trained and tested for regular forms, but never used during training for irregular forms. Since no general rules apply to the pluralization of irregular forms, one cannot simply introduce new objects which take irregular forms in the plural and see if the child correctly transforms them. One must train and test for each form individually.

Manual I: Recall

The object of this manual is to enable the child to transmit and record past events in a manner comprehensible to all so that these records and transmissions may then become functional stimuli for persons not present when the event occurred. As such they will control the behavior of both the speaker and the listener. The program requires that the child have most, if not all, of the skills outlined in the previous manuals. The training procedure on recall involves three steps. Step 1 centers on the recall of the immediate past (e.g., within a minute) and is taught much like transformations (see Manual G). Step 2 involves the verbal reproduction of events with a somewhat longer delay than in Step 1 (e.g., from 1 to 60 minutes old), and Step 3 involves recall of events which have occurred hours or days in the child's past.

Step 1. Immediate past. E selects at least 12 and up to 15 simple behaviors which S has already learned to label. E instructs S to perform the activity, for example, "Close the door." When S has completed the activity and returned to E, E asks, "What did you just do?" and prompts S to answer, "I closed the door." (If S has completed the program for verb transformations, he should be able to answer such questions.) When S is able to give the correct response for a least six simple activities, E begins combining two activities. For example, E instructs S to close the door and then walk to the bed. At first, E may have to instruct S to do one activity, wait for S to complete it, and then repeat the additional instruction. It is often useful for S to label his activities while he is performing them in the first stages of training. S returns to E when he has performed both activities, and E asks "What did you just do?" and prompts the answer (e.g., "I closed the door and then walked to the bed."). As always E fades his prompts as soon as possible, from the complete statement of S's answer to partial prompts, relying on S to "fill in" the answer as best he can ("I do . . . ," waits for S, if no answer, "I closed the . . . ," and on to prompts like "I closed the door and then . . . ," and so on). At this stage in the child's training, it should be possible for E to change the two activities on each successive trial, provided that S is able to label the activity and transform the verb to the past tense. Changing the two activities allows S to discriminate the appropriate stimuli sooner, which may not occur if E stays with the same activities throughout. E continues combining two activities in this fashion until S can reliably recall both without prompts. At first, *E* may not require the child to recall the activities in the correct temporal order. However, the child should be held for temporal order for two activity combinations before moving to the next phase. The next phase involves the combining of three activities, then four, and so on. The child should be held for temporal order for three activities before combining four, and so on.

During these first stages of training, *E* will want to select activities which have concrete objects associated with them, such as closing the door or playing ball. *E* will then be able to prompt the child's response by merely saying "and then . . ." and pointing to the cue (i.e., object) associated with the next activity. *S* should be allowed to look at the objects at this point when questioned; however, one cannot consider the training of Step 1 complete before the child can recall the activities in correct order without prompts, which ideally means that he doesn't have to look at the objects associated with the activities he has performed. When the child can reliably recall five or six activities in order without prompting, *E* may move on to Step 2.

Step 2. The less immediate past. In this phase, the child will be taught to recall what he has just done when that activity involves more complex behaviors than in Step 1 and when concrete cues may not be available. The child is now expected to "think back" a short period in time.

In the initial stages of this phase, *E* selects a number of common activities which require an extended period in time to perform as compared to the activities in Step 1. Some examples are riding in the elevator, getting a drink, and greeting another person. It is best to select activities at this stage which require walking some distance, performing the activity, and returning to the original starting point. As the various behaviors are performed, it is recommended that *E* ask *S* to verbalize what he is doing. Upon returning to the starting point, *E* asks, "What did you just do?" and *S* is prompted to respond, "I rode in the elevator," "I said 'Hi' to John," "I drank water in the fountain," and so on. If *S* responds correctly at first with no prompts, *E* may immediately begin combining two activities or may hold *S* for recalling the first activity in more detail, e.g., "I opened the door and then I rode in the elevator." If *S* does not respond correctly at first, another single activity is selected and trained until *S* is recalling single activities without prompts. *E* continues combining activities and requiring more specific recall until *S* can recall a sequence such as "I opened the door, walked downstairs, then got a drink, and talked to someone. We looked at the fountain and went up in the elevator."

It is extremely important during Step 2 to immediately and profusely reinforce all instances of spontaneity. In the course of performing the selected activities, E will require S to label what he is doing, or E will label it himself. For example, E may say "We are opening the door, now we are walking downstairs, now we are getting a drink." If, upon returning, S answers E's questions with a sequence like the following: "We opened the door, we walked downstairs, SAW A DOG, got a drink, and CAME BACK," S may be considered to have given two spontaneous responses. These should be immediately reinforced. As in Step 1, E may not require correct temporal order when first training a combination; however, before another activity is added to the combination, S should be required to recall the correct temporal order.

Step 3. The remote past. During this step of training, S will be taught to recall events which took place several hours before at first, and eventually those that happened days and weeks before. E begins, for example, by requiring S in an afternoon session to recall what occurred that morning. E concentrates on common, daily activities during the initial stages. For example, E may begin with the question "What did you do today?" He prompts S to say "I got up." E then says, "Then what?" and prompts S to say "Ate breakfast." The question "What did you do today?" is then repeated and S is required to answer "I got up and ate breakfast." Training continues by expanding S's responses until S can recall a sequence such as "I got up, ate breakfast, then played with my toys. After that I went to school, ate lunch, and came to UCLA." Spontaneous responses are immediately reinforced. Training in recalling the "remote" past proceeds best when E is sufficiently familiar with the child to know the nuances of what specifically has happened on a particular morning, or on a particular trip the day before, to "extend" the child's verbal behavior to as many parts of his existence as possible. Most of the time parents are the only persons who have that kind of familiarity with the child, so that the term E here as often as not refers to the child's parent.

At this point, training in recall merges completely with training in spontaneous speech and conversational speech. When the child gets to this stage, it becomes extremely difficult to separate the programs and specifically define the procedures E uses. The child is being taught in much the same manner as the normal child is taught at home. Training becomes part of his everyday life, and every day life becomes training.

Manual J: Spontaneity Training

As we described it in the basic text, the training regime, with its experimental laboratory setting, its use of "unnatural" reinforcers, and the like may have been responsible for producing the very situation-specific, restricted verbal output which we observed in many of our children. To attempt to "open" the children up more, to help them talk more often and more freely, we devised a specific program in spontaneity training. Keep in mind that it may be possible to teach spontaneity, but not in the kind of structured program we describe here. Perhaps spontaneous speech comes about when the child feels accepted and liked by his grown-up friends, which does not occur when he is continuously monitored as to the correctness and incorrectness of his language, as we have done. Even though some of our data support the notion of increase in spontaneous language, we do not have the data we needed to show that our spontaneity training program produced an overall, generalized use of everyday spontaneous behavior. The reader may want to test the empirical value of this program himself, and here is what we did.

For convenience, we divided the program for spontaneity training into four parts: (1) describing pictures, (2) describing body parts and personal belongings, (3) describing everyday events, and (4) expressing desires. In general, the principal intent of the program, with the exception of expressing desires, is to have the child learn to give more and more extended descriptive accounts of his environment with fewer and fewer requests to do so by his *E*s. We came to define spontaneous speech which occurred in the absence of experimentally manipulated cues, i.e., the child speaks without being specifically requested to do so. Spontaneous speech also refers to speech that occurs in a stimulus situation in which that particular behavior has not been trained; it may consist of a novel response, a novel combination of old responses, or an old response in a new stimulus situation.

Part 1. Training in extended descriptions of pictures.

E makes up a number of posters for use in this procedure. These posters consist of pictures taken from magazines, of objects which the child can label. *E* begins by holding up a poster on which is pasted a picture of one object. *E* asks "What do you see?" and prompts the answer. If the child does not respond well to the question "What do you see?" *E* may use "What is this?" at first to prompt the desired response (example: *E:* "What do you see." *S:* No response. *E:* "What is this?" *S:* "Car." *E:* "Good. What do you see?" *S:* "Car."). The posters (each poster showing a different object) are changed from trial to trial. When the child is reliably labeling posters showing one picture, *E* introduces a poster with two pictures on it. *S* must now label both pictures before being reinforced. *E* asks *S* "What do you see?" and then points to or labels the pictures for *S* in order to prompt his response, or *E* may simply say "and. . . ." In fact, it is generally useful to include "and . . ." along with other prompts so that later "and . . ." may be used alone. A new poster with two different pictures on it may be used on each trial. The number of objects per poster is gradually increased until *S* can label as many as a dozen objects in response to one general question like "What do you see?"

It is often useful to prompt *S* to name the objects from left to right and top to bottom. As this gives *S* an organized way to scan, he does not repeat the same labels over and over again while omitting some completely. It will also help in later programs, such as reading, where scanning in an orderly fashion becomes quite important.

A number of posters may be reserved for generalization testing. Another approach to generalization training and testing involves describing real stimulus arrays, for example, *E* may say "Tell me what you see on the table," or "Tell me what you see in the room." At this point, the procedure begins to overlap with the procedure for Part 3, describing-accounting.

Part 2. Describing body parts and belongings.

The procedure for teaching the child extended descriptions of his own person is very similar to that for describing pictures. The major difference is that *S* is required to respond to a larger stimulus, only parts of which are visible. *E* will say to *S*, "Tell me about yourself," and require *S* to respond by describing his body parts and clothing. Thus *E* begins by saying "Tell me about yourself," and prompting *S* to say something like "I have a nose." *E* responds with "Good, and . . ." or "Good, and what else?" and prompts (e.g., by pointing) the child to say "I have eyes." *E* then repeats the S^D "Tell me about yourself" and prompts the child to say "I have a nose and eyes" (perhaps initially E may point to the child's nose, then eyes). E gradually requires S to make more and more responses to the S^D "Tell me about yourself." The most important aspect of Part 2 is that it is more likely that S will give a spontaneous response in describing his body parts and belongings than in responding to the posters and pictures. At this stage in the training, S should be able to label a large number of body parts and belongings. If S uses one of these labels, and it has not been specifically prompted, S is immediately reinforced generously.

A spontaneous response is reinforced immediately regardless of where in the chain it appears. Again, a spontaneous response is one that has never been prompted or required that day. It may be necessary at some point to simply wait for the child to give such a response before reinforcing him. S may go through the entire list of responses that have been prompted, E may then say, "And what else?" and wait for the child to include some new label. More and more, E's reinforcement is made contingent on novel responses, such that S acquires novelty in his repertoire. Generalization may be tested by asking the child to describe E or a third person.

Part 3. Describing-accounting everyday events.

Describing-accounting of everyday events takes up, in a sense, where poster and picture training ends. In poster and picture training, the major goal is to have the child learn to give longer and longer chains of responses to a general request. However, poster and picture training is somewhat limited as a base for the generalization of spontaneous speech. Describing-accounting utilizes the everyday experiences and environment of the child and thus provides unlimited novelty of stimulation and opportunity for the child to make new responses. The object of the procedure, then, is to have S give a detailed description of an array of stimuli or an activity in response to a very general request.

The procedure involves asking S a general question like "What are you playing?" or making a request like "Tell me about your toys," and then presenting a number of prompts (such as pointing to objects, asking specific questions or saying "and . . .") designed to evoke specific information, eventually fading these prompts. E tries to keep prompting as general as possible, even in the first stages of training (e.g., asking "What else?" or saying "and . . .") rather than suggesting a certain kind of response (e.g., "What color was it?" "How big?"). Specific prompts are given only if S does not give the desired response to more general stimuli. E gradually reduces the number of specific prompts and requires more and more responses per general prompt. Eventually, the goal is to drop all prompts and have the child emit a long, detailed chain of responses to one general request.

In many ways this procedure overlaps with that for recall, as it often involves the description of events and activities in the past. The difference is in the emphasis. In this program, one is particularly concerned with the number of responses and the degree of spontaneity rather than the accuracy of description and temporal order. Responses which are not specifically prompted are generously and immediately reinforced.

Part 4. Expressing desires.

In this procedure, one is concerned not so much with the number of responses the child makes to a request by E as with the number of responses the child can make without any requests whatsoever. The object is to have S be able to tell E and others what he wants in hopes that the child will become aware of some of the everyday reinforcement properties of language.

In the initial stages, the procedure is quite similar to simple labeling. Nonverbal pretraining based on receptive speech, as described in Manual A, may be useful. E would ask the child "What do you want?" and have S point to the desired object. In the beginning, it is recommended that one use food items. At all levels of training, E must be fairly certain that S actually desires the object or activity in question.

To begin expressive speech training, E selects several foods or toys which S appears to enjoy. We recommend beginning with food, as E can be fairly certain about S's likes and dislikes and his level of satiation. E asks S "What do you want?" and prompts S to label the desired item, e.g., "milk." S is then given some milk as reinforcement for making the desired response. The procedure proceeds much like labeling, except it is useful to have S indicate, e.g., by pointing, what he wants on each new trial, as his desires may change during the session. Thus, one cannot be as consistent about training item 1, then 2, then 1, and so on. The objects or foods may have to be changed on every trial, to avoid building a stereotyped sequence. In general, we have begun training in expressing desires as soon as the child is able to label three or four food items. It is apparent, then, that certain aspects of spontaneity training were started very early in the language training (already with Program 2) and were practiced informally as part of all programs. The early introduction of this program reflects our desire to have the child learn from the beginning that language is an important tool for obtaining reinforcement.

Generalization

Generalization is probably the most important step in this manual. One should begin generalization training very early in the learning process, for instance, as soon as S can express his desires for three or four food items. E and others around the child should require that the child begin to ask for everything he wants, even though S may only be able to label the item in the most elementary way. At first, E asks "What do you want?" each time he notices that S appears to be desirous of some object or activity (such as going outside or getting a toy.) Eventually, as one wants the child to learn to request such items without being asked, E will have to stop asking and start waiting at some point. This often requires much patience and persistance. The importance of consistency is high. One cannot require speech sometimes and not others and expect to get very far with these children.

As the child moves through other programs, such as pronouns, verb labels, colors, and conversation, these are incorporated into demand training. For instance, one may begin to hold the child for "I want tickle" and later "I want you to tickle me" as he learns to make these longer responses in the course of other programs. At first, of course, "tickle" will suffice. After yes-no training is completed, "I don't want" may be trained using an informal procedure such as E: "Do you want me to hit you?" S: "No." E: "Good. Say no, I don't want you to hit me." S: "I don't want you to hit me."

The most important point to be remembered in pursuing demand training is that any and all spontaneous requests are to be reinforced generously and immediately if at all possible. At times, it will not be possible to give the child exactly what he is asking for. For example, he may ask to go out on a rainy day.

Such requests can be reinforced socially with such phrases as "Good talking. Good boy," and hugs and tickling.

Sometimes it may be impossible to specify the reinforcer which underlies a child's speech. In this regard we have an interesting observation to relate about one of the children who was undergoing training in "extended" descriptions of his own person and immediate environment and who also had an extensive repertoire of self-stimulatory behavior (he was continuously twirling, gazing, and the like). As the child's father began to suppress the self-stimulatory motor behavior (through disapproval and punishment), he spontaneously began describing his environment, apparently as a substitute for the motor self-stimulation. We took this to mean that the child was substituting an acceptable form of self-stimulation for one that seemed bizarre and psychotic. The establishment of self-stimulatory verbal behavior may be seen as one of the ultimate goals in the program, but we don't know as yet how this can be accomplished at will.

Manual K: Storytelling

The object of this manual is for the child to tell a detailed story about an event which goes beyond the concrete stimuli available to him in his physical environment at the time and uses what is commonly called "imagination." That is, the program demands that he verbalize events which he has "internalized" and which are not physically available to him in his present external environment. This training builds upon all previous programs. It is similar to the spontaneity program, particularly describing-accounting, in that it involves giving an orderly, detailed account of some particular subject matter, and in that novel and untrained responses are heavily reinforced. It has obvious similarities to the program on "recall." But the program on "storytelling" is different from the other programs in that *E* is beginning to teach the child to talk about events which are not physically present in the child's current physical and external environment. The events which the child now is taught to verbalize may not even have occurred in his past but may in fact be verbal descriptions of events which he is constructing for himself. That is, he is responding to events which truly do not have an exact external referent but which nevertheless are made up from what experience he has to date.

To the extent that storytelling is similar to accounting, a similar procedure can be followed. This involves an initial presentation of a general stimulus, e.g., "Tell me about this picture," followed by presentation of increasingly specific questions necessary to obtain the appropriate amount of detail. Pictures of persons or animals engaged in some activity are particularly useful. Once the child has described the people, objects, and events depicted, *E* begins asking questions which cannot be answered directly from stimuli in the picture. Thus *E* moves from questions like "What is this person doing?" to "What is this person's name?" As training continues, questions become even less concrete, e.g., "Where does he live?" "Where is he going?" "Why is he going there?" "How does he feel?" *E* should encourage and reward longer, more detailed response sequences and gradually decrease the number of specific prompts.

One of the best settings for generating "stories" arranges for the child to simply "pretend" that he is engaged in some activity he likes. Suppose he had a good visit to Disneyland, and suppose that *E* has helped him verbalize ("talked to him about") the various events that took place at Disneyland. Then, the next day seat *S* in a chair, take a seat beside him, and pretend to go down the Matterhorn ride. Perhaps it is easier to start "pretending" with a more immediate event, like eating food. If *S* likes ice cream with chocolate sauce, one can of course gradually fade those components and retain the behaviors (eating ice cream and feeling good) to a stimulus like "let's pretend we are eating ice cream," while going through the motions of "pretending" to pour chocolate sauce over the ice cream, holding the spoon, and so on. If *S* likes car rides, one can pretend to drive a car, turning sharp corners and so on. Similarly, *S* can pretend to be *E,* and one can help prompt that when *S* wears some of *E*'s clothes, *S* trains *E* on some task, feeds him, and disapproves of his errors. Many of the children we saw were extremely reinforced by gaining such explicit control over *E*.

Manual L: Some Further Problems in Teaching

Throughout this book we have described a number of "special" problems, or learning peculiarities, and our attempts to deal with them. Let us now attempt to complete a description of the difficulties we have encountered. Very often during the early stages of training, the children show great losses in material they have previously mastered. At times, these losses can be attributed to the introduction of new and somewhat similar demands or to generally negative behavior. But often one can cite no directly antecedent condition. We shall discuss some of the problems we have typically encountered in the course of label training, but analogous problems occur in almost all the early programs at times.

In addition to these seemingly spontaneous losses, the children may show marked deterioration in pronounciation or the lowering of the voice to a point where they become inaudible. Let us begin to look at these difficulties with an example drawn from the logs kept on Chuck, one of our first patients, an initially mute five-year-old boy. We began training on June 26 and on August 31, Chuck began losing some of the words he had previously mastered. He seemed not to look at objects he was to label, and his voice became inaudible at times. He had difficulty switching from one response to another. On September 3, "attention training" was instituted as a separate part of several sessions. Chuck was required to point to and look at the object he was to label and was reinforced for gradually increasing the length of his gaze. This procedure appeared to work for a while, and by September 9, Chuck was making four out of five responses correctly during meaning training. However, during the next week, he again showed signs of deterioration.

The staff tried placing each bite of food on a white towel before asking what it was, in an attempt to focus Chuck's attention on the stimulus to be labelled. This seemingly led to some improvement in the accuracy of his labelling. Another technique which seemed to result in some improvement, consisted of asking Chuck to attend to objects held by the therapist at a distance of six or more feet. This required a more active "attentional search" on Chuck's part. Obviously, then, we tried a number of different solutions with more or less success. In the case of Chuck the most successful technique seemed remedial training on receptive speech, but we have not had the opportunity to systematically evaluate this step. That is, Chuck was told to give the therapist a particular object or to point to an object and was asked "What is it?" only after he had correctly identified the object nonverbally.

Eventually, the nonverbal demand was faded out. Remedial training on receptive speech was instituted on September 19, and by September 22, Chuck had made substantial improvement.

The reader should note that expressive speech training was not discontinued altogether. Rather, several minutes of remedial training were employed at the beginning of each session or at points where Chuck appeared to have particular difficulty. The amount of time spent in receptive speech training was gradually reduced over sessions until only expressive speech training remained (September 22, morning). During the afternoon of September 22, Chuck showed a slight relapse in performance, was briefly given remedial training involving a nonverbal identification task, and again showed immediate and substantial improvement.

These procedures may be used when the child begins to offer incorrect responses or no response at all during drill on material with which he is already familiar. Another approach is necessary when attempting to raise the child's volume. For example, Chuck was speaking very softly when answering the question "What do you want?" The staff was able to raise his volume simply by asking him questions such as "What is it?" which he had already mastered. The procedure seemed to reinforce the child's confidence in his own responses and seems to be successful in some limited number of cases. In general, however, two more easily explicable procedures have proved most fruitful.

The first of these is volume imitation. This procedure has been used with a number of children. The therapist begins by saying "loud" in a very loud voice. Note this, that although the child has gone through extensive imitation training, and now can imitate most words with minimal if any training, he still cannot imitate E's loudness (volume). That is, loudness did not become a functional stimulus during imitation training, probably because we did not differentially reinforce the child for imitating E's decibel level. (We found scant evidence for a large range of "general imitative behaviors" during our imitation training.) Anyway, we proceeded to teach the child to imitate loudness, by differentially reinforcing the child for matching the adult's level. We also taught him to raise his voice to E's "loud," by E saying "loud" in a loud voice, then gradually lowering his voice level, leaving the command "loud" as the functional cue. Once the child has mastered this response, E introduces the word "soft" using a near whisper, and again the child is held for imitation of volume as well as of the word "soft." When the child is shifting easily from loud to soft, the experimenter introduces other words. He may raise his own voice volume and hold the child for imitation, or he may use the word "loud" as a prompt to increase volume. Drill is maintained until the child is imitating the new words in the appropriate volume. The use of "loud" as a prompt generally means that E says "louder" and then gives the second word. The child is reinforced for repeating the second word, but not the word "louder." Of course, the child must give the second word in the appropriate volume. Gradually, the second word is faded. For example, let us say the word to be imitated is "cat." The E would say "cat," and the child would imitate. If his volume is too soft, the E says "louder, cat," repeating "cat" in a very loud voice. The child would be held for imitating "cat." Eventually, the therapist should fade the word "cat" and use only the word "louder" to increase the child's volume.

The second method depends for its success upon the child's current repertoire. Very often the child is consistently making some responses in a loud voice spontaneously. For Chuck, this response was an Indian war whoop, with all the concommitant pounding on the chest. In Billy's case, E noticed that Billy was consistently louder after he had just been tickled. In both cases, the staff began by briefly reinforcing the children for any loud responses. Then the activities were used as stepping stones for raising volume in training sessions. When the child's volume dropped, the therapist would initiate one of these activities and follow it up closely with the task on which the child's voice was too soft. Activities which serve this purpose usually involve a large nonverbal component, such as tickling, pushing, chasing, and jumping. Rough-and-tumble play is a good place to begin looking for the appropriate activity.

The final problem which we will cover in this section involves poor pronunciation. This may be a continuing difficulty for the child or may occur in connection with a particular task and appear to be a transient problem. Often, simply holding the child strictly for the best pronunciation of which he is capable is the best cure. However, with more recurring difficulties in this area, the suggested procedure varies with the specific deficiency.

Billy, for instance, displayed much difficulty in making the silibant sounds. The therapist drilled on these, taking Billy's hand and putting it in front of the therapist's mouth, and then Billy's mouth, so he could feel the expulsion of air, in the hope that this additional stimulus would facilitate his discrimination. In addition, words on which Billy had much trouble were broken down into component sounds and drilled separately.

Here is another, similar, procedure. One may regain clarity in the production of the sounds "pa" and "ba" by suspending a piece of cotton on a string so the child can see the cotton swing in the air expelled by E when making the sound, or by himself, if he makes the sound correctly. The gutteral sounds may be prompted by having the child imitate coughing, a response with a large nonverbal component which some children seem to enjoy. One must remember always, however, that any artificial means of getting the child to make the correct response must eventually be faded. These methods serve the purpose of making the correct response more clearly discriminable, something very difficult for the therapist to demonstrate, since so much of pronunciation is virtually unobservable from the child's point of view, and difficult to explain verbally to the most lucid adult.

The basic principle in all of these procedures is to discover what sort of remedial training is necessary, and then drop briefly to drill on the simpler task, building back as quickly as possible to the more difficult ones. One must be able to sort out attentional problems from real losses and volume difficulties from pronunciation or just general confusion and to see compounds of several problems. From there, the methods are a combination of awareness, common sense, and trial-and-error in a reinforcement framework.

Manual M: Stopping Echolalia

Echolalia is one of the most interesting and frustrating symptoms associated with autism. Basically, one is faced with the fact that the child echoes everything you say. You cannot afford to completely extinguish echolalic behavior, for imitation is a basic tool in every procedure; but you must teach the child to discriminate between those words he is supposed to imitate and those he is not. The two procedures we have used most frequently for facilitating this discrimination are "volume cueing" and the use of the command "don't echo."

The goal of the procedure is to have the child echo only the desired response and not the prompt, question, or instruction which precedes it. For example, one needs to be able to say "What is it? . . . car." and have S repeat only "car," or E might verbalize "Say, my name is Ricky," and want S to omit the word "say." Volume cueing is one way to facilitate such discriminations. One repeats the questions very softly and the responses quite loudly. The child will usually repeat only the loud words. Over successive trials, one gradually increases the volume of the question and, of course, fades the vocalization of the desired response (the prompt) until the two are equal in volume. One then proceeds to fade the prompt further until it is dropped altogether. Time out may be made contingent upon incorrect imitations, that is, verbalizations in which the question is entirely or partially repeated. When such a response occurs, E may say "Don't echo" immediately before instituting a time out.

There are many kinds of programs where verbal imitation is entirely inappropriate, for example, where a command is involved. An important example is receptive speech training for pronouns (it can be disastrous if the child echoes the words "my nose" when pointing to E's nose.) At these times, E gives the command "don't echo" and presents time out contingent upon echoing.

In many programs, E will need to be able to include the word "say" just prior to a word or phrase in order to indicate to the child that he is to take a prompt directly. This technique saves a good deal of time once the child learns that he is not to echo "say." When the child has learned this discrimination, "say" may serve as a cue that what comes next should be imitated. If one were to consistently reinforce imitation after the word "say" and not at other times, the child should learn that "say" means "now you are to imitate" and that imitation is inappropriate in other circumstances. However, we usually do not train "say" until the child has been in the program for some time. Remember, the rule at first is that the fewer words the better. However, in later stages of training, it is often useful to teach the child this discrimination, particularly where E and S are making extended responses and interchanges as in recall, conversation, and storytelling.

Chapter VII
CASE STUDIES: LANGUAGE ACQUISITION IN THREE AUTISTIC CHILDREN
By Dean Alexander,
Paul Dores,
and Paula Firestone

C hapter VII is presented by three therapists who participated in the treatment of three autistic children. These cases are
representative of three different kinds of autistic children. The
first child, Reeve, functioned at a very low level and for practical
purposes he had no language at intake. Stimultaneously he
showed an excessive amount of inattention, tantrums, and self-
stimulatory behavior.

The second child, Tommy, was not quite so undeveloped; he
could follow simple commands and showed sporadic imitation of

vowel sounds. He was not as inattentive as Reeve and showed less self-stimulatory behavior; in general, he was easier to manage. He had no play and only limited or nonexistent social behavior.

The third child to be described, Linda, is a "high functioning" autistic. She had echolalic speech, could label simple objects, and could follow simple commands when properly motivated. She had no understanding of abstract terms such as time or prepositions and pronouns. She would play with simple toys but showed no interest in her peers. Her self-stimulatory behavior was delimited and fairly easy to control, as were her tantrums.

Each child was started in therapy prior to 40 months of age, partly because of the reversibility of treatment gains which had characterized our earlier efforts with older autistic children (Lovaas *et al.*, 1973). Each child received more than 15 hours of treatment per week, and most of that treatment was conducted in the child's home. This treatment, although supervised by a professional was conducted by a graduate student in psychology or education who, in turn, had from four to six undergraduate students working for him. Additionally, the child's parents were taught how to treat him, to observe and participate in all therapy sessions, and, keep logs and take data. In this manner, the child received treatment (i.e., lived in a relatively intensive educational environment) for almost all his waking hours. The involvement of the child's parents was intended partly to overcome the situationality associated with the treatment gains in our earlier work (Lovaas *et al.*, 1973). That is, we wanted some assurance that improvement in the children would not be limited to the clinic but would also extend into their day-to-day functioning in their homes. The parents, of course, greatly expanded the efficiency of the project in a number of ways.

The current autism project from which these three cases have been taken is run as a joint effort by Drs. Laura Schreibman, Robert Koegel, and myself. The chapter begins with a description of Reeve, the least developed of the three children.

Reeve

Reeve was 2 years and 3 months old at the onset of treatment. He was the product of a normal pregnancy, but had been delivered through Caesarean section for breach presentation. A congenital cleft of the velum, which extended approximately half an inch into the hard palate, had been successfully repaired at the age of 18 months. He suffered from frequent ear and respiratory infections, colic, and allergies. He also had a bilateral hernia and unilateral cryptorchism (the failure of the testes to drop into the scrotum). A small overgrowth of skin on the lower portion of his ear may suggest a genetic defect, of a type usually not associated with autism. Extensive medical examinations showed no evidence of neurological disease and no indication of brain damage or other cerebral dysfunction. There is no family history of neurological or genetic disease.

Developmental milestones were reached within normal limits. He sat up at 8 months, crawled at 9 months, and walked at 16 months. Teeth erupted about 12 months of age. He would grasp at objects at about 8 months, but stopped doing so after several months.

His parents became aware that he was definitely different from other children when he was 3 months old, when he seemed to avoid social interaction or contact with adults or other children and was content to remain alone for long periods of time. He would respond to other people's attempts to show him affection by screaming and crying, particularly when picked up. Later, his use of toys was generally inappropriate (e.g., he would repeatedly throw them on the ground), and he would not play on equipment such as slides or swings. When first seen by us he was physically very lethargic, moving with seemingly great effort. He could not dress or undress himself, open doors, or climb into chairs without help. He was only partially toilet-trained and had only recently been taught to feed himself. He still resisted solid foods.

Both parents report him as having been unresponsive when spoken to his first year of life. He vocalized rarely and never mimicked. He failed to laugh or smile, and he seemed insensitive to pain. His mother reports that he sat up on the operating table during hernia surgery (when he was 26 months of age) and attempted only a few days after the operation to walk up the stairs of his home.

He engaged extensively in self-stimulatory activities such as gazing at his hands, at lights, or off into space. He chanted to himself continuously, ran or stomped in small circles repeatedly, and rocked himself frequently in his crib, on the floor, and particularly next to the vacuum cleaner. He smelled and licked both objects and people. He refused to eat objects of certain colors, for example, he would not put anything red into his mouth. He violently refused to touch sand or grass. In addition, he compulsively lined up papers or toys in particular patterns. He was often extremely fearful of new toys or activities and of any intrusions into his environment. He showed some self-destructive behavior, consisting of head banging concentrated on sharp corners of furniture.

When his language was tested at 2 years of age by a clinical psychologist (two months before he began treatment at UCLA), Reeve was characterized as totally nonverbal with minimal receptive speech exhibited only when properly motivated. He tested at only 8 months on the language area of the Gesell Developmental Schedules; the test results revealed an "inability to formulate words or imitate sounds." Reeve's vocalizations consisted primarily of primitive grunts, screams, and squeals; and only rarely did he vocalize a repetitive series of reduplicated consonant vowel syllables ("no no no," "na na na," or "do do do," for example). These reduplicated syllables were only sporadic, occurring with low frequency, and like many other aspects of Reeve's behavior tended to appear briefly and then disappear for prolonged periods. Many of his sounds never reappeared after being heard once or twice. He would never imitate these sounds when they were presented by his mother for him to mimic. Reeve's parents initially suspected a hearing deficit because he seemed oblivious to verbal commands and comments. Subsequent testing, however, showed Reeve's hearing to be normal. At intake his developmental index on the Bayley Scales of Infant Development was less than 50.

Month 1. Much of the first three to four months of therapy focused on eliminating his incessant high-pitched screaming, squealing, and crying when people approached him, particularly when the therapist placed demands on him or spoke to him or touched him. We tried initially an extinction procedure, consisting primarily of ignoring his screaming. In addition, any momentary subsiding of his screaming and tantrums was praised, and food was given as a reward. However, he responded to all these efforts with increased tantrums. Incidentally, his tantrums were physically quite passive; for example, he screamed, squealed, and cried continuously, yet his body simultaneously remained limp. He seems incredibly physically lethargic and unresponsive.

During sessions when we try to teach Reeve to lift his arm on command ("raise arms" while therapist simultaneously raises his), the therapist manually lifts Reeve's arm up for him, verbally praising him for having his arms up, but as soon as his physical support is withdrawn, Reeve's arm falls limply to his side. During the first month we also began to build eye contact in response to the command, "Look at me." There has been no progress on either task during this month, and no reduction in his tantrums.

Month 2. Reeve was sick most of this month with massive ear and throat infections. There seems to be no decrease in his tantrums. His spontaneous verbalizations remain at zero. Because time-out procedures were ineffective in reducing his tantrums, we have decided to "work through the tantrums" and keep delivering our requests despite his objections. Also, since food and social reinforcement did not maintain his response to the therapist's "raise your arm" (Reeve typically would barely and lethargically raise his arms a couple of inches, or fail to do so altogether), we have decided to harshly (and probably painfully for Reeve) raise his arms when we prompt him (we abruptly raise his arms by physically moving our limbs under them). That is, he has been shifted more to a reinforcement schedule by which he avoids or escapes aversive stimulation (in addition to receiving positives) when he complies. These are extremely trying times for his therapists as well; they are fatigued after one or two hours of such treatment. His lethargy and apparent negativism are astounding.

Month 3. Reeve underwent surgery to correct his bilateral hernia this month and is ready to continue therapy three weeks later. He is beginning to master some simple sounds in the therapy sessions. These sounds, primarily "Aee" (which may be Reeve's word for "light," since he points to it when he makes the sound) and "Mmmm," are not spontaneous but are emitted upon command. When the therapist points to the light and says, "What is it?" Reeve sometimes says "Aee," and when the therapist says, "Reeve, say 'Mmmm,' " he sometimes says "Mmmm." (That is, these sounds are not under consistent S^D control but occur sporadically.) We are beginning to see some progress in his response to our commands.

Month 4. We are hearing more sounds during therapy sessions. Although these sounds are often animalistic, spoken in very throaty grunts, they are of the type we have seen before, multiple chains of syllables; for example, "mah mah mah mah," "me me me me," or "lah lah lah lah." If we present the S^D,

"Reeve, say 'me,' " we may hear "me me me me," although we are just as likely to hear him say "la la la la." As the first step in our language program, every verbal response of Reeve's is considered correct and is reinforced heavily. We are encouraging vocalizations of any kind in any context, but they are still scarce.

Reeve is now making some progress in receptive speech training, which has prompted us to accelerate his receptive speech training to commands such as "give me the book," "touch your foot," and the like. His responses continue to be quite random; he does not appear to be listening to what is being said.

Months 5 and 6. Reeve's little brother was born, but Reeve seems very quiet and remains unresponsive to him. (This brother and a subsequent one both developed normally; the parents were amazed at the difference.) Reeve now has a very small repertoire of sounds upon which we base a daily verbal imitation drill. We continue to reinforce all vocalizations in an effort to increase his frequency of responding. Reeve's inability or unwillingness to move his mouth and tongue flexibly inhibits his further progress. This, associated with his failure to chew and swallow hard foods and the trouble he shows swallowing liquids, along with the problems inherent in the repaired cleft palate, suggests that Reeve's problems with his tongue and mouth are not simply related to a low motivation to perform.

We are expanding his receptive speech drills, and he is doing well with simple tasks and will retrieve and deliver many labeled objects. He has an affinity for receptive labels and now appears able to remember as many as are taught with only minimal exposure. Finally, the tantrums have definitely subsided. While expressive speech creeps along, receptive speech is flourishing. It is apparent that Reeve's earlier tantrums and self-stimulatory behavior were masking his potential receptive abilities.

Month 7. This month Reeve started half-day sessions at a regular temple-connected nursery school in his neighborhood. He seems to like the school, and we are encouraged. The elimination of his disruptive tantrumous behavior at the beginning of treatment and his early successes in receptive speech help him adjust to school. We are engaging daily in formal verbal imitation drills, using sounds we have overheard him say in earlier drills or sounds which are similar to those which we have heard, such as "we," "lah," "nah," "mah," "Mmmm," and "do." In these drills, while the sounds are presented as single syllables, we continue to receive responses from Reeve in multiple reduplications such as "we we we we we" or "lah lah lah lah lah."

Reeve shows an increasing spontaneity with music. He hums songs he has learned, such as "Happy Birthday" and "It's a Small World," and has begun to sing the songs using his syllables, such as "bah bah," "do do," "nah nah," "lah lah." This allows us to practice his sounds in an informal, spontaneous context and allows him to experience his sounds in rhythm, which will hopefully have some effect on his learning of intonation. "Ahmah" has now become his stock answer, replacing most of his other sounds during verbal imitation training. His perseveration on the "ahmah" response is remarkable, and he is even singing with "ahmah" as the lyric.

Reeve has made rapid progress in his receptive speech development in the last month. He is now able to discriminate, point to, or retrieve any number of objects, responding to the verbal S^Ds, "Point to _____," "Touch _____," "Give me _____," "Pick up _____," and "Bring me the _____" accurately and consistently. We are concentrating on objects around his bedroom such as the table, chair, bed, and books and on body parts such as head, tongue, and arm. He is able to discriminate and point to his leg, knee, sock, and shoe. These receptive speech activities are not without problems. Reeve has a tendency to become sloppy when asked to point to objects.

He is learning color concepts quite rapidly. He will identify and retrieve red, blue, and green objects. He is also able to respond over two dimensions, discriminating both color and shape; for example, a red square from a red circle, a yellow triangle from a blue triangle, or a yellow circle from a red square.

Reeve has shown a fascination with alphabet letters. He has a small set of plastic magnetic ones that he plays with constantly. He can now identify and point correctly to the letters "A" through "F" when presented before him. It appears that we may have an avenue here to exploit. When a child such as Reeve shows little motivation to learn, it is extremely important to find an activity that is at once rewarding and potentially educational.

Month 8. In addition to language training, Reeve's therapy time includes a number of varied activities designed to sustain a higher activity level, including playground activities, catching a ball, dancing, and crafts such as painting. We work them into the speech drills. We have begun to withdraw all attention and reinforcement for the response "Ahmah" in an effort to extinguish it as Reeve's stock verbal response. From all indications it appears that this extinction procedure will be effective. Throughout the month, Reeve's verbal imitation responses are consistently high and accurate for a variety of sounds. His verbalizations are becoming more accurate and much more distinct and easier to understand.

During a therapy session at UCLA, one of the therapists engaged in a new type of dialogue with Reeve. An initial verbal S^D was presented to which Reeve responded. The therapist then imitated Reeve's response back to him with an intonation characteristic of conversation. Every response Reeve made became the therapist's next verbalization. We observed an immediate increase in his frequency of vocalizations during this interchange. Also during this same session, Reeve said "Do do" spontaneously, without any verbal S^D or prompt, during a verbal drill. He has rarely spoken spontaneously during therapy, and this is the first observation of the type of spontaneity that has been reported by the parents in the home journal.

Reeve is now saying "mama," but we can't be sure that he is making the connection between the word "mama" and his mother. Because he appears to enjoy seeing his mother, we have begun to make "mama" functional, pairing its emission with an opportunity to see Mama.

In his receptive speech activities he continues to progress in the same directions as last month. Often those commands that Reeve completes quickly and consistently in therapy he will not complete for his parents. We have given the parents five commands to use with him. They are: "come here," "sit down," "bring me shoes," "go to bed," and "close the door." The parents are concentrating on achieving consistent compliance to these five commands, using punishment if necessary.

Month 9. Reeve went to Seattle for one week with his parents at the beginning of the month. Upon his return, his mother reports to us that he is more verbally responsive at home. However, in the therapy sessions he is more tantrumous, more uncooperative and noncompliant. His attention is poor and both his verbal and receptive speech responding seem depressed. He shows signs of pain and, feeling that he is perhaps ill, we have become more lenient, decreasing demands on him in therapy.

We have moved into more play and begun receptive speech drilling with active toys such as "go down the slide" and "climb over the hump." Reeve is participating voluntarily and appears to have fun.

Month 10. Our school observations are alarming. Reeve is gazing and does not orient to his name. He is continually engaged in running back and forth along a fence as self-stimulatory behavior. He runs with his head bent over and his tongue out.

His overall behavior in all contexts seems poor. Whenever therapy demands are placed upon him, he holds his genitals, doubles over as if in pain, begins a tantrum, and demands the toilet. However, once placed on the toilet, he refuses to go. This type of noncompliant behavior has continued since just before the trip to Seattle. We had interpreted it then as possibly due to physical illness and had been sympathetic and lenient toward it. A doctor's check, however, proved us to be wrong. There appears to be nothing physically wrong with Reeve. Probably our lack of discipline and withdrawal of demands has allowed Reeve to seriously regress.

We decided that Reeve's substantial nonperformance is to earn him sharp punishment (a slap on the bottom). After only a few days of such punishment and reinstated accentuated positive contingencies, he is responding much more quickly and consistently. His verbal imitation is more accurate, and his overall awareness of the total environment has improved.

As we had hoped for earlier, we are hearing two more partially reduplicated syllables in Reeve's repertoire, "nonah" and "dodah." We can now assume that his use of "ahmah" (in Month 7) was not merely a fluke. In using "nonah" and "dodah," Reeve appears to be contrasting the vowel sounds "a" and "o," mixing them while he keeps the consonant context constant. As the predominance of these partial reduplications subsided, Reeve's other verbal repertoire reappeared, with his vocalizations consisting almost totally of syllables formed with consonants and "a," while the sound "o" has virtually disappeared. Reeve is saying "ah," "pah," "mah," "bahbah," "mahmah," and "nahnah," and yet "o" sounds such as "no" and "do," which were previously strong, have decreased in frequency to almost zero.

In these aspects, Reeve's verbal behavior continues to be consistent with linguistic observations of normal children. His use of partial reduplications, contrasting sounds within identical contexts, and his predominate use of the vowel sound "ah," the vowel most commonly used first by normal children, are encouraging examples of normal language development. As long as Reeve continues to develop along the same lines as normal children, we will be encouraged about his future language possibilities.

We are using two methods to loosen Reeve's mouth and tongue, facilitating his tongue movements, lip formations, and sound production. He is asked to blow out matches held in front of him. A puckered blow is modeled for him by the therapist, and then Reeve is asked, "Blow out the match." He is imitating some minimal mouth movements. A more effective and enjoyable method is "mirror imitation." We are now modeling facial expressions for Reeve while sitting next to him in front of a mirror. We are modeling such responses as an open mouth, a closed mouth, a blow, puckering the lips, tongue out, a smile with teeth together, and a frown. Reeve enjoys this mirror imitation and will respond in short spurts, moving his tongue and lips quite flexibly.

We are introducing receptive speech commands throughout the house, using S^Ds such as "turn on/off the TV," "put the newspaper on the table/chair," and "open the record cabinet." We agree that the parents are almost continuously to ask him to carry out behaviors, on their requests, in all situations, throughout the day. We have begun work on the concept "same," asking Reeve to pick up the same object as the therapist. We are having only moderate success.

Reeve's parents report in the home journal that Reeve can now identify most of the alphabet letters and is saying the letters "A" through "F." We have not worked on alphabet letters in therapy, and because Reeve appears to be learning them on his own, we have no immediate plans to include them in formal drills.

Month 11. Reeve has made great progress in verbal imitation, but he is no longer using many of the sounds he once did. This is apparent from a review of a typical list of verbal drill sounds. He is accurate 60 to 90% of the time for the sounds "lahlah," "nahnah," "mahmah," "mah," "bahbah," "bah," "pahpah," "pah," and "ah." He is accurate less than 30% of the time for "lolo," "nono," "dodo," "do," "dudu," "dahdah," "du," "da," "na," "ee," and "baby." Apparently, Reeve's vocalizations are now predominately of the form of consonant and "ah." All other vowel sounds seem to occur with very little frequency. The "d" sound is now virtually nonexistent in his repertoire. While Reeve says "nahnah," he cannot or will not say "nah." We have begun to use contingent access to music as a reinforcer in the verbal drills.

The parent's home journal reports Reeve's use of words which we are not hearing during therapy, and an increased frequency of spontaneous verbalizations at home. We have noted during the month a small amount of spontaneous vocalizations during

Reeve's free play time. We are hearing the spontaneous sounds, "ah," "ae," "yah," "mahmah," "mah," "lahlah," and even "dodo," which he does not use during verbal drills and will not repeat when asked directly.

Month 12. Reeve's behavior seems erratic this month. At the beginning of the month, he seemed inattentive and sloppy and noncompliant and was doing poorly on tasks we knew he had mastered. Therefore we sharpened our consequences, increasing both positive reinforcement and punishment. The effects were immediate and positive. He is now discriminating his body parts from the therapist's, responding to commands like "touch Reeve's hand" and "touch (therapist's) hand." No personal pronouns are used as yet.

Reeve is becoming more disruptive and physically assertive outside the formal drills, which we welcome and encourage. He shows great fluctuations in the rate of his vocalizations and frequency of spontaneous speech; one day they are excellent, the next day poor.

Although Reeve had little luck with the sound "f" (made by placing the top teeth on the lower lip and blowing out), he did use the sounds "tu" and "we" for the first time during the drills this month. We have begun to use flash cards of alphabet letters and pictures to facilitate verbal imitation (in part because he likes these objects so much).

Month 13. With minimal work (using the mirror) we observe a significant increase in the flexibility of Reeve's mouth and tongue. Once again, necessary punishment for inattention during verbal drills is bringing clear, animated verbalizations. He is now reciting the alphabet and numbers 1 through 12 in the correct order, leaving a space where he can't reproduce the sounds. Verbal drills continue, generally comprised of four sounds at a time. In an effort to increase the length of Reeve's sound "ah," we are introducing into the drills the shorter sound "eh eh" to provide a length contrast for the longer sound.

Now that the sound "f" has been shaped, Reeve has begun to use it as the initial sound in many vocalizations, insisting upon keeping his teeth out on his lower lip. While this is an interesting example of overgeneralization, it is obviously inappropriate. We hesitate to extinguish the sound as it took so long for him to learn it, and he likes it so well. We are using the presentation of some of his high frequency sounds ("bah," "mm," and "mahmah," for example) in the verbal drills as reinforcement for the emission of the more difficult, less frequent sounds. This variation of the Premack principle appears effective in maintaining Reeve's interest.

It is becoming apparent that Reeve is watching our mouths for visual clues in both the receptive and expressive speech drills, perhaps ignoring the auditory ones. We have experimented by covering our mouths during the presentation of S^Ds. While Reeve's accuracy of responding did not decrease, his eye contact disintegrated completely. Because a decrease in eye contact may increase the probability that Reeve would become inattentive, we have decided not to remove the original cues.

Month 14. Due to vacations both in the university and in Reeve's nursery school, he was without therapy for most of this month. He has regressed in both his verbal responding and in his overall behavior. However, as always, his receptive use of language remains relatively undisturbed. He continues to respond consistently and correctly to commands such as "stand up," "sit down," "jump up and down," and "hug the doll."

He has once again lost several sounds that he once used. Specifically, "buh," "puh," "me," "nah," and "i" are gone. We are drilling alphabet sounds now, pairing the presentation of a verbal S^D with the presentation of a plastic letter, the letter drawn, or the letter on a flash card. We are drilling both "a" and "ah," "be" and "bah," "mm" and "mah," "pe" and "pah " and "el" and "lah," for example. To put Reeve back into shape in his expressive speech, we have reintroduced into the drills "nahnah," "dodo," and "nono."

Month 15. Reeve is now using all of his vowel sounds, although the "o" sound occurs infrequently. Having begun to label, Reeve is now combining simple sounds into a small functional labelling vocabulary. His "words" occur in several categories: as single consonant-vowel segments approximating words, such as "du" for juice, "wah" for want, "teh" for ten, and "te" for teeth; as fully reduplicated segments, such as "cheche" for cheese, "nono" for nose, "mahmah" and "pahpah," "nahnah" for banana, and "tete" for Reeve; as partially reduplicated segments, such as "Ayah" for Allen, "Tahtee" for Scottie, "ahpah" for apple; and as formally drilled sound segments that are themselves words, such as "me," "knee," "two," and "eye." In all of these cases, by presenting the object and then the verbal S^D for imitation, we are able to make the labels functional.

We are finding, in addition to the obvious oversimplification of these words, that Reeve is leaving the endings off most of his words as in his approximations for juice, ten, teeth and his use of "orah" for orange. The sound "te" appears as a frequent substitute for the "c" and "s" sounds, as in his approximation for Stevie.

We have wanted to start Reeve on elementary (preschool) drawing exercises, and after several futile attempts at drawing lines and figures by nonverbal imitation, we asked Reeve to draw the letter "M." He drew an "M" and labeled it, then drew an "I" and labeled it. His fascination with letters is again an obvious advantage. We will begin to work on his drawing letters as a way of introducing him to other kinds of drawings.

Month 16. We are continuing verbal drills with variations on alphabet sounds, for example, "a," "be," "i," "ce," "de," "da," "do," "du," "di," and drills of words. Reeve can now also label "tute" for cookie, "tetah" for tickle, "nor" for more, "ahm" for arm, and "beh" for bed. Reeve's approximation of his own name has changed from the original "tete" to "weebe." We hope that Reeve will clear up his articulations as he develops, and we are satisfied to allow his approximations to words at this time.

Reeve is not maintaining a constant repertoire of vowel sounds. While the vowel sound "ah" continues to dominate, all other vowel sounds come and go. The "o" sound occurs in context but rarely in isolation, where it does occur as a grunt. Consonant and "e" sounds were strong a month ago, yet they virtually disappeared by the end of this month. Consonant and "i" sounds are all ending in "n" or "m," as are many of Reeve's verbal approximations. He has now substituted "y" for "l," and the word "leg" is transformed in his repertoire to "yem."

We have received an evaluation of Reeve's speech from a speech clinician who tells us many things we have already observed: the predominance of "ah," although other vowels exist in isolation, and the elimination of end consonants and the substitution of some initial and end consonants. She suggested several prompts to encourage certain sounds: the S^D "a-o" to prompt the vowel sound "o," the S^D "e-u" to prompt the vowel sound "u," and the manual prompt on the tongue to facilitate vocalization of the hard "k" and "g" sounds. The vowel prompts are effective while the consonant prompt seems ineffective.

During free play, Reeve engages in a peculiar verbal play, speaking in patterns, keeping one unit of a two-unit phrase constant while varying the other almost like advanced partial reduplications, for example, "ahmah," "ahtah," "ahbah," and "mahnene," "tahnene," and "bahnene." We encouraged this babbling because it is spontaneous, because it provides practice, and because it may provide the opportunity for Reeve to hear the contrast of different sounds in identical contexts. We have even begun formal drilling of partially reduplicated sounds such as "ahmah," "ahnah," "ahdah," "ahpah," and "ahlah."

Reeve is now using a sentence, "I wah," which is his approximation for the sentence, "I want." Beginning with "I wah che," for cheese, it expanded quickly to demands for juice, cookie, tickle, mama, daddy, and so on. He has even added the words "some" and "more" to the sentence. It has generalized rapidly over situations, people, and objects.

Reeve is now able to receptively discriminate and then label with verbal approximations about half a dozen colors. He understands the concept of counting, responding verbally to the S^D "How many?" when presented with a number of objects. He responds to the S^D "What does this animal say?" when presented with a picture of an animal, by giving the appropriate animal sound. He is responding to commands that include prepositions, putting his foot, his hand, or his arm on, under, or near the bed, the chair, or other furniture in his room.

Reeve's letter and drawing repertoire on the blackboard now includes the letters "m," "i," "o," "h," "x," "e," and "a." He recognizes the word "me" drawn on the blackboard. He can write it and label it, and as he labels it, he points to himself. We are using the blackboard to teach the concepts of "big" and "little," having him draw big and little lines or letters. He is learning the concepts of "same" and "other" and "first" and "second," using structures he has made with his building blocks. After two identical structures are built, two objects are placed in the *same* structure, or one in the *first* and the *other* in the second, or one in the *first* and the *other* in the *same,* and so on, using all of these concepts.

Month 17. We are concentrating our formal verbal drills on the vowel sounds "a," "e," "i," "o," and "u," using the "a-o" prompt for the sound "o" in an effort to facilitate Reeve's consistent use of all of his vowel sounds. We are also drilling combinations of these vowel sounds, for example, "a-e," "a-i," "a-o," "a-u," "e-a," and "e-o." Reeve is doing very well in all of these vowel drills.

Reeve's "m" and "n" endings persist on consonant-"i" and consonant-"ah" sounds; for example, "bi" becomes "bine" and "ba" becomes "bame." He is substituting "b" for "v" sounds. We have begun drilling the "s" sound that Reeve has never used before, introducing it as a hiss. We have yet to have any success with the hard "k" and "g" sounds, even with the use of manual prompts on his tongue.

Reeve continues to expand his use of the "I want" sentence and is now saying, "My name is Weebe." He has begun to use the word "bye-bye" to expressively signify the absence of an object or his desire for an object or a person to be removed.

In all aspects of language training now, the emphasis is upon Reeve's verbalization of that which is going on around him. Objects are presented to him and labeled for him to imitate. Picking up such labels rapidly, Reeve then responds with the correct word when presented with an object and asked, "What is it?" Reeve is now labeling clothes, body parts, objects around the room, and figures drawn on the blackboard. He is now using two word phrases quite naturally, saying "two eyes" rather than just "eyes" and "red shirt" rather than just "shirt." He is verbalizing all receptive speech concepts concerning color, number, and size, answering "two cookies" to the question "How many cookies do you want?" answering "blue book" to the question "What color is it?" and even labeling as "big" or "little" letters and figures he draws on the blackboard. One day in response to the question "What color are your pants?" Reeve answered "red and blue and white."

On the blackboard Reeve is now drawing a big "o," a little "o," a big line, a little line, letters "m," "i," "h," "a," "n," "e," and the number "10." He can draw and identify "me" and "ma."

Month 18. Problems related to Reeve's current school situation have resulted in severe behavioral regressions, inattention, unresponsiveness, and apathy. Apparently, he was placed in a class way above his level of functioning, with a "nondirective" teacher, and he is falling apart. It also becomes obvious to us that our decrease in use of food reinforcers was premature. Social reinforcers alone are not yet strong enough to maintain Reeve's behavior. It takes us one month to correct these problems, asking that he be reassigned to a more directing, "consequating" teacher, and we reintroduce exaggerated reinforcers in our treatment. He recovers nicely.

We are beginning to reduce the formal verbal imitation drills, concentrating now on the use of dialogue as expressive language therapy. We continue to demand Reeve's verbalizations of objects and activities. He responds to most of our requests and needs only to be given one verbal prompt in order to remember any word or phrase. If asked, he will repeat his verbal responses, often cleaning up his articulation significantly by the second or third repetition. If his articulation does not improve naturally in this informal therapy situation, as consultants have suggested it should, we will reinstate formal imitation drills into the therapy.

Combining receptive exercises on the blackboard, Reeve is drawing and labeling big and little letters, inside and outside squares, triangles, and circles after these figures are drawn and labeled. It is as much an exercise in expressive speech as an exercise in concept formation. Reeve is connecting a circle and a line on the blackboard, labeling it as a lollipop, and then licking the palm of his hand, pretending to eat the candy. He has forgotten how to draw letter "E," becoming confused as to how many horizontal lines should be drawn. Reeve is now counting on an abacus, moving certain numbers of colored beads and then answering, for example, "two red and three blue" when asked what he has done.

Month 19. There is little forward progress this month. Therapy continues in much the same direction, using pictures from Reeve's lotto games and flash cards to expand his expressive vocabulary. His new words include tunnel, water, hammer, bird, and baby, all spoken quite intelligibly. Unfortunately, the rest of Reeve's verbalizations continue to be quite sloppy and hard to understand.

We have decided to work on S^D control over Reeve's verbal volume, to be able to tell him to talk loudly enough to be intelligible, which he often does not do now. Also, he is responding "yes" or "no" to simple questions of volition, for example, "Do you want a cookie?" or "Do you want to erase the blackboard?"

Month 20. We are beginning to notice a significant increase in the spontaneity of Reeve's speech and the clarity of his articulations, while he continues to label nouns and is now labeling activities in response to the S^D "What are you doing?" Reeve is now using three sentences, " I want _____," "I am _____," and "It is _____." It is possible to hold a simple conversation with him now. A typical conversation might go as follows: Therapist: "Do you want something, Reeve?" Reeve: "Yes." Therapist: "What do you want?" Reeve: "I want juice." Therapist (holding juice): "What is this?" Reeve: "It is juice." Therapist: "What do you do with juice?" Reeve: "Drink juice." Therapist (after giving Reeve juice): "What are you doing?" Reeve (after drinking): "I am drinking juice."

Reeve's use of the "I am" sentence has generalized more quickly than the "I want" sentence. He will now perform an activity and spontaneously say, "I am swinging," "I am sliding," "I am running," "I am jumping," or "I am walking." While on the playground, Reeve will label his activities; while on the swing he will spontaneously say, "I want off."

We have Reeve constantly moving about his room, responding to commands and questions about objects and people in it. In response to the SD "What is in your room?", Reeve gives us lists of objects and people that he sees. In response to the S^D "Tell me about Reeve," Reeve gives us a list of his various body parts, as he points to them. We are finding that during Reeve's recitation of these objects, our confirmation of his response acts as a motivating factor, increasing the number of objects he will list during these exercises. In other words, if we respond, "Yes, Reeve, that is a table and what else?" Reeve apparently responds better than if we simply say, "Yes, and what else?"

We have brought into his home some of the songs that Reeve has been hearing in his nursery school. These are songs with lyrics that can be acted out by Reeve as he listens. In addition to performing the activity suggested in the lyrics, Reeve often sings along with the records. We do this "school homework" in part to facilitate his school adjustment.

While sitting at the blackboard now, Reeve responds to the question, "What are you doing?", with the answer, "I am drawing." Reeve now draws letters A, C, E, F, H, I, J, L, M, N, O, P, R, S, T, U, V, X, and Z, and numbers 1, 2, 3, 4, 5, 7, and 10. He is now drawing houses, trees, cookies, lollipops, and faces.

Month 21. Having mastered drawing the numbers 1 through 20 and almost all of the alphabet, Reeve can now spell his own first and last names.

He is improving on his verbalization. He is spontaneous, maintaining a good articulation, and he is building a fine vocabulary. While his use of the few sentence structures (i.e., "I am" and "I want") continues to expand and generalize beautifully, these sentences comprise most of Reeve's conversational speech. That which he learns receptively about the conceptual nature of his language seems confined to those few receptive speech exercises we can conduct with Reeve on the blackboard. Now that he has acquired the fundamentals of expressive speech, he must learn what to talk about, how words are used in relation to each other, and how he can generate novel sentences to express new ideas. We are therefore moving into a new formalized language program, emphasizing language concepts such as pronouns, one of the first concepts we will work with. Along with pronouns, this month we are introducing prepositions and the time concepts of "first" and "last."

Introducing the concept of pronouns, we concentrated on a mastery of the receptive discrimination of "my" and "your," using body parts, before moving into the expressive discrimination. Reeve had had informal contact with pronouns while learning body parts, and within a week he had reached criterion on this receptive discrimination, responding to S^Ds such as "touch *my* nose" and "point to *your* ear."

We began the expressive discrimination, concentrating on the pronoun "my," using a contrast prompt such as "point to your nose" and the corresponding S^D, such as "whose nose is it?" Reeve quickly worked to criterion, and we then introduced the pronoun, "your" in an identical manner with the contrast prompt before the S^D. As of the end of this month, Reeve is responding to criterion for the pronouns "my" and "your" but not for the pronouns "your" and "my" when they are mixed. This lack of success in mixed drills is explained in part by observing Reeve's data. Having learned each pronoun separately, Reeve is simply persevering on one response, switching only when the prompt changes or he receives no reinforcement. If the prompt is removed or the S^Ds are mixed, his responses are consistently wrong.

Reeve has had much better luck in preposition training. He reached criterion on six prepositions: "in," "under," "next to," "on top of," "in front of," and "behind" in less than two weeks, responding to S^Ds such as "Put the pen under the book" and "Stand next to the door." We are able to mix all six of the prepositions together within any drill, and we are using many objects and locations. No verbal responses are required of Reeve as yet, and we will not move into the expressive use of prepositions this month, having decided to generalize and strengthen the concept receptively.

The concepts of "first" and "last" are entirely new to Reeve. We place five objects on a table, asking Reeve to touch and label three of them, one at a time. We then introduce the S^D "What did you touch last?" Our initial attempts were met by complete failure. Several attempts at various prompts were also unsuccessful. We decided to use only three objects on the table, and two of the six therapists report reaching criterion by the middle of the month. By the end of the month, he is performing differently for each therapist. For some he is giving ten correct responses out of ten presented S^Ds, while others may receive ten correct responses out of forty presented S^Ds. As we are unable to identify the areas of inconsistencies among our therapists, we are unable to explain the erratic nature of Reeve's responding. It does not appear that he has mastered the concept "last."

Month 22. Reeve has begun to babble and sing incessantly, which is good. But it also may have become a good avoidance behavior for him during language drills.

Those therapists who had reported success with the concept "last" decided to introduce the concept "first." Reeve's responding is consistent, 100% wrong. He is persevering totally on the last object rather than the first. With excessive verbal and positioning prompts, some therapists are able to achieve minimal responding, yet this success is once again inconsistent over therapists. We are finding also that any success with the concept "first" is faithfully accompanied by a loss of Reeve's fragile mastery of the concept "last." We are as yet unable to explain our inconsistencies, and the drill has become so aversive to Reeve that he engages in strong avoidance behaviors when it is introduced each day in therapy. It is decided that the possible advantages of learning this concept are all outweighed by the problems we are having teaching it.

As we have found no successful solution, we are dropping the time concept drills from our language program after somewhat less than two months of trying.

Working with pronouns at the beginning of the month, we were able to mix the pronouns "my" and "your" together in a drill with the contrast prompt. As this prompt was faded, however, Reeve's performance deteriorated drastically. He was obviously hooked on the prompt. We decided to retrain the concept "your" alone without a prompt, as Reeve already knew the pronoun "my" without one. Having done this, we went back to interchanging the pronouns within a drill. Reeve's responses fell at chance level. He continued to persevere on the response "my," switching only when he is told he is wrong, and often not changing at all. These drills have also become aversive for him. He cries to avoid them and when he does work, he appears totally confused. We too are confused. It is hard to say what we are doing wrong.

Fortunately, Reeve's initial success with the receptive use of prepositions are followed by similar successes in their expressive use. We point to an object or have Reeve place an object, and then we ask, "Where is (the object)?" Initially, Reeve responded to this command by pointing to the object rather than by telling us where it was. We had to use the prompt, "Reeve, say 'in the hat,' " for example. We faded this prompt quickly, and Reeve now responds 100% to questions involving all six of the prepositions we have taught him.

We are also asking Reeve to place himself in relation to other objects, and then asking him where he is. He responds with the correct preposition spontaneously, often before the question is asked. We will now concentrate on review to maintain performance and a generalization of the response to many environments. He enjoys these tasks.

We now have begun a series of exercises designed to test Reeve's memory of events outside his immediate perceptions. In the first, we verbally present Reeve with several letters, numbers, or words and then ask him to repeat them. For example, we say, "Reeve, say A, R, 7" or "Reeve, say red, B, X." In the second series of exercises, we draw three or four similar letters, numbers, or figures on the blackboard, then cover them up and ask Reeve, "Write what I just wrote."

The third series of exercises involve the sequencing of activities—giving Reeve two commands within one S^D. He must complete both before reinforcement. We say, for example, "Reeve, bring me the book and then stand by the door."

Reeve's responses to all of these exercises are good, around 90%, with minimal prompting. Our immediate goals therefore are to (1) increase the number of letters or words presented verbally for Reeve to repeat, (2) increase the amount of time between our covering the letters drawn on the board and asking Reeve to write them, and (3) increase the number of activities for Reeve to complete within one S^D.

The eventual goal of these memory exercises relates directly to Reeve's language abilities and conversational skills. Often conversation concerns events that have already occurred. These exercises that require Reeve to process and store bits of information for retrieval at a later time involve the skills that are prerequisites to this advanced conversation.

We began a new activity with Reeve involving memory. Four objects are placed on a table. Reeve labels them and then is told to turn around while the therapist removes one of the objects. Reeve is then asked to look again and respond to the question, "What is missing?" Our initial attempts suggested to us that we had expected too much from Reeve. He was totally unaware of what was going on, responding randomly and often not even looking at the objects. We retraced our steps, beginning with only one object, allowing Reeve to watch it being taken away, before we asked him what was missing. While this worked, the introduction of the second object resulted in 50% responding, even with excessive prompts. He is simply not paying attention. In this case it appears that Reeve could learn if he had any interest in performing. We, however, are unable to identify the effective reinforcers.

Month 23. By the end of last month, Reeve had lost his pronouns and could not or would not respond in the "What is missing?" and "first and last" exercises. His ability or willingness to learn new concepts appears to be decreasing rapidly. He seems disinterested. He has even begun this month to respond incorrectly to preposition drills that he has done so well on before.

We may have identified the underlying problem this time: Inconsistencies over the six therapists assigned to Reeve may have led to his confusion. In our enthusiasm we became frustrated easily, so that if a drill did not produce immediate results, we changed it rather than assuming that a consistent pattern of differential reinforcement would be effective. We became innovative, expecting Reeve to learn magically, rather than being persistent and patient.

For these reasons and also because it seems that Reeve is learning more in informal sessions than in formal drills (which had become so aversive as to prompt screaming tantrums), we began searching for new and consistent language activities to supplement the conversational activities that have continued throughout the last two months and have continued to be successful.

In particular we are now concentrating upon Reeve's decription of his room, house, and himself; exercises designed to build vocabulary; and exercises designed to emphasize Reeve's conversational use of verbs to describe his activities. As an example of one activity, we asked Reeve to draw a face and a house. We then erased them and asked Reeve what he had done. His response was "Draw face and draw house."

Every day we read Reeve a story, asking him questions about characters and pictures, prompting answers when necessary. We tried a competitive "group approach" to story reading. One therapist reads the story to Reeve who sits on the floor with two other therapists. After a statement has been read, questions are now posed to Reeve and the therapists, and each person can now respond and get reinforcement. For example, one therapist reads a statement to the effect that a blue bird is sitting in a tree. He then asks the persons present about that statement ("What color was the bird," and so on). If one person fails to answer, another person gets a turn. Reeve's initial response to being incorrect and observing another person receiving reinforcement is to whine, cry, and attempt to take the reinforcer. Again, this is a good example of an exercise which may help Reeve learn better in school, because he is trained to listen more closely to his teacher and other children in a group and to what other group members are doing. In general, we try to rehearse many of the verbal tasks his teacher will demand of him in the clinic and home before they occur in school, so that he becomes more successful.

Month 24. Reeve's voice level is appropriately high, and his sounds are becoming increasingly intelligible. He has close approximations to all of the sounds now, except "K" and "G."

Reeve's spontaneous speech is becoming excellent. He is spontaneously describing his own activities, making his desires known, and labeling objects. He responds using these sentence structures, "I want _____," "I need _____," "I have _____," "It is _____," "I am _____," "You are _____," and several incomplete fragments of sentences, especially those containing verbs, for example, "drawing nose," and "standing up." We are engaged in exercises designed to emphasize Reeve's use of the adjective-noun pairing in his descriptions of objects around him. We want Reeve to say "little red book" instead of simply "book." While he is doing this to some extent now, it is not consistent.

We are continuing our story reading, using the competitive student-therapist approach that we began last month. While we are reading, we show Reeve pictures and ask, "What do you see?" He uses the sentence "I see _____" and the word "and" in listing what he sees. Remembering that confirmation of his response is a reinforcer, we say "yes, you see (that) and what else do you see?"

We have begun coloring with crayons with Reeve. Reeve picks a color, saying, "I want the _____ one!" Either Reeve or the therapist draws a figure, and then they talk about it. If the figure is covered, Reeve can remember what it is; and even after several pictures have been drawn, he remembers who drew which picture. As we wanted him to ask us to draw things, we employed the S^D "Reeve, say, Paul, draw airplane." He spontaneously said, "I want Paul draw airplane." This sentence structure quickly expanded to various situations, for example, "I want Bruce read me story," and "I want Paul tickle tummy," and "I want Nitza give me juice," and even "I want Paul draw red airplane."

We began a formal drill of the concept "yes" and "no" to test once again Reeve's ability to learn in a formal setting. He responds yes or no to questions concerning volition, but not to those concerning facts. We began a drill using the question "Is this a cookie?" while holding up either a cookie or a glass of juice. Even with this simple task, Reeve fails.

Month 25. Reeve's spelling vocabulary has blossomed to over twenty words within a matter of days. This vocabulary includes his own full name and phone number, the names of his brothers, parents, and the therapists who work with him, and the words "cat," "dog," "yes," "no," "up," "down," "all," and "baby." He will spell words presented to him verbally, either drawing them on the blackboard or reciting them back, and he can recognize these words when they are written in front of him. He has learned to spell the sentence "I want" and now adds to it the words "Mama," "juice," "hug," and "book." He can now upon request write a full sentence on the blackboard, expressing his desire for a person or object. One day upon arriving at school, Reeve immediately went to the blackboard and spontaneously wrote, "I want book." When he finished he went to the bookcase, picked up a book, and went to the table to read.

Reeve continues to expand his use of the sentence form, "I want Paul draw airplane!" Rather than remaining a simple response to our request for Reeve to ask us to do something, this sentence form is now his response when we ask him to do something he cannot do. For example, if we say "Reeve, draw a rhinoceros," Reeve will respond "I want *Paul* draw rhinoceros." He has even approached us to ask us to draw objects that he has heard mentioned in nursery school and to spell for him on the blackboard words that he has heard. We are encouraging his use of the shortened command form of this sentence, for example, "Paul, draw a rhinoceros," or "Paul, give me juice," rather than using "I want _____" at the beginning of each request.

Reeve's reaction to the use of other therapists during story-reading time has changed completely. He now really enjoys the activity, and he smiles, laughs, and touches another person when

gets a reinforcement. As our questions to Reeve now
rmation given by the other therapists in earlier ques-
must now listen to the other people's responses. This
efore has become a program involving Reeve in the
nformation among a number of people. It seems ideal
pretraining for school, where he has to learn from other children's
behavior.

After a year and a half of trying, we have finally succeeded in
finding a prompt effective in facilitating Reeve's use of the sounds
"K" and "G." It has always been our goal in this area to hold the
tip of Reeve's tongue down so that the back would rise into the
position necessary for the production of these hard velar sounds.
However, lollipops, pencils, pens, and fingers have been unsuccessful. Reeve would never allow us inside his mouth. We are
now placing a small piece of cheese on the end of a tongue depres-
ser, putting it on the tip of his tongue, then giving the S^D,
"Reeve, say 'cat' (or 'car' or 'go')." With his tongue so confined,
the "k" and "g" sounds are produced correctly, and he is immediately reinforced by the cheese in his mouth. This is the first
time Reeve has the opportunity to hear himself say the "k" and
"g" sounds correctly and be reinforced. It is obvious now that this
is what we should have done all along.

Beginning this summer, Reeve will be attending an all-day
camp, five days a week. Home therapy sessions will be temporarily reduced until camp is over. We expect to maintain Reeve in
therapy for another year, with treatment activities emphasizing
his receptive understanding of the language, continued practice
in conversational speech, and increased spontaneity and appro-
priateness of speech while in social environments with his peers.

Reeve's continued progress in language learning will depend
largely upon his acquisition of a greater social awareness of his
peers. It is our hope that the camp experiences Reeve brings back
to therapy at the end of the summer will facilitate his further
progress with us. Reeve's last year of therapy will be of the same
intensity as the first two years, and we plan no major changes in
our treatment of him.

Tommy

Tommy, a black male child, began therapy at the age of 3
years, 4 months. He exhibited a variety of autistic behaviors. In

particular, his language development was quite slow. While he had evidenced some expressive speech (such as "dog," "light," "mama," and "bye-bye" which he used fairly consistently) at about two years of age, he had stopped talking by the age of three, except for an occasional "mama" or "dada." He frequently used pointing or other gestures to substitute for his lack of expressive speech. Similarly, his receptive speech was grossly delayed. He displayed no comprehension of concepts such as size, color, and form. However, he did understand a few simple commands such as "sit down," "come here," and "open the door."

His eye contact was fair. While he frequently looked into the eyes of people around him, he rarely looked upon demand. Although he sometimes climbed into a person's lap and sat there for a few minutes, he resisted being held or cuddled when he did not initiate the interaction. His peer interaction was limited to occasionally following around a group of neighbor children. He did not play *with* children. He did play appropriately on tricycles and scooters and with some mechanical toys such as a "record-player" music box. He occasionally played appropriately with cars and trucks but usually preferred to line them up in neat rows.

He exhibited a variety of psychotic behaviors, in particular self-stimulatory behaviors such as rocking, lightly banging his head, spinning wheels and ashtrays, turning faucets on and off repetitively, and jumping in one place for long periods of time. In addition, he engaged in considerable verbal self-stimulation, usually screeching or saying, "ba-ba-ba" repetitively. Occasionally, after hearing a statement, Tommy said "ba-ba-ba . . . ," echoing the inflection of the phrase, as in partial echolalia.

He was characterized by apparent sensory deficits. At times, for instance, he seemed not to hear his name when he was called. His parents had at first been quite concerned about his hearing and had had it tested. The tests, however, showed that his hearing was normal. He was sometimes insensitive to pain and appeared often to act as if he were blind. Finally, his tantrums were excessive, and he would scream for long periods unconsolably; his parents kept him out of stores, restaurants, and other public places to avoid the excessive commotion he caused.

Tommy at intake obtained a Social Quotient of 78 on the Vineland and a Mental Age of 21 months on the Bayley. His chronological age was 40 months.

Month 1. Tommy, within a few trials on the first day of therapy, caught on quickly to verbal imitation. With food reinforcement he would quickly imitate a number of sounds: "t," "da," "me," "be," "p," "eye," "wa," "s," and a few words: "mama," "dada," and "bye-bye" (ba ba). But he was also unable to imitate some sounds that most three-year-olds could say: "k," "g," "n," "l," and he could not imitate two different sounds in succession, such as "wata." For the first two weeks of training Tommy was drilled on the sounds and words that he could already say, to insure that he would consistently perform them (we could "get control" over them). In the third week of therapy, Tommy was manually prompted to imitate a "k" sound by holding down the front of his tongue. After three prompted trials, he was able to say "k" spontaneously and with great enthusiasm. For the first few days after this prompting, Tommy confused "t" and "k" on verbal imitation trials, but by the end of the third week, he rarely confused the sounds.

In the fourth week, Tommy began to work on putting different sounds together. By the end of the week he could imitate two new words: "up" and "eat," when presentations of these words were randomly alternated with words and sounds he could already imitate.

In the first days of therapy, Tommy did not swallow his saliva during the verbal imitation drills. The saliva filled his mouth, preventing him from imitating efficiently. Tommy was therefore taught to swallow on command. The swallowing response was at first manually prompted by massaging the throat, but it soon came under verbal control. By the end of August, Tommy was usually swallowing without being reminded to do so.

During the first month of training Tommy rarely used the words he knew spontaneously. Only one instance of spontaneity was recorded: He ran to his front door and called out "mama" when he saw her approaching. However, Tommy's babbling changed considerably during the first month of therapy from its initial repetitive "ba-ba-ba-ba." He began to incorporate most of the sounds worked on in the verbal imitation tasks into the babbling at home.

In the first week of therapy, Tommy was not taught any receptive language. However, he was periodically asked to perform various commands that he understood, such as "close the door," "turn on the light," and "kiss daddy," as a change of pace from his verbal and nonverbal imitation drills. During the second week, training was begun to shift the nonverbal imitation to verbal control. By the end of the month, he could make the following responses to a verbal command: clap hands, raise arm, and touch knee, nose, mouth, head, ear, pants, and shoes.

He initially exhibited little self-stimulation or tantrums during the therapy sessions. During the second week of therapy, however, these behaviors began to increase in frequency. He clicked his teeth and let his attention drift between trials in the sessions. Punishment, shouting "no" or "pay attention," and occasionally slapping his arm or leg, decreased the frequency of these behaviors. Punishment was not effective in stopping a tantrum once it had begun. A highly effective strategy, however, was to "work through" the tantrum by presenting S^Ds and reinforcing Tommy for appropriate responding just as though he were not having a tantrum. Tommy usually quieted down within one minute when this "working through" strategy was used. However "working through" proved ineffective the first time that Tommy's father did therapy with him. Instead, as Tommy refused to respond to his father's requests, he was placed, chair and all, into a corner and "timed out." There he continued the tantrum for 15 minutes, the longest tantrum ever seen in his year of therapy, before he became quiet. Time out was rarely needed to control his tantrums after this incident.

Month 2. Tommy learned to differentially imitate "k" and "g" and began to learn to imitate two new words, "water" and "cookie." He initially had difficulty in sequencing the two different sounds in each word. Water tended to come out as "wahwah," while cookie was "keekee." He was able to say "wahtah" (for water) consistently, but "cookie" still required two S^Ds, one for each syllable. No therapy was conducted in the second and third weeks of Month 2, when the Autism Project staff took their vacations. Tommy regressed slightly over this break. He had dropped the "t" from his imitation of "eat," and he could no longer imitate "water" when a single S^D was presented. By the end of the first session he again was able to imitate "eat" appropriately; his imitation of "water" to one S^D returned by the end of the week. In addition, by the end of the week he was able to imitate "cookie." Tommy was taught his first expressive labels: water and cookie. These words were learned quickly (within the first one-hour session). He was also required to say "up" before he could get up from his chair. By the end of one week of training he spontaneously asked for "wahtah" and to get "up." Tommy's parents noted that he spontaneously began to ask for "cookie" and "wahtah" at home at this time.

Tommy's receptive language continued to increase. He learned to touch his teeth, shirt, shoes, and tummy. At home, he began to comply more readily with his parents when they asked him to come to them, sit down, or put his toys in his room.

At the end of this month, we began to see that Tommy had substantial trouble with complex demands. Thus, he could not perform a task in which he was asked to give one of two available objects to one of two people present. If either component, object or person, was held constant across trials, he could follow the instructions. The processing problem occurred only when both components were unlimited within a single command.

Month 3. Tommy learned to imitate a number of new words, such as "car," "keys," and "out," composed of sounds that he could say separately. The learning of a new word frequently temporarily disrupted the pronunciation of a previously learned word. For example, just after being drilled on a new word, "key," he began to pronounce "out" as "ouk"; the error was corrected with a few trials of prompting. Tommy also learned to say two new sounds, "f" and "l," and words containing these sounds. "L" was difficult for Tommy. He was first taught to place his tongue properly to make an "l" sound.

As soon as Tommy could say a word fairly well, he was taught to label the corresponding object and find the object when it was asked for by name. He frequently used the words that he learned spontaneously. At the clinic, he picked up a doll and labeled the features on its face. At home, he frequently tried to label the things he saw on television. He often asked for cookies or milk and the like. Since Tommy was verbally asking for things regularly, he was taught to use "I want _____" sentences. Within a week, Tommy had mastered this sentence form. A second phrase, "Hi, (person's name)" (in response to the greeting "Hi, Tommy"), was added at this time.

Tommy learned receptive labels quite easily. He seemed unable, however, to learn to discriminate between cup and spoon. After three weeks of trying numerous variations of discrimination training (both Tommy and his therapists were pretty frustrated) we stopped working on the discrimination. It seemed pointless to spend so much time on one discrimination when Tommy learned other receptive labels very easily. We felt that, later, he would probably learn these labels easily or on his own. (In fact, a few months later, Tommy did learn these labels in less than 10 trials).

We began to teach verbs receptively. The first verbs we chose were "run," "jump," and "walk." Tommy was asked to perform the action named. These verbs were chosen primarily because the actions involved in carrying out these verbs were very reinforcing to him, and he learned them quickly. Furthermore, after teaching him a label for the behavior, we were also able specifically to instruct him to "stop jumping," an activity which he engaged in excessively for its self-stimulatory properties. That is, we were beginning to gain verbal control over his self-stimulatory behavior (later, we may tell him to stop twirling, to stop spinning, or to stop acting bizarre). At home, Tommy is now sent around his house to find objects and perform simple tasks. He enjoys these tasks because he can be quite active and because a task is very game-like at times.

Month 4. Tommy finally learned to make the "n" sound this month. We had tried unsuccessfully to teach him to imitate the sound last month. During a break in the therapy session, Tommy asked the therapist for the toy gun she had by saying "gah." The therapist refused to give it to him and told him to say "gun." To her surprise, Tommy did so, breaking the word up into two distinct syllables, pronouncing the word as "gu-n." For a few days, Tommy was unable to say "n" except as part of "gun," but he eventually learned to say the "n" sound separately and in other words.

Tommy's vocabulary of names continued to increase. He learned more body parts, object names, and verbs. A new task, labeling pictures in books, was added to the sessions. Tommy learned the names of a number of animals and also the sounds that they make. For instance, when asked what sound a cat makes, Tommy answered "me-ow" using the appropriate inflection. Tommy also began to recite, by rote, the numbers one through five.

Tommy spontaneously began to label the people he knew: his parents, his relatives, and the therapists. Without being taught, he used these names as modifiers of objects. He called his father's car, "dada car," and a therapist's car, "Larry car."

Given this spontaneous use of names as adjectives, we systematically began to teach Tommy other adjectives. He learned some of the adjectives quite easily; others were difficult for him. He learned big versus little discrimination using blocks in about 50 trials. He generalized the relational terms to other pairs of items with few errors. In contrast, Tommy acquired color names slowly. He learned to label blue quickly, but he was still having trouble with yellow and green at the end of November.

Tommy was taught how to match identical items to each

other. He began matching objects to objects, went on to matching photos to photos, and finally to matching objects to photos. We planned to use this matching response later in teaching more complex concepts.

We also started to work on Tommy's memory. Tommy labeled an object, then put it into a bucket. The opening in the bucket was covered, then Tommy was asked what was inside. Within a week, he could usually answer correctly even after a 30-second delay between the action and the request, even if he had performed another task during the delay interval.

At this point, Tommy began a program of learning to process complex demands. In the first task, he was asked to give the therapist two objects from a five-object display. To our surprise, in the first session he began to say the names of the objects out loud a few times before picking them up. He did not echo the entire S^D; rather, he seemed to be verbally rehearsing the names before picking up the objects.

In the middle of this month (i.e., four months into training), Tommy began showing less eye-to-face contact, dawdling when complying with demands, and his rate of self-stimulatory behaviors went up. Verbal punishment (like a loud "no") had little immediate effect in reducing the frequency of the off-task behaviors, so physical punishment (his therapist slapped his leg) was used. The physical punishment was effective almost immediately. This temporary rise in psychotic behavior showed us that, although Tommy had been improving rapidly, he was still far from normal.

Month 5. Tommy finally learned the names of four colors: red, yellow, blue, and green, receptively and expressively. When his correct responding became consistent, he was taught to discriminate between the questions, *"what* is it?" and "what *color* is it?" Since the word "color" was heavily emphasized whenever that question was asked, he spontaneously began to repeat "color" before proceeding to answering the question. Soon after he began echoing or rehearsing the word, he learned to discriminate between the questions. It was very clear in this task that he spontaneously engaged in overt verbal rehearsal.

Tommy continued to learn the names of actions. We used a variety of pictures showing people engaged in various activities. We frequently tested for generalization in other situations. For instance, after Tommy had been taught to "jump" and had learned to command his therapist to "jump," we gave him a toy soldier and asked him to "make the man jump." Tommy lifted the man up and down from a table and labeled the action "jumping." After he had learned verbs such as eating, sleeping, combing hair, and brushing teeth, Tommy began to learn how to pretend to perform the actions. He learned to pretend quickly and enjoyed it very much. After about one week of training, he began to act out the pretending behaviors which he had been taught spontaneously and to label the behaviors he acted out.

The program for teaching Tommy to process complex demands was resumed. Tommy was to give one of two available objects to one of two people present. He had been unable to learn this task three months ago. He now learned the task within one hour. The second type of complex demand that Tommy worked on was more difficult for him. He was asked, in one S^D, to touch two different parts of his body in sequence. A typical S^D was: "touch nose and touch ear." His problem in this task was that he did not wait for the complete S^D to be given before beginning to respond. The therapists therefore began to hold Tommy's hands down until the S^D was completed, and his performance improved.

This month, Tommy learned his first shapes and prepositions. He acquired a receptive discrimination between circle and square in one 50-minute session. He similarly learned a receptive discrimination between "in" and "on" in one session. "Under" was later added to his repertoire of prepositions.

Some simple social games were added to the therapy session. The first game was "knock, knock." Tommy knocked, the therapist asked "Who's there?" and Tommy answered "Me!" Another game was "patticake" to a song. Tommy performed the clapping part and tried to sing along. "Gimme 5" was a third game. The therapist held out his hand, palm up, and said "Gimme 5"; Tommy then slapped his hand. The "Gimme 5" game was used to teach Tommy to discriminate between "easy" and "hard" in his hitting. He was asked to "Gimme 5—*easy*" or "Gimme 3—*hard.*" In addition, because he greatly enjoyed all of these games, they were used as reinforcement for working on less-preferred tasks. For example, after working on his prepositions for five minutes, Tommy was allowed to play the games for two minutes.

Month 6. Tommy worked on generalizing "in," "on," and "under" to a variety of situations. He became confused at one point when he was placing objects "on" or "under" a chair. The therapists soon realized that Tommy was not discriminating between the instructions "on chair" and "under chair" because he imitated both instructions as "under." He was taught to discriminate the instructions using verbal imitation drills, where he was first taught to *imitate* the instructions accurately. He then performed the responses correctly with no further training. By the end of the month he could put objects "in," "on," or "under" just about anything and tell the therapist where it was.

Tommy's repertoire of verbs continued to expand. He was taken to a playground a few times by his mother, where he learned "swinging" and "sliding." His pretending became more elaborate. He learned how to "make pancakes" after his parents cooked some for him one weekend. He added three more colors, orange, brown, and pink, to his repertoire with little trouble. He also learned a third shape, triangle, easily.

Tommy learned to count by rote from one to five this month. After he mastered the first task, he worked at counting objects. At first, he was asked to touch each object as he counted. He had trouble, however, in coordinating his verbal and motor responses. He tended to count faster than he touched the objects. The task therefore was modified. The therapist placed the objects on the floor in front of Tommy, one at a time, banging each object against the table to make a loud sound; Tommy counted each object as it was placed on the floor. He quickly mastered this task. In the next step, the blocks to be counted were all placed on the table at once, and the therapist pointed to each block while Tommy counted. After this step was mastered, he returned to the original task, touching and counting simultaneously. He successfully coordinated his motor and verbal responses most of the time.

Tommy learned to imitate the pitch and loudness with which words were spoken. He learned to vary loudness and pitch very quickly. He thought that whispering was very funny, laughing as he imitated the therapist's voice. He treated the whole task as a game, which of course is ideal.

Tommy began attending a nursery school. His second day at school, he and another child picked up the receivers of two toy phones and began "talking" (babbling) to each other. After a few days at school he spontaneously began to sing along with the other children during the music period. He could only say a few words clearly, and they were said a little too slowly, but he tried to keep up, and he enjoyed participating. In his first month at school, however, he engaged in little real verbal interaction with his classmates.

Month 7. This month Tommy learned to use "yes" and "no" to indicate volition. He learned to say "yes," he wanted cookie, and "no," he did not want vinegar, in one session. The response generalized to other foods and to activities such as playing and getting spanked, with few errors.

Tommy continued to work on counting. He learned to count by rote up to 10 and to count up to 10 objects. He then began to learn how many he had just counted when he was asked to do so. He also began working on a new memory task. At first two pictures were placed in front of him. After he labeled the pictures, he closed his eyes, and the therapist removed one of the pictures. Tommy was told to open his eyes and was asked, "What's missing?" He learned this task very quickly. By the end of this month, he responded correctly when five pictures were used as stimuli. He now began sponanteously to play therapist in this task. He, acting like the therapist, laid out and took away the picture himself, then waited for the therapist to ask him what was missing.

We began to teach pronouns. He was first taught "your" and "my" receptively. A typical demand was "touch *your* nose." Tommy learned this task quite quickly.

When Tommy first learned to use prepositions expressively, he said only the preposition in response to the question "where is it?" For example, if asked, "where is pen?" when the pen was on a table, he answered "on." This month, he learned to expand his answers to phrases. In the above example, for instance, his response became "on table." He began to do this task all by himself. He placed an object somewhere, then told the therapists where it was.

We are expanding his use of sentences. First, he learned to say, "I am done," when he finished a task or game such as a puzzle. He also learned a new sentence form, "I am_____ing," with which he described his current activity. He learned to use this sentence form within a week. Lastly, he was taught to give his therapists commands, such as "Larry, jump" or "Susan, move," so that he could exercise more verbal control over his environment.

Tommy's mother noted that his spontaneous speech at home increased rapidly this month. She commented that he was trying more often to put words together in phrases and sentences. It was usually hard to understand him, his mother said, but she was pleased that he was trying. One day, at home, Tommy ran up to his mother, yelling, "Sky! sky!" He pulled her outside and pointed to a bird-shaped kite in the sky. Another time, after getting out of the car, he ran up to his mother and said, "Mama car—hand hurt." When his mother asked him to show her what was wrong, he pointed to the hot exhaust pipe on the car. He apparently had touched it and burned himself.

Tommy's parents and therapists are now noticing that he is beginning to learn many words without formal training. For instance, he learned "window," "tree," and "sky" from his father in informal conversation in which his father labeled the objects once or twice. Also, by the end of the second month of nursery school, Tommy, without systematic training, had learned the names of about half of his classmates.

Tommy developed two problem behaviors this month. First, he began to echo frequently. To suppress this behavior, he was taught to echo on command, and was subsequently told "don't echo" when he did so inappropriately. Second, he became quite noisy at his nursery school. We again dealt with this behavior by teaching him a label for it. He was taught to "make noise" on command. After he learned this response, he was told "don't make noise" when he was disruptive in the classroom. This procedure was effective in eliminating the echoing and the noisiness.

Month 8. Training on the expressive pronouns began; it did not progress easily. Tommy learned to use "your" and "my" expressively, but in doing so, he lost the receptive use of the words. When training was reinstituted on the receptive use of "your" and "my," he became even more confused. He finally acquired the receptive and expressive forms of "your" and "my" after two weeks of drilling. After his "your" and "my" responding stabilized, he began to learn "you" and "I" receptively. Tommy and his therapist each held an object. The therapist asked, "What do you (I) have?"

He is mastering counting. For example, he can tell the therapist that there were one, two, or three blocks in the display without counting them out loud. To generalize his counting skills, other tasks were introduced. For example, he was taught to clap or jump or tap a designated number of times. By the end of the month he could make up to five motor responses accurately. In other tasks, he was asked to count blocks and tell how many he had counted. Then, one block was removed and he was again asked, "How many?" To go along with his counting, he learned to recognize and label the numerals in order. Like many other autistic children, Tommy enjoyed working with the numerals and learned them quickly. After he had learned the numerals, he began labeling them whenever he saw them, on clocks, license plates, or whatever.

During this month we also began to teach him the functions of objects. He was asked, "What is _____ for?" For instance, a bed was "for sleeping," a cookie "for eating," and milk "for drinking." He also learned new memory tasks. Three or four pictures were displayed in front of him in a line. After Tommy labeled the pictures, they were turned face down. The therapist then asked for one of the pictures by name. He learned this memory task with few errors, and he quickly began to play therapist. He would turn over the pictures himself and name one for the therapist to pick out.

Tommy began work on a task designed to improve his descriptive speech. We began teaching this by showing him a picture and asking him to tell about it. At first, he labelled just *one* item and then stopped. When asked what else he saw, he repeated his first response. The therapists began to prompt him to name different items by pointing to them, then fading this prompt. By the end of the month he had begun to extensively describe pictures.

Tommy learned two new sentences this month. He learned to answer "I am four" to the question "How old are you?" and to answer "I am fine" to the question "How are you?" In addition, he learned to say "stop" when he did not like what someone was doing to him. He was taught to use the word by having a therapist tickle him until he said "stop." This response generalized to the nursery school, where he used it when a child was bothering him.

Tommy continued to use language spontaneously. At home, he told his mother, "Give me gun." He had never been taught to say "give me," although the therapists often used the phrase. At school, he frequently began to ask for foods at lunch, for instance, "I want milk" or "more juice."

Month 9. As Tommy had mastered the pronouns "you and I" receptively, he was taught "you" and "me" expressively, using a game. The therapist placed a block between himself and Tommy. He then said "Ready—set—go!" When he said "go," they both grabbed for the block. They each got the block some of the time. The therapist then asked Tommy, "Who has the block?" Tommy loved to play this game. He would put the block in position, say "go" himself, and later spontaneously tell the therapist who had the block. Some further training was conducted with the pronouns "your" and "my" because it was found that the presence of a third person in the task disrupted his responding. Tommy did not understand that the receptive "my" and expressive "your" referred only to the person speaking to him. First, Tommy, Tommy's therapist, and Tommy's teddy bear worked in the task. The therapist asked whose body part had been touched. Tommy mastered this task quickly. A person was then substituted for the teddy bear. Tommy made few errors. In later sessions, the person who gave instructions and the other adult in the task switched roles half way through the session. Tommy was able to change his responding appropriately.

Tommy learned new prepositions this month. He learned to place objects in front of, behind, and next to other objects, each with less than 10 prompted trials. A generalization task was taught next. Tommy was asked to position himself in relation to various objects. A typical command, for instance, was "stand behind chair" or "sit under table." Tommy mastered this task in one session.

Tommy also learned a new use for "yes" and "no." An object or picture was held up, and Tommy was asked, "Is this a _____?" Tommy learned to say "yes" when the object was correctly named and "no" when the name was incorrect. Tommy was trained with one object or picture until he mastered the task with it, then another picture was used. After training on about five pictures and objects, Tommy generalized the responses. He answered questions correctly about new objects with no training. After he mastered "yes" and "no" for object names, some generalization tasks were conducted, using actions, adjectives, and prepositions. Typical S^Ds were: "Are you sitting?", "Is the boy (in a picture) running?", "Is this a blue square?" and "Is the block on the table?" Tommy mastered these variations of the task with few errors. He also learned new concepts this month: "More" and "less" were taught at first by showing him two sets of blocks, with a different number in each set, and asking him to point to that which had "more" or "less." To teach "same" and "different," in one task, three objects were placed in front of Tommy; two were identical, the third different. Tommy was asked to give the therapist the "same" or the "different." He also learned a new sentence form this month, "It is a _____," in response to "What is it?" when an object was held up or pointed to. By the end of this month, Tommy was occasionally using the sentence spontaneously.

Tommy's spontaneous speech increased noticeably, and his speech became much more varied. During a therapy session, for instance, after Larry, a therapist, slapped his hand, Tommy said, "Larry hit me." At school, he tapped a girl who had her back to him and told her "around," for turn around. Tommy had never been taught to say or use the word "around." He began to spontaneously use colors as modifiers. A few times during the month he said, "I want blue càr" or "I want orange car." When he was placed in time-out (a corner) at home for crying, he stopped crying, turned to the therapists and said "done." At school, he held his jacket out to the therapist and said "I want on." The inflections that he used in talking became more normal during this period, and he picked up certain mannerisms such as shrugging his shoulders. We concluded that he was learning these behaviors from the children at his nursery school.

Month 10. Tommy learned a number of sentence forms this month. In answer to the question, "What color is (*item*)?", he learned to answer "(*item*) is (color)." He learned this sentence quickly, but he used it only in response to the specific question. He also learned to say "you are _____ing" to describe a person's actions. At first, he tried to substitute "am" (from "I am _____ing") for the "are," but within a week he was able to use the sentence appropriately without prompting. Finally, he learned to say "I have _____" and "You have _____" to describe objects that he and a person speaking to him were holding. Tommy soon began to use these sentences spontaneously. His main problem with his sentences was that except for the "I want _____" sentence, he said other sentences more slowly than normal children did. Part of the problem was that he said many individual words slowly. A speed drill was therefore begun which relied on his imitating different rates of speech.

Tommy continued to work at describing pictures from books and magazines. Two elements were added to his responses. First, he was taught to say "and" between the items he named. Second, he was taught to say "I see _____," at the beginning of his response, to make the response a sentence. Thus, a typical description of a picture was "I see man and dog and tree and house." By the end of the month, Tommy generally would mention all of the items in a picture without a prompt.

Tommy learned a new variation of "What's missing?" The therapist drew a face, but he omitted one element such as the eyes or the hair. Tommy was asked to identify the missing part.

Somewhat to the therapists' surprise, he never made an error on the task. In the other "What's missing?" task, which involved pictures, he began to play therapist much more elaborately. He removed one of the pictures, then asked "missing?" If the therapist answered correctly, Tommy showed him the picture and said "good." If the therapist was incorrect, Tommy got a puzzled expression on his face, said "no—wrong" thoughtfully, and again asked "What's missing?"

Tommy's knowledge of the functions of various objects was expanded to include the functions of his body parts. A typical question was "What do you see with?" to which he answered "eye." Tommy acquired the responses quickly. About two weeks after the training of the task was begun, he approached one of his therapists and spontaneously began to name the functions of certain body parts. He pointed to his nose and said "smell," then to his eye, saying "see," and finally to his ear, saying "hear."

A number of tasks were designed this month which combined elements of language which had previously been worked on separately to facilitate his understanding of everyday speech. One task combined the use of pronouns, color, and the conjunction "and." Tommy and the therapist each held a few colored blocks. The therapist asked, "What do you (I) have?" A typical answer from Tommy was "I (you) have yellow and blue and red." A second task combined the use of pronouns with yes and no. The therapist and Tommy again held objects. The therapist asked, "Do you (I) have _____?" and Tommy answered yes or no. Tommy mastered these tasks quickly.

Tommy began work on new number tasks in May to generalize his use of numbers and counting. In one task, he was required to count a set of blocks and then point to the numeral which corresponded to the number he had counted. By the end of this month, he could perform this task correctly for up to four blocks. A second task required him to give the therapist a designated number of blocks from a larger set of blocks. Tommy could give up to seven blocks correctly. He spontaneously played therapist in this task. Tommy gave the therapist the S^D "give me _____ blocks." At first he asked for the same number of blocks on each trial. By the end of the month, however, he asked for a different number on each trial without prompting. In a third task, blocks of one color and blocks of a different color were presented to him in one display. He was asked how many blocks of each color were present. A typical set of questions was "How many red?" followed by "How many yellow?" As Tommy mastered this task quickly, different shapes were substituted for different colors. Tommy still required prompting with the shapes at the end of the month.

Tommy started to learn the alphabet this month. By the end of the month, he recognized and labeled "A" through "K," and he could put these letters in the correct order. He also learned the first half of the alphabet song. He was often playful during the alphabet task. One day when he was reciting the part of the alphabet that he knew, he took one step backward as he said each letter.

The amount and variety of his spontaneous speech this month surprised both his parents and his therapists. He began to make more demands of people, for instance, he told one therapist, "Laurie, dance." He told his mother "Mama, clap," when he wanted reinforcement. He began to comment more frequently on his environment, using sentences. At home, he said phrases such as "Phone is green," "Mama wash dishes," and "Dada on chair." He made some attempts to use the past tense in verbs. After his father gave him a record, he said "Dada give me record." He began to engage in more prolonged verbal interactions. At a restaurant, the therapist allowed him to order for himself. He said, "I want hot dog and milk." When the milk was brought, Tommy said, "No, I want chocolate milk." He later said, "Thank you," when the waiter brought him the chocolate milk. At a therapist's home, Tommy took a dollar from the therapist's mother, and said "Bye-bye—store." The therapist asked him, "What do you want?" Tommy answered, "Ice cream, ice cream, bye-bye," and then added, "Laurie car—store."

Tommy's therapy is expected to continue for another year, with the treatment focusing on his understanding and use of conversational speech, increasing his spontaneous speech, and improving his social interactions with peers. He will attend a normal nursery school full time, five days a week. Most of his therapy will be conducted at the nursery school, as this setting will provide Tommy with a variety of opportunities to interact with his peers and to use the language which he is learning.

Linda

While motor development appeared normal, both her parents and a pediatrician suspected Linda to be partly deaf and blind. She showed no startle response to a loud clap behind her, yet

Picture F. Tony is with his parents and his therapists, "giving them orders," which can be very reinforcing for some of the children. To build variety, Tony tells his father to touch his nose, another therapist to open her mouth, the third therapist to touch her hair, etc. It is probably critical that the child acquire early and extensive verbal control over his environment for language to "take hold."

would react to the sound of the opening of a gum wrapper. She would hold her hand in front of her face much of the time, stare at the lights on the ceiling or at a point on the wall, and not look at people who approached her, but "look right through" them, even when they attempted to distract her.

In addition to these apparent perceptual disturbances Linda showed considerable self-stimulatory behavior. She rocked from foot to foot in her crib so incessantly that she wore out several mattresses. She also spun bar stools and toy wheels, twirled her hair and the strings on her blanket, closely examined minute pieces of dirt and lint, giggled, laughed, and clapped her hands inappropriately, and rubbed her own skin, ground her teeth, and looked out of the sides of her eyes. She was also very concerned with maintaining order. Thus, she would have a tantrum until all objects were returned to their proper places, until her father's briefcase was closed, until the Cheerios box was shut, and until the washing machine lid was closed. Given a series of objects, she would line them up in ordered rows. She also remained unusually afraid of falling and of elevators and was fearful of new and unpredictable things.

By the time she was seen by us at intake, Linda could label a few common objects, and she would follow many common commands when properly motivated (e.g., "sit down," "give me the cup," "raise your hand"). Yet she would not respond to her name when called. She had no understanding, receptively or expressively, of abstract terms. She could not converse, but instead would echo others. That is, she would respond to the questions "What day is today?" or "What's your name?" by echoing back the question.

She began treatment with us when she was 3 years, 4 months of age. At that time she obtained a Social Quotient of 72 on the Vineland, and a Mental Age of 30 months on the Bayley.

Month 1. Linda had a tantrum and struggled "to get away" during portions of the first three sessions. That is, she would not sit in a chair when asked to, but would instead scream and cry, struggle to get out of the chair, and resist the therapist touching her. The first step with Linda, as with the other children, was to bring her under this elementary control: to sit in a chair for brief periods of time, to look at the therapist's face when asked to do so ("look at me"), and to remain reasonably free from screams. This was relatively quickly established with Linda, being reasonably well accomplished within the first month in the clinic.

Second, steps were taken to bring Linda's echolalia under the control of the therapist. Her imitation (echoing) of the therapist's verbalizations was unreliable in that she sometimes would not echo him, or she would echo his previous verbalizations (as in delayed echolalia), or her enunciation would be poor. We tried to accomplish this by reinforcing her for echoing him when he said "say _____," or "say what I say: _____, or "say this: . . . ." At the same time she was taught to inhibit her echolalia when the therapist said *"Don't* echo" by giving her verbal disapproval for echoing at those times. Finally, she had a peculiar intonation to her statements, in the sense that each of her statements ended with a rising inflection, as if she was asking a question. The therapist also brought this intonation under his control, in a similar manner as he gained control over her echolalia.

Already during the first month Linda showed us several appropriate verbal behaviors; for example, she thanked a therapist for giving her a toy, replied "O.K." when asked if she wanted candy, and correctly labeled several toys and objects. For the most part, however, her speech remained inappropriate. She persisted on echoing commands and often used either garbled or "singsong" speech.

Month 2. The most important work in this month centered on the reduction of echolalic speech. Linda continued to echo and mimic the words and gestures of her therapists when imitation was not called for. Linda's extensive echoing made her appear very abnormal. We now began to pair the command "Don't echo" with a finger over the mouth each time Linda started to echo. At the same time, we rewarded Linda with candy for not echoing our commands. Echolalia decreased sharply.

Second, we introduced functional speech exercises. Specifically, we began to build the first "I want _____" phrase, starting with "I want candy." Similarly, Linda learned to use the action-based verbs "see," "take," and "go." She acquired these behaviors very quickly.

Also during this month we began to teach her the beginnings of conversational speech ("How old are you?" "How are you?" "What's your name?"); the pronouns "my," "your," "his," and "her"; color, shape, and size, the prepositions "in" and "under"; and the concepts of "same" and "different."

Month 3. Already during this month we felt that we could branch out into different areas of language training without worrying about special problems of motivation. During the first

month we had depended upon food rewards to keep Linda motivated to learn. Already during the second month she had become
interested in many of the teaching materials themselves, and by
the third month of training she began to demonstrate a concern
for getting the right answer by herself and obtaining our social
approval.

We continued to develop both receptive language and functional speech. Linda would be asked to give us two or three objects from one group (e.g., of toys), and perhaps *all* of the objects
from another group (e.g., *all* of the marshmallows). The functional speech training focused on verbs (have, do) that were not
obviously action-based. Linda soon mastered "have" as it applied
to parts of the body, but "do" was perhaps confusing. Asked
"What are you *doing*" she would respond "I am doing jump up
and down" rather than "I am jumping."

A memory task called "What's missing?" was also introduced
as a first step in teaching terms relating to past and present. She
was asked to identify several objects on a nearby table and then to
cover her eyes. The therapist then removed one (or more) objects,
rearranged the position of the others, and asked, "What's missing?" Linda did quite well (about 75% correct) after only one
prompt.

Another exercise, which proved more difficult, helped Linda
learn to ask questions about unfamiliar things rather than talk
about then inappropriately. She was taught to say "I don't know"
when asked to identify an unfamiliar object and also prompted to
ask attending adults, "What's this?" Teaching such children to
ask questions (such as "What's this?") is a very important skill
because it helps the child to obtain information about the environment.

In addition to training on memory tasks and asking questions, we started teaching concepts of number. She quickly
learned to count to ten and to use singular and plural forms correctly. Identification of quantity ("How many?"), however, remained difficult. During this month she also learned the alphabet
through "G," to use "yes" and "no" in statements of fact, to use
the connective "and," and to use pronouns and prepositions together in functional speech.

Month 4. Linda's speech was becoming much clearer, her
inflection was improving, and she had begun to use complete,
well-constructed sentences spontaneously and appropriately. We
were both surprised and encouraged by the large amount of

generalization which emerged from our specific drills. Intonation exercises corrected and sharpened speech inflection. Description of story-book pictures and picture cards provided an opportunity to use newly acquired speech. She spontaneously began to describe her own activities, which we could clearly observe during breaks in the speech drills. A classification exercise helped Linda to talk about concrete objects at a more abstract level: e.g., a cow is an animal, cookies and raisins are foods.

A second step in teaching past-present relationships was introduced this month. Using at first only verbs with regular "ed" endings, the therapist would model a past-tense construction (e.g., "Say, 'You closed the door' "), and then ask "What did I do?" after closing the door. During this month she also learned more extensive pronouns (such as "we are" and "they are") and to recite the entire alphabet. The concept of "last" was particularly hard for her, and training on it was temporarily discontinued. Linda's use of questions improved considerably, and she seemed to generalize the concept of "I don't know." Occasionally, however, she would respond with a familiar but incorrect answer if she could not answer a question correctly.

Month 5. We attempted to strengthen and stretch newly acquired skills such as use of past tense, spontaneous speech, receptive speech, and plurals. We began to expand her use of the past tense. The therapist and Linda together performed various actions around the room. The therapist would then ask her "What did we do over there?" pointing to a particular location in the room. Somewhat later they carried out a series of actions in different parts of the building. Linda was initially required to recall all of the activities regardless of order, and later to recall the activities in their proper sequence. In a supplementary exercise an adult would enter the treatment room and carry out an action in front of Linda and the therapist. Then at increasingly longer intervals, the therapist would ask Linda what action the adult had performed. All of these past-tense exercises worked together to clarify the relationship between the immediate past and present. Linda was learning that actions taken together formed sequences and that order was important. At the same time, these exercises were preparation for a later exercise that would teach her to integrate events of the more remote past with present and future functioning.

During the previous month we had noted the appearance of spontaneous speech, particularly relating to structured tasks and activities. We then started to consider possible exercises that would allow spontaneous speech to emerge through some kind of structure. At first several of us exchanged single statements found in everyday conversation. Linda seemed confused by the exercise and echoed one of the statements in turn. Next, one of the therapists began some activity, and each therapist in turn described what he was doing. Linda appeared to understand the exercise, but found it difficult to add to our descriptions. Our third attempt, however, met with success. Individual foods or toys or picture cards were passed around to each member of the group. One therapist would then announce that he was holding a baby doll, or that his balloon was red, or that he was eating a raisin. Since the other group members had objects from the same class (foods or toys or jewelry), the structure for that trial was already defined. If the first therapist said "My balloon is red," Linda could readily say, "My balloon is green," without any further prompting and without echoing. Moreover, this form of the "spontaneity exercise" allowed us to build spontaneous speech more systematically. Two statements could be required from each group member rather than one. Different sentence constructions, tenses, and parts of speech could be employed. Objects from different classes could be used to encourage individual forms of response. Subsequently, we observed substantial increases in spontaneous speech not only within the exercise but in Linda's everyday functioning.

Continued work on receptive speech exercises appeared to help Linda's expressive speech. Linda would spontaneously ask for two green candies after a therapist had earlier asked for objects according to number, color, size, and class.

Month 6. To allow Linda to express herself freely and frequently we began to reduce the structure of earlier exercises. Instead of asking her specific questions about pictures in a story book, we would ask her simply to tell us about them. The therapists also involved her in pretend play where Linda could describe ongoing imagined activity sequences and help make up the story as it went along.

The word "and" was used to connect series of objects in the "What's missing?" and spontaneity exercises, and to link prepositional phrases together and also verb statements in both the present and past tenses.

Moreover, Linda learned the preposition "through" and the adjectives "open" and "closed." She improved rapidly on identifying quantities and learned to respond correctly to the past tense of "do" ("What did he do?"). Finally, she entered the clinic one day and proudly showed us that she could read and spell her name and her sister's name.

Month 7. As we entered the second half-year of treatment, Linda began to demonstrate increasing initiative in speech as well as spontaneity. After we had practiced a simplified "Simon says," Linda started to give the commands. Soon afterwards she insisted on leading the "What's missing?" exercise, doing so without error and with great satisfaction.

Similarly, she began to ask or comment about everything at the clinic. Handed a broken peg she said, "It's broken, it scratches." Her more detailed observations corresponded nicely with "attribute exercises," which had been recently introduced. Here a therapist would ask Linda if a particular animal had four legs or if an airplane flew in the sky. Alternatively, the therapist would set out a group of objects and say, "Give me all the animals with four legs"; "Give me something that flies in the sky." Also this month we began to practice discrimination of number forms and children's songs such as "Old MacDonald."

Month 8. Throughout this month many of the exercises were combined in various forms. These variations strengthened Linda's performance in different areas and helped maintain motivation. Our log frequently notes spontaneous, clear, and appropriate speech.

At this time we began to work on a concept of the more remote past. Linda's mother would note events of the morning or the preceding day so that we could question Linda at the clinic ("What did you eat this morning?"; "What did you do yesterday?"). Prompting was necessary at first. Linda did best when we questioned her about something of significance—a birthday party, a special visit, a favorite cartoon. Occasionally she would answer appropriately but incorrectly (e.g., eggs rather than cereal for breakfast), and we would correct her with her mother's help. Linda's face would beam each time we talked about her birthday party or a trip to Grandma's house. She also learned that a consideration of past events could be very useful in making decisions about the present and future. After talking about falling out of a wagon, Linda declared that she did not want another ride.

All along we were expanding her use of receptive language. In one exercise a therapist would make a statement, or a series of statements, followed by a question based upon the content. For example, the therapist would state: "The black horse jumped over the fence. She ate oats and hay." Then, he may ask: "What color was the horse?" "What did the horse eat?" A second exercise required that Linda not only comprehend what was said to her but also transform it from receptive to expressive speech. Linda was told, for example, "Go ask Dan what he is wearing today," or "Go ask Rich how old he is." Beside remembering the information Linda would have to transform the pronoun and verb forms when she returned the information to the therapist ("Dan said he is wearing jeans.").

Month 9. The few sessions run this month focused on variations of earlier exercises. Having learned the concepts of number and matching, Linda used her memory skills in playing the card game "Concentration." She learned several new songs with accompanying motions. She pretended to be the different animals which she labeled and described. As the immediate past exercises (i.e., activities conducted around the room) were reviewed, irregular verb forms were introduced. Not surprisingly Linda attempted to regularize them (e.g., "blowed" instead of blew).

The only new concept was causality. Here, for example, the therapist would knock over a block and ask, "Why did the block fall down?" The therapist then prompted Linda to say, "Because you pushed it." "Why did the door shut?" "Because you closed it." Linda mastered the concept quickly, and she correctly used the "ed" endings for past tense.

Month 10. We introduced variations of the attribute and classification exercises, several new pronouns, and some new games. A variation of the attribute exercise (i.e., "Give me two animals with horns.") tried to draw out similarities expressively: "How are a ram and a bull alike?" "They are both animals. They both have horns." The classification exercises (i.e., "Cows and pigs are animals." "Cookies and raisins are foods.") led into the concept of belonging: "Where do these animals belong?" "They belong in this barn."; "Where do these foods belong?" "They belong in the cupboard." Linda did well on both of these variations.

Several new pronouns (everybody, nobody, it) were next introduced in a new pronoun exercise. One therapist would work with Linda while one or two adults sat nearby. The therapist would ask, "Who has a brown shirt?" and prompt, *"He* does." This kind of training proceeded until Linda had mastered "he does," "she does," "I do," and "you do." The therapist then asked, "Who has green hair?" and prompted the response, *"No-*

body does." Similarly he asked, "Who has two eyes?" and with physical and verbal prompting cued Linda to say, "*Everybody* does." Having learned to use "nobody," Linda, when asked who has a nose and mouth, replied "Yes-body!"

Moreover, Linda learned several new games this month. One in particular—the card game "Go Fish"—not only allowed Linda to practice many new skills (number, matching, functional speech, asking questions) but also led to considerable play with her older sister. She also learned a trading game, which exercised functional speech. Teaching her to rhyme, however, proved difficult.

Other exercises included story-book description and comprehension, immediate and remote past drills, pretend conversations on the telephone, and numbers up to 20.

Month 11. All of our attempts to teach specific speech skills would be quite meaningless if Linda were not able to integrate them into her everyday speech. Thus, this month we worked on integrating order and causality relationships into Linda's descriptions of stories and situations.

At the same time, we worked carefully on reducing the structure which had helped to shape Linda's conversational skills. Rather than pressing her with questions, we encouraged Linda to talk freely. Conversations led by Linda about yesterday and the weekend, preschool activities, and the colors, functions, and initial letters of various toys helped Linda to practice her speech naturally while we provided only minimal guidance.

While making up stories by herself was too difficult, Linda confidently directed games like "Simon says" with such commands as "Simon says, 'Touch your eyebrows.'; 'Blink your eyes.'; 'Lie on the floor.' " In a game where one person hid an object and a second person guessed at the location Linda was happy to assume either role.

In addition, she began to learn the days of the week and "right" and "left" during this month.

Month 11 and 12. It was apparent to us several months earlier that Linda would not need a second year of intensive treatment. She already had acquired the most important skill which we could teach—the ability to learn from her natural environment. Thus, our efforts in these two months were aimed simply at refining such skills as asking questions, classifying, listening, and conversing.

Linda practiced asking questions as she was told, "Go ask

Cory what color her car is?" After several "refresher" trials Linda was encouraged to ask her own questions ("Go ask Linda a question," or "Ask me a question"). A constant "barrage" of spontaneous questions during subsequent sessions and at home indicated that Linda had appropriately learned to request information.

Matching and classification skills were integrated in an exercise where Linda had to match picture cards according to class. A fireman and a policeman, or a cow and horse, represented a match.

An addition to our simplified version of "Simon says" helped to develop listening skills. If Simon gave a command, each player had to obey. However, if Ralph gave a command, no one was to obey. In another exercise Linda had to listen carefully to descriptions of picture cards and then guess what the picture was. Her performance was perfect.

By placing different-colored candies in identical paper cups a therapist began to teach Linda the demonstrative pronouns "that" and "which." Linda was prompted to say, "give me the cup *that* has a *red* candy." She learned this quickly and exhausted our candy supply.

Finally, we continued exercises where Linda could use her speech flexibly and spontaneously. We developed a group exercise to simulate a classroom setting where one therapist would ask, "Who can tell me about _____?" Another person would raise his hand and say, "I can!" and would then talk to the group. As Linda raised her hand excitedly to speak, we all knew, in fact, that she could.

Since Linda had entered treatment as a higher-functioning autistic child the gains in language—while nonetheless dramatic—were not unexpected. Our present emphasis is to shift the training from the clinic to the preschool classroom. We have carried out extensive observations in her classroom in order to assess and subsequently remediate any language problems. We have observed, for example, that Linda is more grammatical in the clinic settings than in the classroom. Also, Linda uses more commands with children and more descriptive and conversational speech with adults. Presently we are working to help Linda converse as easily with her friends as she does with her therapists. That is, we have become heavily involved in peer therapy. At the same time, the differences between Linda and her peers are quite small. We believe that a naive observer could not today single out Linda from among schoolmates as an exceptional child.